Hare Krishna Transformed

D0863382

THE NEW AND ALTERNATIVE RELIGIONS SERIES
General Editors: Timothy Miller and Susan J. Palmer

Hare Krishna Transformed
E. Burke Rochford Jr.

Hare Krishna Transformed

E. Burke Rochford Jr.

NEW YORK UNIVERSITY PRESS

New York and London

NEW YORK UNIVERSITY PRESS
New York and London
www.nyupress.org

Library of Congress Cataloging-in-Publication Data
Rochford, E. Burke, 1949–
Hare Krishna transformed / E. Burke Rochford, Jr.
p. cm. — (The new and alternative religions series)
Includes bibliographical references and index.
ISBN-13: 978-0-8147-7578-3 (cloth : alk. paper)
ISBN-10: 0-8147-7578-0 (cloth : alk. paper)
ISBN-13: 978-0-8147-7579-0 (pbk. : alk. paper)
ISBN-10: 0-8147-7579-9 (pbk. : alk. paper)
1. International Society for Krishna Consciousness—History.
2. Krishna (Hindu deity)—Cult—United States. 3. Family—
Religious aspects—International Society for Krishna Consciousness.
4. Hinduism—United States. 5. Hindu converts—United States.
I. Title.
BL1285.835.U6R63 2007
294.5'512—dc22   2006038031

New York University Press books are printed on acid-free paper,
and their binding materials are chosen for strength and durability.

Manufactured in the United States of America
c 10 9 8 7 6 5 4 3 2 1
p 10 9 8 7 6 5 4 3 2 1

To the followers of
A. C. Bhaktivedanta Swami Prabhupada

Contents

Acknowledgments

Even though I have studied the Hare Krishna movement for more than thirty years, I could not have written this book without the contributions of many people. Most important, of course, were the many Hare Krishna devotees who graciously gave their time to further my research interests. It has been a wonderful, if sometimes bumpy, journey for all of us. Although I would like to thank many of you here by name, doing so would break my pledge of confidentiality. I have been inspired by your determination, pained by your sorrow, and envious of your spiritual growth. I pray that this book brings understanding to what has proved to be a difficult period in the lives of many.

From the world of academia, I first want to acknowledge my friend and mentor, Bob Emerson, who taught me the skills as well as the love for field research. I also want to thank a number of colleagues for their help and support along the way: Eileen Barker, Jim Beckford, David Bromley, Jean Burfoot, Bob Ferm, Kim Knott, Tim Miller, Peggy Nelson, Paula Nesbitt, Susan Palmer, Jim Richardson, Ted Sasson, Darren Sherkat, David Snow, and Bill Waldron. Kendra Bailey, Ian Burfoot-Rochford, Mateal Lovaas, Doug Rogers, and Marina Zaloznaya provided invaluable assistance in researching and writing this book. My colleagues in sociology/anthropology and religion at Middlebury College have supported me continuously over the past twenty years. I couldn't be more grateful. Special appreciation goes to my colleague Peggy Nelson, whose friendship, encouragement, and considerable sociological insight have been an inspiration. I am especially grateful to Charlene Barrett, coordinator for sociology/anthropology and religion, who has made my life easier in countless ways. I also want to thank Middlebury College for providing funds to support my research.

Jennifer Hammer at New York University Press saw the possibilities for this book before I did. She proved to be a capable editor who was nothing short of a pleasure to work with. This book is better because of her interest and thoughtful advice.

Finally, I want to thank my wife, Jean, who for years has endured an ongoing medical disability with a degree of grace and dignity that reveals her inner strength as well as her deep love for her family. To Holley and Ian, thank you for your love and good humor. Love to you all.

Introduction

It is the end of July 1991 on the Westside of Los Angeles. The park is teeming with visitors. Besides the usual number of families picnicking and kids throwing frisbees and riding bikes, a large gathering of perhaps 150 young men and women are enjoying the summer day as well as one another's company. As a group, they appear very much like other young Californians with their colorful shirts and shorts, long hair, and youthful manner. Many are sitting in groups of five or six socializing while others, mostly the young men, are throwing footballs, shooting baskets on the nearby court, wrestling, and generally having a good time. In the distance I can see several barbecues with smoke billowing from them. One would have to get up close to realize that there are no hamburgers or hot dogs on the grill, only veggie burgers and other vegetarian food. From my perch on the hillside looking down, I am struck by the fact that the reunion festivities before me appear so ordinary. I look hard without success to find any markers that might reveal the collective identity of this group of young people enjoying the summer afternoon.

As I sit observing, two young men from the group walk toward me and sit down. At first I think they might recognize me, but I soon realized that they are merely looking for a safe place to smoke marijuana. One of the young men refers to me as "Jerry" as he sits down a few feet away, presumably because my long hair, bushy gray beard, and large frame remind him of Jerry Garcia. I am surprised by their choice to sit so near, given their intentions, but then I am reminded that this is California after all. At one point the young man who calls me "Jerry" reaches over to offer me a "taste" of his neatly rolled joint. When I decline, he responds, "What's the matter Jerry, too early in the day for you?"

I have returned to Los Angeles after a ten-year absence to research these young people in the park. In the late 1970s, when the majority of their generation were five, six, and seven years old, I was living down the street and conducting research for my dissertation on Los Angeles's Hare Krishna community. With me now are a few of the young people I had chaperoned to this very park, or to the beach just five miles away. As I sit here observing these second-generation Krishna devotees, I am reminded of how, in different ways, we grew up in Krishna Consciousness together, me as a graduate student clumsily trying to understand their religious world and they as children growing up in a controversial new religion. I am reminded, too, of the many things I learned from the devotee children I met during the movement's formative years. Being a novice in every sense of that word, I had much to learn, and the young children I met took special delight in teaching the person they called "Bhakta Burke."[1]

In 1989, I began recalling fond memories of the boys I had come to know years earlier. I couldn't help but think about what had happened to them over the previous decade. I wondered whether they had managed to escape using drugs and alcohol, something most teenagers find reason to experiment with and occasionally abuse. I considered as well where their lives might have gone. Were they still devotees of Krishna and members of the movement? Were their girlfriends or spouses devotees or *karmies* (nondevotees)? Where were they living and working? In short, I thought about the nature of their lives, given their experiences growing up in the Hare Krishna movement. Many of my questions, of course, formed research topics even while expressing personal interest in and concern about the boys. Being a student of new religions, I realized that those born into Hare Krishna and the other new religions of the 1960s were important, given their collective inability to capture the imagination of a new generation of converts. I wondered and even worried about how the changing fortunes of the Krishna movement had shaped the lives of the children and parents I had come to know during the 1970s. My observations of the young people who had come together for a reunion in Los Angeles suggested that much had changed over a decade, and I was drawn to studying what had happened and why.

Studying the Hare Krishna

The Hare Krishna movement, formally known as the International Society for Krishna Consciousness, or ISKCON, is a religious group founded in New York City in 1966 by A. C. Bhaktivedanta Swami Prabhupada.

It is based on the Hindu Vedic scriptures and represents a Western expansion of the Bengali *bhakti* (devotional) tradition, or Krishna Consciousness, which emerged in the sixteenth century. Members practice an ascetic lifestyle that includes vegetarianism and a life devoted to the Hindu god Krishna. Essential to achieving spiritual enlightenment is the practice of chanting the Hare Krishna mantra. ISKCON spread to other cities in North America and to Europe, Australia, Latin America, India, and, in more recent years, eastern Europe. Since the death of its founder Prabhupada in 1977, the role of authority, heresy, and dissent in ISKCON has been debated, especially women's rights and leadership in the wake of highly publicized scandals. What is most striking is the transition from a communal structure that actively discouraged marriage and the nuclear family, denigrated women, and viewed the raising of children as a distraction from the devotees' spiritual responsibilities to a movement that now embraces the nuclear family and is becoming more accepting of both women and children, steps taken out of necessity to sustain itself as a religious movement into the next generation.

Focusing on the second generation of Hare Krishnas, this book is the first systematic attempt to understand how marriage, gender politics, and family life have influenced the development of this group and its prospects for the future. I also consider the implications for the movement of its recent outreach into the India-born American Hindu community. I have been studying the Hare Krishnas for thirty years and have visited and conducted research in virtually every major ISKCON community in the United States. Significantly, this book studies a new religious movement over the two generations since its founding. I focus on the interplay among individuals, families, and the inherent volatility of new religions as they progress from their radical beginnings to accommodation with the mainstream society.

In order to continue my research of the Hare Krishnas into its second generation, in 1989 I contacted a longtime devotee friend who had risen to a position in the ISKCON leadership in the years since we had last spoken. I told him of my interest in studying the movement's second generation. He gave me a cautious but still largely encouraging response and recommended that I contact two leaders involved in educational issues. Shortly thereafter, I spoke with the devotee who served as ISKCON's minister of education. He, too, seemed cautious but asked me to send him a copy of my book, *Hare Krishna in America*.[2] He said that he would speak to me again about my project after reading the book. Several weeks later he called to say that he was willing to talk further about my research plans. Clearly, my book had passed the test, although I remained unsure exactly what that meant. He told me early on in our conversation that the second generation represented a sensitive issue to the movement and one that might well prove difficult to study. At first I interpreted his words as indicating an existing generational divide, not unlike that found in other communities and society more generally. I thought this in part because he suggested that it would be difficult to gain the trust of ISKCON's young people. Therefore, he recommended that I begin my research by interviewing parents about ISKCON's children. Such a strategy would allow me to learn some of the issues relating to the movement's children before I asked them directly for interviews.

In the summer of 1990, I interviewed seventy first-generation parents in four ISKCON communities in the United States (Detroit, Los Angeles, San Diego, and Three Rivers, California). I also interviewed a dozen teachers and other devotees directly involved in educating ISKCON's young people. My initial interviews revealed some startling information. One teacher and mother told me that some of the children had been abused in the movement's *ashram*-based *gurukulas* (boarding schools). Some parents also acknowledged that their children, or those of other parents, had been neglected and abused in the schools. At first I remained cautious in my assessment because I had no way of knowing how extensive the abuse had been. Moreover, the unfortunate fact is that large numbers of children face abuse and neglect in American society. The reports I was hearing did make me realize, however, that this was likely one reason why ISKCON's young people might be hesitant to speak with me about their experiences growing up in the movement. My suspicions were indirectly confirmed when I spoke informally with a young, second-generation woman in Los Angeles who told me in 1990, "You have to understand the kids have a lot of things they are working through. Many of them won't talk with you because they haven't fully understood and processed their own experiences in the *gurukula*." Yet she never mentioned abuse, and at that point, I hesitated to push the issue any further.

My interviews with parents made me realize rather quickly that I needed to broaden my research focus to encompass family life more generally. Many parents, both men and women, told me that ISKCON's leaders had neglected the needs of families. Others mentioned that women had endured particularly troubling lives in the movement and that many continued to do so.

Initially, I did have a difficult time gaining the trust of the second-generation youths I hoped to study and, in the end, probably was able to do so only because *they* began to make public what had happened to them growing up in ISKCON. This happened only after members of the second generation began holding "*gurukuli*" reunions beginning in 1990. These reunions, which I attended in the early 1990s, began as consciousness-raising affairs for the youths involved but in time grew to include their parents' generation as well. I became one voice among others in the discussions that emerged during this period. One way I became a participant was in my role as a member of ISKCON's North American Board of Education during the early and mid-1990s. Seeing me as involved in generational issues, a number of young people expressed interest in speaking with me. In the end, I was able to interview forty-seven second-generation youths about their experiences growing up in ISKCON. Many of these interviews were conducted at the four gurukula reunions I attended in Los Angeles and at ISKCON's rural farm community in West Virginia (New Vrindaban) between 1990 and 1994.

My qualitative research was supplemented by three surveys conducted in North America during the 1990s. My qualitative research was supplemented by three surveys conducted in North America during the 1990s. Where appropriate, survey results are reported in the body of the text inclusive of the data tables. In other cases, I have placed tables in appendix 2, to avoid disrupting my discussion.

During the fall of 1991 and early winter of 1992, I conducted a nonrandom survey of ISKCON members, and 268 devotees responded. The survey targeted first-generation devotees affiliated with nine ISKCON communities in the United States. In the end, however, because the ISKCON members distributed the questionnaires widely, nineteen communities in the United States and three in Canada were represented. My questions focused primarily on family issues, children and education, and organizational and religious commitments.

In 1992/93, I conducted a second nonrandom survey of eighty-seven second-generation ISKCON youths in North America. This survey was aimed at the older members of this generation (eighteen to twenty-five years old), although several high school age youths also took part. My questions were about their experiences in the gurukula, their transition into public education, their views of ISKCON, their current life circumstances, and the degree to which they continued to identify with ISKCON and Krishna Consciousness.

Finally, the North America Prabhupada Centennial Survey was conducted in 1995/96 with a total of 556 respondents,[3] of whom 251 were full-time members, 145 were congregational members (who are less committed and involved in ISKCON), 94 were former ISKCON members, and 66 claimed to have never officially joined ISKCON. The survey addressed a wide range of issues, including opinions about ISKCON's gurus and international governing body, family life, the place of women in the movement, education of the young, cultural development, types and levels of involvement in the conventional society, individual religious practice, and commitments to and involvements in ISKCON.

As a new religious movement, ISKCON has distinctive qualities that have influenced its development in North America, which reveal the types of struggles the movement encountered in its mission of converting America to its Krishna conscious beliefs and way of life.

Radical Protest and Religious Culture

New religions are one of the significant carriers of the 1960s counterculture and the spirit of protest associated with that era (Judah 1974; Kent 2001; Rochford 1985). New religions tend to be prophetic movements challenging the legitimacy of the existing social order while at the same time distancing them from it (Bromley 1997, 2004). Particularly in their formative stages, new religions tend to be antistructural, seeing "corruption" and "contradiction" in what others view as a normative reality (Bromley 1997). New religions thus exist "in relatively contested spaces within society as a whole" (Melton 2004:75) and face an ongoing potential for tension with the dominant society (Bromley 2004; Mauss 1994; Stark 1996; Wilson 1990). New religions therefore are not aligned with either the dominant cultural patterns or the dominant societal institutions (Bromley 2004:94).

Because of their radical quality, new religions must construct oppositional religious cultures to support their unconventional beliefs and lifestyles. In crafting these cultures, new religious groups create structures, practices, and symbols meant to integrate followers into their unconventional religious worlds while simultaneously segregating them from the supposedly corrosive effects of the secular culture. Collectively, they tend to foster highly robust and strict religious cultures that place considerable demands on their members (Iannaccone 1994; Lofland 1987;

Stark 1996). Reflecting these characteristics, they usually are isolated from the mainstream culture and favor communalism as a form of social organization (Bromley 1997).

Like all cultures, religious cultures are strongly influenced by the changing social contexts in which they operate. Their cultural expression is driven as much or more by the situations that people and organizations confront as by their beliefs and values. As Swidler argues in reference to culture generally, "Variations in the ways that social contexts bring culture to bear on action may do more to determine culture's power than variations in how deeply culture is held" (1995:31).[4] As the institutional challenges faced by new religions changed over time, the contexts in which they operated required new repertoires of action, or cultural "tool kits" (Swidler 1986). These tool kits have often provoked social conflict between supporters of traditionalism and those favoring a more progressive cultural agenda (Rochford 2007), and the outcomes of these internal conflicts have helped determine how new religions develop over time.

ISKCON's history in North America has been one of ongoing conflict over the nature of its religious culture. Most significant has been the growth of family life and its challenge to the movement's non-family-oriented origins, radical goals, and way of life. Beginning in the early 1970s, renunciate leaders vigorously opposed marriage and family in an attempt to preserve ISKCON's goal of transforming American society through preaching and conversion. This denigration of family life led to the abuse and neglect of women and children. Then in the early 1980s, ISKCON changed dramatically when the revenues from its literature distribution plunged and the communal structure that served as the foundation of its oppositional way of life disintegrated. Thereafter, ISKCON became a congregationally based movement composed of independent nuclear families. It was further changed when the legitimacy of ISKCON's leadership was widely challenged. Pro-change women wanted equal rights. Children sought justice in the courts for past abuse. And long-time members joined other Krishna-based organizations or pushed for change within ISKCON. On the verge of organizational failure, ISKCON attracted substantial numbers of Indian-Hindu immigrants to its communities at the expense of its traditional religious culture and identity. These changes continued as its long-standing members began accommodating to America culture and sought to reshape the movement's religious culture to reflect these changed realities. By the turn of the new millennium, the Hare Krishna had given up its radical beginnings in return for a place in America's pluralistic religious landscape.

Overview of the Book

This study of the Hare Krishna movement in North America is meant to contribute to the sociology of religious organizations. It focuses on organizational change, the politics of religious culture, and human tragedy, each of which I consider by tracing the development of marriage and family life during ISKCON's history. In essence, this is a story about how radical religious protest is tamed and transformed and how a new religious movement survives by reinventing itself in the midst of decline and crisis.

After a discussion of ISKCON's origins and early development in North America, the text is organized into the following chapters:

Written in the first person, chapter 1 (Growing Up) is a narrative describing the experience of one young man who grew up in ISKCON. Dasa's story, both compelling and tragic, foreshadows many of the issues covered in the remainder of the book.

Chapter 2 (Family, Culture, and Change) examines in detail the history of marriage and family life from the movement's early days in the 1970s through the early 1990s. Marriage and family life expanded during a period of economic decline, resulting in the collapse of communalism and the emergence of a congregation of independent householders.

Chapter 3 (Child Abuse) presents a sociological framework to show the reasons for child abuse in ISKCON's ashram-based gurukulas during the 1970s and 1980s. In important respects, this child abuse resulted from the firm commitment of renunciate leaders to ISKCON's radical goals and way of life, at the expense of householders and their children.

Chapter 4 (Public Schooling and Identity) considers the transition of adolescents educated in ISKCON's boarding schools into public education. Because it had no system of secondary education, most of ISKCON's young people were forced to attend public schools during their teenage years. Here I look at the devotee youths' experiences and the consequences of this transition for their later identities.

Chapter 5 (Women's Voices) addresses the emergence of ISKCON women's collective voice and the struggle by pro-change women for gender equality. Because renunciate leaders perceived women and family as threatening ISKCON's mission, they vigorously campaigned against both, leaving women powerless and subject to neglect and abuse. Women's voices rose in protest against their own abuse and that suffered by their children.

Chapter 6 (Male Backlash) explores the response to women's advancement. Like other religious groups, ISKCON experienced a backlash by a small but vocal group of male traditionalists determined to turn back gender reforms and rid the movement of feminist influences. To traditionalists, gender reform represented compelling evidence that ISKCON had abandoned its goal of building an oppositional religious culture based on Vedic ideals.

Chapter 7 (Moving On) traces the paths of the many devotees who left ISKCON during the leadership controversies of the 1980s and 1990s. Because most of those leaving ISKCON remained committed to ISKCON's founder and to Krishna Consciousness, they sought new environments in which to pursue their beliefs. In essence, the Krishna movement spilled beyond the borders of ISKCON and its temple communities, leaving the organization with an uncertain future.

Chapter 8 (Hindus and Hinduization) looks at the growing importance and influence of Indian Hindus in ISKCON's North American communities. As large numbers of devotees left ISKCON, the leadership began a campaign to revitalize its failing communities by expanding local Indian-Hindu congregations. Unintended consequences resulted, however, as ISKCON's religious culture and overall identity became subject to "Hinduization."

The concluding chapter (World Accommodation) describes ISKCON's long-standing members as they try to become established in conventional American society. This worldly accommodation has given rise to new forms of cultural production on behalf of families and the broader devotee community.

Hare Krishna's Origins, Religious Beliefs, and North American Growth

A. C. Bhaktivedanta Swami Prabhupada founded ISKCON in New York City in 1966. Bhaktivedanta Swami, or Srila Prabhupada as his followers called him, traveled to the United States in 1965 at the age of sixty-nine to make good on a promise to his spiritual master to bring Krishna

Consciousness to the West (Goswami, Satsvarupa 1993:1). With little more than forty Indian rupees (about seven U.S. dollars) and a trunk of books containing his translations of the ancient Vedic literatures, Prabhupada set off to bring the message of Krishna Consciousness to the United States and ultimately to the world (Goswami, Satsvarupa 1993: 7–8). No one could have imagined that this elderly *sadhu* (holy man) from Calcutta would create a worldwide movement in little more than ten years.

Prabhupada represented a religious tradition that began in Bengal, India, during the sixteenth century. Although it is aligned with the more prevalent forms of Hinduism, the Krishna Consciousness preached by Prabhupada traces its beginnings to the Krishna-bhakti movement founded by Caitanya Mahaprabhu (1486–1533). A distinctive feature of this tradition is that Caitanya is believed to be an incarnation of Krishna (Rosen 2004:63–64).[5] In fact, Caitanya elevated Krishna as the supreme manifestation of God, instead of being one of several Hindu gods, as was believed in other forms of Hinduism. He preached a devotional form of Hinduism called *bhakti-yoga,* which emphasized love and devotional service to God as the means to spiritual salvation. In a controversial split with Hinduism, Caitanya preached that all people, regardless of their caste or position in life, could gain self-realization by serving Krishna. In keeping with Caitanya's religious philosophy, ISK-CON devotees consider themselves first and foremost Krishna's servants and view human life as a unique opportunity to revive their devotion to God by surrendering to him (Squarcini and Fizzotti 2004:54).

Caitanya also developed another innovation unique to Hinduism, which has become a trademark of the Hare Krishna movement. From his intense religious passion, Caitanya initiated *sankirtan,* a practice requiring his followers to go into the streets to dance and sing their praises of Lord Krishna (Rochford 1985:11). When Prabhupada began his movement in America, sankirtan (preaching, chanting in public, and book distribution) became the principal means of spreading Krishna Consciousness (Rochford 1985:11–12).

By chanting and performing devotional service under the guidance of a spiritual master, a devotee is able to restore his or her eternal relationship with Krishna and thus bring the soul back to the spiritual realm (Squarcini and Fizzotti 2004:54–55). Because of its material contamination, the soul is forced to assume a continuous succession of rebirths (*samsara*). To escape the laws of *karma* and break the cycle of reincarnation, devotees seek to perfect their lives by controlling their senses. As this implies, devotees understand that they are not this material body but spiritual souls.

A Krishna devotee participates in a number of religious practices meant to purify the soul. Central to this process of self-realization is chanting the Hare Krishna mantra: Hare Krishna Hare Krishna, Krishna Krishna, Hare Hare, Hare Rama Hare Rama, Rama Rama, Hare Hare. Consisting of the names of God, the *mahamantra* is believed to be a genuine transcendental sound vibration with the ability to revive our transcendental consciousness (Beck 2004:35–36). Chanting Hare Krishna is ISKCON members' single most important religious practice.

A major milestone in the spiritual career of an ISKCON devotee is the moment of initiation. First initiation, or *harinama-diksa* initiation, is performed as part of a fire sacrifice. When being initiated by a guru, devotees commit themselves to chanting sixteen rounds of the Hare Krishna mantra daily on a string of 108 *japa*, or prayer beads. They also agree to abstain from eating meat, illicit sex (sex other than for the propagation of God-conscious children), ingesting intoxicants (cigarettes, alcohol, tea, coffee, and drugs), and gambling. The new initiate also receives a Sanskrit name from his or her guru. The name links the newly initiated devotee to a particular quality or form of god (Squarcini and Fizzotti 2004:43) and always includes a suffix, or last name, *dasa* for men and *dasi* for women. In each case, this signifies that the devotee is a "servant" before god and guru. A year or more after the *diksa* initiation, a devotee can be considered for "second initiation." On this occasion the initiate receives the status of *brahmana,* symbolized by the sacred thread (*yajnopavita*). Brahmana initiation enables an ISKCON devotee to perform specific liturgical procedures and practices such as cooking for the deities, serving on the altar, and performing sacrificial rites (Squarcini and Fizzotti 2004:44).

Although no longer mandatory, many ISKCON members continue their early-morning worship (4:30 A.M.) at a local ISKCON temple, but nowadays devotees more commonly worship at home with their families. Devotees worship marble or brass deities of Krishna and his consort Radharani on the altar, the spiritual plant Tulasi, and ISKCON's founder Srila Prabhupada. Music accompanies this worship, with a male or female leading others gathered in singing various Sanskrit and Bengali verses to the beat of *mrdanga* drums and *karatals* (small hand cymbals). Between morning ceremonies, or during the day as time allows, devotees busily chant their daily rounds. At the end of morning worship in the temple, a class is held on Prabhupada's commentaries on the Vedic scriptures. The ritualistic routine performed by devotees inside or outside the temple is meant to maintain individual and collective purity by focusing the mind first and foremost on Krishna.

North American Growth and Development

After arriving in New York City from India, Prabhupada, or "Swamiji" as his earliest followers referred to him, turned his proselytizing efforts to the young people living on the Bowery on the Lower East Side (Goswami, Satsvarupa 1993). Initially, Prabhupada attracted the attention of a few young people while chanting in Tompkins Square Park. Rather quickly, word spread about "the Swami" among the musicians and bohemian crowd living in the area. Within a short time, several of Prabhupada's followers helped him establish a small temple on Second Avenue in a storefront that had previously served as a curiosity shop called Matchless Gifts (Goswami, Satsvarupa 1993:102–8). In his new temple, Prabhupada lectured on the Bhagavad Gita and other Vedic scriptures of Hinduism and held *kirtans* (congregational singing and chanting). Visitors often brought harmoniums, flutes, guitars, and other instruments, which they played, often while "high" on drugs. In these early days, ISKCON revealed few of the spiritual practices that restricted the lifestyle of those drawn to Prabhupada. During his first year in New York, Prabhupada initiated nineteen disciples and, in 1966, legally registered ISKCON as a nonprofit, tax-exempt religious organization (Goswami, Satsvarupa 1993:130).

ISKCON radically changed after Prabhupada relocated in January 1967 to the emerging hippie community in the Haight-Ashbury section of San Francisco. At the time, thousands of hippies were migrating to Haight-Ashbury. After situating the temple in the heart of the district, ISKCON recruited an estimated 150 to 200 converts during its first two years there (Johnson 1976:33). Prabhupada and his followers appealed directly to the hippies who literally were at the devotees' doorstep: "Below the large 'Hare Krishna' sign on the outside of the temple was a smaller placard that stated: 'Stay High All the Time, Discover Eternal Bliss'" (Johnson 1976:38).

Because the majority of the hippie recruits drawn to ISKCON had only recently moved to the area and did not have a permanent or stable residence, ISKCON's communal structure emerged to hold on to the young countercultural youths attracted to Krishna Consciousness. Prabhupada then began to insist that his followers living in the temple complex adhere to the four regulative principles (no meat, intoxicants, illicit sex, or gambling) and that they chant and attend worship services in the temple. ISKCON's San Francisco organization served as a model for devotees deployed to other cities across North America to establish Krishna temples and recruit followers (Rochford 1985:159).

The Krishna lifestyle generally afforded few opportunities for members to maintain societal contacts, as the outside was seen as a source of "pollution" threatening the spiritual development of ISKCON's neophyte members. The isolation of ISKCON's U.S. communities accelerated in the mid-1970s as ISKCON came under attack by deprogrammers and other opponents of cults. ISKCON's communities consequently became increasingly closed religious enclaves where interaction with outsiders was limited largely to proselytizing and distributing literature (Rochford 1985:159–60). Anticult propaganda, widely disseminated by the media, helped reshape the public's image of Hare Krishna from a peculiar, but essentially harmless, religious movement to a threatening and dangerous one (Rochford 1987).

ISKCON was largely supported economically by the practice of sankirtan, the public distribution of religious literature. During the late 1960s and early 1970s, devotees distributed incense[6] or *Back to Godhead* magazines to the public in exchange for donations. The strategy of combining the movement's missionary goals with collecting money became standard policy for ISKCON until the early 1980s (Rochford 1985:173).

Prabhupada wrote more than sixty volumes, including *Bhagavad Gita as It Is* (1972), the multivolume *Srimad Bhagavatam* (1972–77), the *Caitanya-caritamta* (1974–75), *The Nectar of Devotion* (1970), and many other books on the Vedic scriptures. These volumes included translations of the original Sanskrit and Bengali texts, along with Prabhupada's commentaries, and have been translated into more than sixty languages. Owing to the work of his nearly five thousand disciples and tens of thousands of followers worldwide, 500 million copies of Prabhupada's books and magazines have been distributed around the globe (Squarcini and Fizzotti 2004:62).

As ISKCON grew and the demands on Prabhupada's time increased, he recognized that his movement needed a more formal structure of governance. In 1970, he created the Governing Body Commission (GBC) to help oversee the movement's affairs worldwide (Rochford 1985:18). The GBC meets yearly in Mayapura, India, to make policies, address problems, and transact any and all business related to ISKCON and its communities across the world. GBC members assume administrative responsibility for ISKCON communities in specific countries and regions of the world.

By 1975 ISKCON had established communities and preaching centers in thirty cities in the United States and six in Canada. It also had eleven communities in western Europe and twenty-nine in other parts of the world (Australia, Africa, India, Asia, and Latin America) (Rochford 1985:277). In 1983 the number of communities in the United States had grown to fifty (Rochford 1985:277), and in 2006 ISKCON had a total of forty-four communities (iskcon.com 2005c). ISKCON has a North American membership of about fifty thousand and claims to have one million adherents worldwide.

In the fall of 1977, the devotees' beloved founder died in Vrndavana, India, at the age of eighty-two. Prabhupada's death represented a major turning point in ISKCON's development in both North America and the rest of the world (Rochford 1985:221–55). Unable to travel in the months before his passing, Prabhupada appointed eleven of his closest disciples to serve as *ritvik-gurus* (ceremonial priests). These gurus were responsible for initiating new disciples on Prabhupada's behalf (Rochford 1998a). When Prabhupada died, the eleven appointed ritvik gurus assumed the position of regular gurus, offering diksa (first) initiation to persons who accepted them as their spiritual master (Rochford 1985: 222). ISKCON's successor gurus effectively led their own independent movements as they assumed control over separate portions of the globe. Within their geographical zones, they exercised exclusive political, economic, and spiritual authority (Rochford 1998a:104). Controversial from the beginning, this structure of authority known in ISKCON as the "zonal *acarya* system" existed for nearly a decade. During that period, the majority of the gurus became involved in scandals, resulting in the defection of many long-standing members from the organization (Rochford 1998a).

Under the leadership of senior Prabhupada disciples, in 1986 a reform movement successfully pressured the GBC to make a number of changes to ISKCON's guru institution. Most significant was expanding the number of ISKCON gurus, which served to undermine the zonal acarya system by eliminating the gurus' claims to exclusive geographical zones (for other reforms to the guru institution, see Rochford 1998a). The number of gurus increased from thirty to sixty in 1990 and to eighty in 1993 (Squarcini and Fizzotti 2004:26), and in 2005, ISKCON had more than eighty gurus throughout the world. Despite these reforms however, controversy remains.

Chapter 1 describes one young man's journey growing up during ISKCON's formative years in North America. Although Dasa's story is uniquely his, it nonetheless speaks to the experiences of many boys and young men who grew up as Hare Krishnas during the 1970s and 1980s. In particular, it illustrates how ISKCON's antifamily stance shaped the lives of a new generation as well as those of their parents. It also chronicles how ISKCON's second generation individually and collectively stood up to contest the past as part of creating a future for themselves and their own families.

1

Growing Up

Defending the honor of the religion is more important than protecting the children.

In 1968 Dasa was born in Ann Arbor, Michigan, a liberal college town considered by some as the "California of the Midwest." Before they met in college in 1966, both Dasa's parents were interested in Eastern and Native American religious traditions. They married one year later. Both were products of the counterculture, leaving their college studies to protest the Vietnam War. Dasa's father went to Canada for a while to escape being drafted into the army. Dasa's mother continued with her studies until his birth, and his father helped start a health food business with several old friends.

A few months after his birth, Dasa traveled with his parents to the Haight-Ashbury section of San Francisco, where thousands of hippies were migrating to take part in the counterculture. As Dasa described it,

> When I was born in '68 they moved, at the end of that year, to California. A lot of people at that time were going to San Francisco, "with flowers in your hair," all that. It was there that they began running into [Hare Krishna] devotees and other religions. They were into Alan Watts and Eastern philosophy and religion. They met the devotees out there in San Francisco and would go to the [Sunday] feast. That's where it started.[1]

Although they were involved in the Hare Krishna movement during their year-and-a-half stay in San Francisco, Dasa's parents refused to move into the temple. At the end of 1969, Dasa returned to Michigan with his parents, where they shared a house with a couple who also were interested in Krishna Consciousness and subsequently were initiated by ISKCON's founder and guru Srila Prabhupada. Within a short time, Dasa's parents also became more involved in the practice of Krishna Consciousness, becoming members of the Detroit ISKCON temple. As Dasa explained, "So I started attending the temple a lot then with my parents. They often would invite the devotees at the temple back to their house for kirtans and to chant. My parents were becoming increasingly involved at this time."

Although his father's involvement in the movement remained less intense and sporadic, Dasa's mother more readily committed to ISKCON and its religious way of life. Consistent with her commitment, in 1972 Dasa was sent off at age four to ISKCON's recently opened ashram-based gurukula (boarding school) in Dallas, Texas. But as Dasa recalled, his mother rather quickly became disillusioned with the school after visiting her son.

> My mother was convinced enough to send me to the gurukula in Dallas. It was a short stay, less than six months. She sent me down there because people thought that was the right thing to do. But the separation was too much for her. And then she came down for a visit and saw that I wasn't being very well taken care of. There were some bruises on the back of my head, ears, neck, something. She pulled me right out.

Finding their son unhappy and not well cared for, Dasa's parents became far less involved in the Detroit ISKCON community.

> That was the break-off point for them from ISKCON. So when that happened with me in the gurukula, my mother was so disgusted. My mother was more the tie to ISKCON at that point than my father. When she was unhappy they just broke off their connection. After that it was just sporadic contact until '78 or '79.

In 1977, Dasa and his family faced a crisis that ultimately led them back to ISKCON. In the spring of that year, after falling into a coma and being hospitalized for three weeks, his mother was diagnosed with leukemia and given six months to live. Although she lived another eight years, she "knew she was going to die soon and thought she had better prepare." As a result, she committed herself more strongly to her religious faith and decided to return to ISKCON.

In 1979 Dasa's mother moved into the Detroit temple with Dasa and his four siblings. By now the temple had relocated to the Fisher mansion.[2] Dasa and his oldest sister stayed in the homes of two different families. Because there was no "real school" in the Detroit community for older children, Dasa worked with a number of artists during the day. After a short period, however, Dasa's mother was given a choice by the temple president: send Dasa to either the gurukula in Vrndavana, India, or the school at New Vrindaban, the ISKCON community in West Virginia. Dasa and his parents found the choice an easy one to make. "I had already heard about the Indian schools. Besides being so far away. So given the rumors [of neglect and abuse within the Indian schools], I just said, 'Send me to New Vrindaban gurukula.'" As it turned out, Dasa's sister went with him to New Vrindaban to attend the girls' school, and in the winter of 1980 the two of them traveled to New Vrindaban by car with another devotee family.

> I remember we were in a station wagon. We had squirt bottle fights because [name of husband] was falling asleep and his wife was spraying him to keep him awake. It was a typical family, fun thing. . . . I remember when we first pulled into West Virginia, we crossed the border from Ohio, and we pulled into a gas station. And as we were putting in gas to go the final leg of the trip up the winding roads to New Vrindaban, another devotee pulled into the gas station. . . . For me, just the fact that I am in the middle of nowhere at a remote gas station and a devotee pulls up. It had never happened to me before. It made a real impression on me. It was like, "Wow, I am in a whole city of devotees."

After arriving at New Vrindaban, Dasa spent the first night in the guest lodge. In the morning he woke early to attend the morning program in the temple.

> It was the first day that I actually made eye contact with all the kids, the boys, from the school. The temple was small; it seemed bigger because I was small. We were eyeing each other. But I didn't talk to anybody. I was just trying to take it all in.

Later in the day Dasa moved into the boys' gurukula, which doubled as both a school and an ashram (place of residence). Over the next week he struggled to establish relationships with the other boys, most of whom were younger than he.

For the first week of school I wasn't really clicking with any of the other boys. There was a gang. I do remember that they were really mean and they would pick on you hard. It was a very abusive situation I was coming into. So they were defending their position in the pecking order, down the line. Verbally mean. Mentally mean. Even at some points, physically mean.

After about a week at the school, there was an incident that proved to be a turning point in Dasa's relations with the other boys.

I remember we were playing out on the front yard. We were playing kickball. Somebody took the ball and just slammed it into my face really hard, to the point where I cried out. And [teacher's name], who was in his classroom, heard it. He came walking out the front door and said, "All right, what's going on here?" I said, "Oh, we were playing kickball and someone accidentally kicked the ball and hit me in the face." That was the turning point; they could see that I wouldn't squeal. . . . Somehow I was suddenly in.

Also during that first week Dasa was faced with an unwanted sexual advance. An older adolescent serving as a monitor for the younger boys in the ashram attempted to transform a wrestling match into something entirely different.

At some point during that week [name of the monitor] tried to make sexual advances toward me, trying to molest me. It was one of those situations where you're in a room and you're asked, "Do you want to wrestle?" "OK." You start wrestling. And it's like, "Oh, God, I'm really hot; I'm sweating. I'm going to take my shirt off." Suddenly you're down to your underwear, and you're wrestling around and suddenly a hand is in a place where it shouldn't be. I looked and said, "Sorry, I am not interested." He didn't initially take no for an answer. He kept trying. Finally I grabbed him by the hair or ear or something and pulled him up and said, "Listen I am going to scream if you don't stop. I'm not into this. Cut this out." And so he stopped. He said, "Oh, I'm sorry." Just backed off. At that point I believed him that it was just innocent. Later on when I found out the extent of stuff that was going on, I said to myself, "No, he was making a move. If I had gone for it, he would have gotten more involved."

With this definitive refusal, Dasa escaped the sexual advances that some of the younger children found more difficult to ward off. As he remembered, "Reflecting back, that was the best move I could have made. The word was out, 'This guy is not into it. He's not easy.'"

Following the morning worship program in the temple, Dasa attended classes until lunchtime, after which he worked in one of the community's businesses. His classroom teacher instructed the ten older boys in his ashram. Although their spiritual training was emphasized, the boys also were taught traditional academic subjects such as English, math, and geography. Yet because of his past academic training in the public schools in Michigan and because he was a talented student, the gurukula had little to offer Dasa academically.

> So when I came to New Vrindaban, the academics were nothing. They had these books from the 1950s. I remember specifically the math books. They were little hard-back books. There was a yellow one, a red one, and a blue one. And I think the yellow one was the most advanced. When I did it, it was all review for me. But they made me go through it three times anyway. I had already gone past this level before I had even come here. So I sat in the classroom, and they made me go through this so I wouldn't cause a disturbance.

Dasa's ashram teacher, who was responsible for overseeing the boys outside the classroom, was a Vietnam veteran. He favored a military approach to dealing with the boys in his charge. In the morning he would awaken the boys by turning on the lights and announcing:

> "You have exactly five minutes, forty-two seconds, to be in the vehicle, or else you will be walking to the temple." And he would sit out in his vehicle and he would time it. It didn't matter if you had one foot in the vehicle. He would just put it into gear and drive away; body hanging out of the vehicle. There must have been fifty kids in this building. There were only ten kids in our ashram, but there was only one shower and one toilet. I remember sometimes there would be five of us standing in the shower with our arms raised trying to get a trickle of water on our body. Sometimes we would skip out on the shower altogether so we could be in the vehicle.

Although there were hardships, there was also ample time for fun and recreation during his early years in the gurukula.

During the day we would play games. We would have rock fights. Draw a line; you go here and others go there. You would just pick up rocks and start throwing them at each other. Sometimes we would call it the battlefield of Kuruksetra [a site recorded in the Bhagavad Gita]. Kurus on one side and Pandavas on the other.[3]

With respect to sports, the boys were limited, as the only sport officially allowed was soccer, because ISKCON's founder Srila Prabhupada had sanctioned it.

The only sport we could play was soccer. Prabhupada had said, "No frivolous sports," but another time he said that soccer was OK. So they would give us a soccer ball, and we would play kickball or whatever. Everything had to be authorized by some quote from Prabhupada. That was the only thing they could ever find. So soccer was the only thing we were ever allowed to play.

After six months, Dasa's mother decided to move the rest of the family from Detroit to New Vrindaban. She hated living away from her eldest son and daughter and wanted to reunite the family. She therefore thought moving to New Vrindaban would allow her time to see Dasa regularly. But as it turned out, she ultimately had few opportunities to spend time with him, as the boys in the gurukula were actively discouraged from interacting with their parents, especially their mothers.

It was coming from the philosophical teaching of that time; families were the basis of binding people to the world. So family was bad. Any interaction you had with a family member was only going to bind you. That was very heavily preached from the top down.

One day, after his teacher inadvertently cut off much of his *shika* (tassel of hair on the back of an otherwise shaved head), he questioned Dasa in a way that revealed his negative attitude toward mothers.

"You're a *brahmacari* [renunciate monk] right? Because brahmacaries don't tell their mother things. You don't talk to your mother. Are you a brahmacari or are you a momma-cari?" Of course I said, "I am a brahmacari." He was manipulating me so I wouldn't tell my mother anything. If she had been told, she might have reacted. There just wasn't communication going on with parents.

The prevailing negative attitudes toward parents ultimately led Dasa to ask his mother to stop visiting him at the school.

> I remember my mother who would make attempts to come. So when it was "parents' day," she would be there every time. I remember the pressure because the teachers made fun of your parents for coming to visit you. Also, the ill feelings it would create among your friends who didn't have parents there who could visit, or wanted to. The unpleasantness that it caused was such that I remember having a conversation with my mother saying, "Don't come anymore." I told her, "It's just too painful for me. It's just easier if you don't come." Her crying and saying, "If that's what you want, that's what I will do." I just didn't want to deal with the aftereffects. It was just easier for me to survive. Suddenly you are dealing with your mother, and all the feelings are there again. You're opening it up again. That on top of some kid making fun of you. Or the teacher going, "Did you talk to your mother today? Why did you talk with her?" All those things combined. So let's just avoid the situation to begin with.

In 1980, Varnashram College was established at New Vrindaban to train the older boys. At the same time, the leader of the community, Bhaktipada, formally known as Kirtanananda, decided to send some of the older boys he deemed *brahmanas* (spiritual leaders and intellectuals) and *ksatriyas* (administrators and protectors) to ISKCON's gurukula in Vrndavana, India. The remaining boys, including Dasa, remained at New Vrindaban to receive training as *vaisyas* (agricultural producers) and *sudras* (skilled/unskilled workers). At first there were only eight to ten boys involved, but in time the Varnashram College grew to nearly one hundred adolescent boys. The training offered little academic instruction, since the boys' primary work was jobs in the community. Often this was fixing up the house in which the boys were living, before moving on to the next house in need of repair.

At this point Dasa became a monitor in the school, responsible for six of the younger boys. His job was to ensure that the boys in his charge got up in the morning, showered, and got to the temple in time for the morning program. He also had to see that the boys' living spaces remained neat, their clothes were washed, and each one carried out his daily chores.

The living conditions at the school were primitive or, as devotees might say, "austere." New Vrindaban was known across the movement for its austere living conditions, a fact that dissuaded many from moving there. As Dasa described it, the boys in the Varnashram College faced harsh living conditions, especially during the West Virginia winters.

The furnace never worked well, and it was always cold in the house. I remember there were times when it was warmer outside than inside the house. So we opened the windows, even though there was snow on the ground. All the pipes were frozen in the house, so we had no water practically all winter. There was some water in the basement, and we could get three buckets a day for bathing purposes, for everybody. I remember that you had to save some of the water [in the bucket] because it was so cold out on the porch that your feet would freeze to the ground. So you had to pour water on your feet to free them so you could rush to get back inside.

In September 1980 Dasa was initiated by his spiritual master, Bhaktipada. When he was living in the Detroit temple, Dasa watched a videotape on New Vrindaban, which showcased Bhaktipada. Dasa remembered thinking, "Wow, this guy looks cool. . . . It showed Bhaktipada standing up tall, looking across the mountains, saying that Krishna is here in the land of New Vrindaban." So I said, "I like that guy. He is the one that I want to be my guru."

Unlike his parents' generation, for whom initiation was a significant turning point in their devotional lives, for Dasa and his peers, initiation had little meaning at such an early age; it was just a matter of "going with the flow."

When you're eleven or twelve, it's hard to know how seriously to take it. I know the day I was initiated I didn't chant sixteen rounds. So that's how serious it was. There were times when I was in a sincere mood where I was chanting sixteen rounds for long periods. But how dedicated was I to chanting sixteen rounds for the rest of my life? The first day I didn't even follow it. . . . I never really aspired to it.

During this period Dasa began taking part in the communitywide practice of "going on the pick." "Picking" was a practice that ISKCON used during the late 1970s and early to mid-1980s. It involved selling products such as record albums, artwork, and stickers and hats supporting sports teams to members of the public. It also entailed soliciting donations for nonexistent charitable causes. Picking generally did not require revealing one's identity as an ISKCON member. Albeit controversial, the practice provided a significant source of funds for New Vrindaban and many other ISKCON communities (Rochford 1985:182–84; Rochford and Bailey 2006). Dasa described some of his early experiences of picking.

> The first time I went out was the summer of '80 when I was twelve. I went out with [name] in a brown K-car station wagon. We went gas station to gas station selling records, pretending we were from some rock-and-roll station. Selling records for $10, $15, or $20 a pop, whatever we thought we could get. We also went to grocery stores. There we claimed we were collecting on behalf of some abused local children. Whatever the line was, some child cause. Other times we would ride around in a car. I didn't like doing it, so he made a deal with me. I was to act retarded. He would pull up to people and say, "Hi, I am collecting on behalf of some retarded school, blah, blah. Would you give a donation?" For every person he hit up while I acted retarded he would give me a dollar toward my score [overall amount of money collected in a day].[4] I would just sit there scrunched up trying to look like what I thought was retarded.

Although the adults were pressured to go on the road collecting funds, Dasa and his peers normally stayed close to the community. Occasionally, he and some of the other boys were taken to Pittsburgh to distribute books and other religious literature. These experiences were memorable because of the negative reactions they often received. As Dasa recalled, "People would be gawking at you and saying nasty things. And you are trying to walk up to people and offer them a *Back to Godhead* magazine, trying to get them to take the magazine. People would spit on you."

While Dasa was serving as a monitor in Varnashram College, he was involved in an incident that troubles him to this day. As he described it, a teacher used him to physically assault another student.

> There was a boy [name] and there were three brothers [names]. And this boy and these three brothers just couldn't get along. The brothers

were all younger. So this boy would individually pick on the three brothers. . . . He was very mean. So [name of teacher] saw it going on over time, and he tried to deal with it. But finally he just said to the brothers, "OK, why don't you three just gang up and beat him up." So they did. Everyone was yelling, "Yeah, yeah." They get the guy down, and they are beating the heck out of him. But he was one of the most stubborn people I have ever met. They were choking him, he was turning purple, and he couldn't breathe. They kept telling him to give up. "Say you give up. Just say it, give up." And he wouldn't say it. Finally they let him go. So he lies on the ground for a couple of seconds, and the brothers are going, "All right." But he jumps up and starts pounding on one of them again. They drag him off, and the whole thing starts up all over again. . . . So he starts screaming, "It's not fair. It's three on one. Let me take them one on one. Then we can see who is toughest." This sort of thing. [Teacher's name] is like, "This isn't the point. This kid just needs to get the snot beat out of him. So he will get a little humility." So he takes me outside and says, "Take this guy out." So I remember I am beating him around, punching him. I knock him on the ground, and I have him around the throat. [Teacher's name] is going "more, more." I am hitting him in the face. His nose is bleeding; blood is gushing all over the place. I remember crying at this point. . . . At some point I got tired of hitting him in the face. So I put my hand on his face and started hitting him on the chest. So he bites me on the hand, biting, and wouldn't let go. My hand started bleeding. So I started whaling him on the side of the head. Finally I am screaming because my hand hurts. So [teacher's name] finally comes up and kicks him on the side of the head. His whole head jerks sideways, and my hand pops out.

Most of the adults knew little or nothing about what was taking place at the school. The majority were themselves busy attending the morning worship program, chanting their rounds, and working all day on behalf of the community. Moreover, as Dasa explained, "They were doing their part, and they assumed everyone else was doing the same. You read the books and hear Prabhupada saying how happy these children are going to be when they grow up. They will be devotees, having been sheltered all their lives."

Dasa's attitude toward what was happening to him and his peers began to change before the school closed. As he pointed out, "When I was younger, I didn't know to think differently." Yet this changed when another teenager joined the school and began challenging what he saw happening there.

> It wasn't until another boy came who was older than me, [name]. He didn't stay long. If you look at the pattern, by the time they were sixteen [years old], they were being thrown out of the community. That was pretty regular because they just couldn't handle them. So he was on the verge of that. He was two years older than me. If I was twelve or thirteen, he was fourteen or fifteen. He came in, and he was standing up for himself. He was going, "You can't do this to me. What do you think you're doing?" I remember [teacher's name] throwing him around physically, like bam off one wall and bam off another wall. I remember him saying, "You can beat me, but I won't change my mind." And hearing someone say that was like a lightbulb going off in my head. I went, "You know what, he's got something there." It was like a spark for me. That got me thinking, "You know I don't just have to stand here and take the smacks that I get." Before, I knew that I didn't deserve it. But you just took it. But then it was like, "You know what, I don't deserve it *and* I don't have to take it." He was the guy who did that for me. He lasted for less than six months. He knew this was abuse, and he wasn't going to take it. I credit him for awakening it in me.

Realizing that the mistreatment he had endured for years constituted abuse, Dasa became more vocal, challenging abusive teachers. In so doing however, he sometimes had to pay a price: "I started standing up and getting beat around more than I did before. When you stand out, you definitely take the brunt." In the following he describes an incident that revealed to him that the leadership of the community was not concerned about the abuse in the gurukula. It also showed him that resistance was a risky strategy.

> During this era I was freaking out because of the behavior of the teachers. I went to Bhaktipada's house and said, "I've got to talk with you. There is some really bad stuff going on down at that school." I was a teenager and didn't express myself very well. He said, "Oh really, OK." And he called [name of headmaster] and they had a meeting. I was there too. . . . Bhaktipada said, "Well [Dasa] is saying this." [Name of headmaster] sat there for a minute, and then he said, "Bhaktipada do

you know what is going on here? With this boy here. . . . You are the guru. I am the gurukula headmaster. I am your representative. What's happening is that I am trying to get this boy to surrender to you as his spiritual master, and he doesn't want to. Because he doesn't want to, he is telling these things and trying to make trouble." Bhaktipada listened to it, looked at me, and got angry and said, "Get down to the school and just do what you are supposed to do." [Name of headmaster] took me down to the school, knocked me around the room, and said, "If you ever do anything like that again you'll get more." . . . That was a big turning point. I went to the top guy. You think if you talk to the main person and tell him what's going on, that something will happen. If he doesn't do it, nobody is going to do anything. When I got a negative response from Bhaktipada, I just said, "OK, no more trying to expose this stuff. It just causes me grief. I've just got four more years until I am eighteen and [then] I am out of here."

After Varnashram College closed in the early months of 1984, a decision was made to begin a school for the older boys at the old Vrindaban farmhouse. The house was in a remote location, away from other devotees and the center of the community. Behind the decision to start the school was an ongoing problem at New Vrindaban: how to deal with the teenage boys who had not gone to India. In the winter of 1984, six months before Dasa was scheduled to leave for school in India, he and four other teenaged boys were "banished" to the old Vrindaban farm.

In many respects, these were some of his best days in the gurukula. As he remembered it, their teacher was easygoing and "by far one of the best teachers" he had ever had in the gurukula. Within a short period, the teacher, his wife, and their children moved into the house with them. The program emphasized the martial arts and physical education, and the teacher enabled Dasa and the other young men to build up their self-worth and respect.

He was the first teacher that showed me that I could use my labor, my endeavor, and my skills to make money honestly, legitimately. Take that money, give part of it as charity, and keep part of it. To that time my only experience was being on "the pick."

Under their teacher's guidance the boys started a business making "burfee" (milk sweets), which they sold at the various summer festivals

that attracted scores of people to New Vrindaban. On a festival weekend, the boys made as much as a few thousand dollars selling their milk
sweets.

> So we paid off all our expenses, and we said, "OK, one-third goes to-
> ward the deities;" and between four or five kids we had like two grand.
> . . . I worked. I made money. Krishna got his money. That was one of
> the first experiences where I felt, "Hey, this feels good. I like this."

With the profits the teacher took the boys to a local shopping mall.
He told them to walk around and make a list of the things they wanted
to purchase, along with the cost. He then distributed the money to each
of the boys for "tennis shoes, pants, Michael Jackson T-shirts, Harley
Davidson hats," and the like. Not unexpectedly, the community authorities were upset that not *all* their profits had gone directly into the community treasury.

The remoteness of their location also allowed the boys a degree of
freedom they had never before experienced. Being out of public view,
the boys' teacher allowed them to act contrary to the movement's religious principles and lifestyle.

> Looking back on it, [teacher's name] wasn't doing what he was sup-
> posed to do. There wasn't a schedule. He would do things like after
> dark we would start a bonfire, and he would get his guitar out and start
> singing. It was "Hare Krishna" all night long to a guitar beat. We
> wouldn't fall asleep until midnight, and we wouldn't get up for the
> morning program. Totally not allowed.

On other occasions the boys were able to "sneak out" at night to en-
joy some of the pleasures of the outside society.

> This is the time when we started to make endeavors on our own to be
> going to the movie theater, outside movie theaters, things like that.
> Mostly this was with the guys. We made a few daring tries with the
> girls too. What we had to do was go to the evening [temple] program,
> eat, dress, and go to bed. When it got dark out, we would run across
> the valley and have an older person with a vehicle pick us up. We'd
> jump in and cruise into town, watch the 11 o'clock showing, get back
> at one thirty in the morning. Run across the valley in the pitch dark,

'cause if you used the flashlight, they would catch you. So you had to navigate the valley up and down in the dark, which by the end we were expert at. Get up at like 3 A.M. We got [only] an hour and a half of sleep, but the movie was worth it. We made incredible efforts to do it.

It was while the boys were living at the old Vrindaban farm that girls started to come into the picture. Certainly there had been those "glances across the temple room" between the girls and boys and the occasional clandestine meeting behind the barn to talk to each other. But now, at the age of fifteen, girls took on greater significance to Dasa and his peers. As Dasa observed, "I like this one and this one likes me" began to have meaning. Because adolescent boys and girls were not allowed to "date," any expression of interest in a particular girl meant "engagement and marriage."

Dating was not allowed, at all. If you showed any real interest in anybody, it was automatically like you are going to be paired off. You are engaged now, very soon to be married. So there was no official intermingling like that. Publicly no one wanted to show any indication of interest in someone else.

At one point Dasa was engaged to a girl six years younger who attended the girls' school. But the pressure to pair off and prepare for marriage ultimately had a chilling effect on their relationship.

I was betrothed to this one girl. Whatever affection we might have had toward each other, by the end of the betrothal period, we almost couldn't stand each other. Thereafter, anytime you thought [about a girl] again it was like, "Oooooo. No. Stop." . . . You look at the other person and say, "You know I really don't like you."

In the summer of 1984, Dasa and twenty-one other young men left New Vrindaban for India to attend the movement's gurukula in Vrndavana. For Dasa and his peers bound for India, the trip was an ordeal. The boys and their gear were packed into an enclosed cargo truck for the ride to JFK Airport in New York. When they arrived, Dasa realized that no adults would be accompanying them to India. As the oldest, he felt the most responsible and did what he could to keep everyone together as they traveled. At the airport they unexpectedly met up with another group of devotee boys from a farm community in Pennsylvania who also were traveling to Vrndavana to attend gurukula.

> Also on the same plane there were like ten other kids coming from Gita Nagari. But we're the New Vrindaban kids. There is an adult with the Gita Nagari kids. He takes all his kids, goes to the back of the plane, and huddles them there. They had to chant two days of rounds because you lose a day in travel. So all they did the whole trip was sleep and chant. They were completely isolated. None of them were allowed to talk with us because we were the New Vrindaban kids. "We are in *maya*" [illusion]. We got our headphones and were watching the movie, listening to music, eating airplane food. They're down back eating their *prasadam*. The Gita Nagari devotees didn't know what to think of us.

They were met in Delhi by a teacher from the school in Vrndavana. From there they took a train to Mathura and finally a bus to the ISKCON community in Vrndavana. When they got there, they were startled to find two teachers at the school who had previously been kicked out of New Vrindaban for abusive behavior toward children and other misconduct.

The school was organized on the basis of *varnas* (social/occupational divisions). The top floor of the school was reserved for the ksatriyas and brahmins. The vaiyas and sudras were housed on the floor below. The first floor was reserved for classrooms and the school kitchen. Dasa was placed in the ksatriya program and lived on the top floor. Academically he faced the same problem he had had at New Vrindaban: little challenge, something that would lead to his departure from the school six months later.

Dasa shared a room with an American boy from San Francisco and three Bengali boys. The two Americans stayed on one side of the room, and the Bengalis occupied the other side. After the second or third week, there was an incident that alarmed the two American boys.

> [Name of American roommate] woke up, and he found semen all over his legs. He was like, "Look." I just said, "Whatever, you had a wet dream." He says, "No. Look." I say, "What do you mean look? It's gross." He says, "Look, my underwear is dry. I have semen all over my legs." And he was a heavy sleeper. . . . Obviously he had slept through

somebody releasing himself on him. So we say, "This is pretty heavy." So I went to [names of two school authorities]. I think I was fifteen at the time. As well as I could, I said, "Look, a guy in my room just got molested. You need to do something." So they say, "OK, we will look into it." Nothing happened that day. They didn't move anybody anywhere. So it was like we are going to be in there another night.

The two American boys devised a plan to protect themselves. They pushed their beds closer together and kept each other's hands touching during the night. If something should happen, they would quickly awaken the other. Dasa had also told several of his friends about the incident. One gave him a knife to take to bed just in case there was more trouble. Dasa described what happened.

Every once in a while we would tap each other and say, "You still awake?" We did like that for hours, and at some point we obviously both fell asleep. So I woke up feeling this poking in my side. I wiggled my hand, and he was not wiggling back. He was asleep and I felt another jab in my side. So I rolled over and looked up and it was one of the Bengali boys there with a pen knife. He was poking it in my side and smiling at me. I forget how he said it, but basically he was saying, "I am going to have sex with you. And you are going to just sit there and take it." [Name of American roommate] was asleep. He was out of it. So I reached under the pillow and pulled out the knife [name] had given me. I already had it open. I pulled it out and said, "You are going to kill me or I am going to kill you." "Over my dead body," sort of thing. He saw the knife, stood back, and went over to the corner of the room and sat down. And that's pretty much what we did all night. I sat in my corner holding my knife, and he sat in his corner just staring at me.

The next morning Dasa again went to the school authorities explaining that he had been physically threatened with a knife during the night by one of his roommates. He was assured that something would be done to rectify the situation. Yet for the next two nights Dasa remained in the room with his other roommates. Nothing else happened while all five boys stayed up watching one another during the night. Finally, Dasa was moved into another room with two other Americans.

That is all they [the school authorities] did. They just shuffled. Didn't change the situation. Didn't break it up. Just shuffled. The guy who actually poked me with the knife, I think they moved him to the guesthouse around the corner for maybe a week. Then he came back in the ashram. That was the extent of it. So that was one heavy experience.

This was not the last incident in which Dasa was party to threats and abuse. The next involved a teacher at the school with a reputation for physical violence against students.

At some point during the meal someone took a piece of potato and threw it. It hit someone else, and everybody just started throwing them around, back and forth. Ten or fifteen kids were involved in it. But what happened is my friend, whom I sat with most every meal, threw one that hit this kid, [name], at the other end of the hall. So he threw one back and hit my friend. . . . Everyone saw [name of teacher] coming around the corner. But because my friend wasn't paying attention, he threw the last chunk as the teacher was coming around the corner. The chunk hit his left leg. Everybody started to scatter. That was it. They knew what was coming. . . . He knew it came from our direction. So out of all the kids that were there, he pointed to the three of us. And he said, "You, you, and you, stand where you are. Don't move." It was me, [name of friend], and [name of another student]. So we are standing there and he comes up next to us. We have our hands folded, looking straight forward, and he just starts going [loudly], "Who did it? Who threw that potato?" So we are there looking straight forward, nobody wanting to say anything. 'Cause you know what is going to happen. This guy is notorious. You know what's going to come because you have seen it happen to others. No one says anything. Looking forward, just shaken. Finally he says, "If you don't tell me who did it, I'm going to beat all of you." But [name of friend] stepped forward and said, "I did it, Maharaja." So he moves right up into him, right up into his face, and pushes him up against the wall. Just starts beating him. It's hard to describe because you can't describe blow for blow, but it was a typical [name of teacher] beating where he would smack you in the face. You would cover your face, and he would bam you on the back of the head with his fist. From there, whatever direction your body moved, he would counteract with a strike. I don't know how long it lasted—thirty seconds. Whatever it was, it was intense. Really intense and violent.

After the boys returned to their room to care for their beaten friend, the abusive teacher arrived at the door looking for the boy he had beaten. Dasa lied and told the teacher that he had gone to the infirmary. Soon after, the principal of the school appeared at the door having heard about the incident. Reluctantly they allowed him in. He immediately escorted Dasa and his beaten friend to the office.

> So we went to his office and he locked the door, bolted the door. Closed the windows, closed the curtains, and we were sitting in the room and he started going, "OK guys, I know this was very traumatic, what just happened. You are feeling really upset. But I think you should wait one week before you tell anybody. Before you communicate this to anybody about what happened." While he was saying this, suddenly there was pounding on the door, "bam, bam." "[Name of principal] let me in. I just want to talk with him. I just want to talk with him. Let me in." Pounding at the door. We are all sitting there in complete silence. Staring at each other, not saying a single word. [Name of principal] starts going, "Go away [name of teacher]. Go away." Teacher: "I just want to talk with him." Finally there was just silence and he went away. [Name of principal] starts going, "You have to promise me, you won't say anything to anybody until you have digested it all." . . . We sat in his office for what seemed like hours until we were finally like, "OK, we promise we won't say anything to anybody about what happened."

According to Dasa, the students had little power to get someone to intervene on their behalf. In short, the boys felt they had no place to turn to for help.

> You had no outside support. The family, whom you didn't get much support from even when you were at home, was way over there. When we were in India, it got to the point where we were consciously saying, "Nobody wants us. We are unwanted and we don't give a crap anymore. Do what you will." Literally that was the attitude during that time in India.

It quickly became obvious to the principal that Dasa was getting little out of the academic training provided. Moreover, by remaining uninvolved in the academic program Dasa was undermining the morale of the other students.

At this point [name of principal] knew I was not doing anything at the school. He saw me there, just a body living there. He knew he couldn't force me into the classes because I took all the test-out exams and passed them all. They could force me to read the Bhagavad Gita because you can never have enough Bhagavad Gita! Also physical education. But other than that, he knew I was just sitting around not doing anything, not going anywhere, not gaining anything. . . . So it wasn't conducive to keeping the other kids in line. So he was like, "We want to get you out of here."

In December 1984, Dasa flew back to America, arriving at JFK airport in New York "without a penny." He called Bhaktipada's house at New Vrindaban and Bhaktipada arranged for him to work and live with a devotee in Brooklyn who had a business making and selling scarves. Dasa stayed there over the Christmas marathon season selling scarves before returning to New Vrindaban at the beginning of January.

Within weeks after returning to New Vrindaban, Dasa's mother died. She had been experiencing a variety of health problems related to her leukemia. Dasa told the story of his mother's death with despair, but as he said, "It's indicative of what went on around here [New Vrindaban]."

So she woke up early in the morning in her room, having heart problems, or something. All the devotees who had been helping her, watching her, said, "OK, time to go." They put her in a car and drove to the hospital. She went unconscious on the way there. She never regained consciousness and died later that day. In the meantime, I woke up and went to the morning program. My mother was not there, and somebody said, "Oh, your mother went to the hospital." So I said to myself, "This is serious." Usually when she goes to the hospital, it's a scheduled thing. This is unscheduled, early in the morning. So I said, "I need to get to the hospital." But of course ISKCON theology is "family is binding." Family contact, especially at the moment of death, is just going to rebind you to this world, etc. etc. So what happened is that from the top down, no one would give me a ride to the hospital. This was so she could die with the devotees chanting around her and not be attached to family. So I was running around trying to get a ride from anybody I could. Nobody would give me a ride. I didn't know why at the time. "No sorry." "My mother is dying at the hospital, and you are telling me no." It was unbelievable for me at the time because I didn't understand.

Later I understood it was because they would have gotten into trouble had they given me a ride. So finally I started walking down the road. I was going to get there if I had to walk to Wheeling. So I started to walk down the road, and this [devotee] girl, who was older than me, drove by, stopped, and asked if I needed a ride. I said, "Great," and she gave me a ride to the hospital. But of course, I got there too late. She had died like an hour before. She was unconscious the whole time, so it's not like it would have made a difference. But yes, I would have liked to have been there.

Adding to Dasa's shock and despair was the reaction he received upon returning to New Vrindaban. As he explained, "They were all freaking out because I got a ride with this woman who was two years older than me. . . . That was the scandal."

A few days later a funeral was held for Dasa's mother. Her body was placed in a wafer-board box, made by a local woodcrafter. Her coffin was then placed in the back of a Chevy Blazer, and devotees chanted as the body of Dasa's mother was taken for burial. As he recounts, "They buried her like that in a shallow grave. I remember the grave was already filling up with water. The casket was floating as they were dumping dirt on it. It was a half-ass effort."[5]

After his mother's death, Dasa's father "came back into our life." He immediately took Dasa's younger brothers and sisters back to North Carolina, where he was living at the time. Soon afterward, Dasa's father decided to return to New Vrindaban to raise his children. "He brought everyone together. It was the first time we were all living under one roof in five years."

Later that year Dasa was in a serious automobile accident with several other New Vrindaban devotees. The group was going out to collect funds when suddenly the driver lost control of the van and it plunged one hundred feet to the bottom of a ravine. No one was killed, but Dasa was seriously hurt, with three vertebra broken. Dasa spent the next three months strapped to a board to stabilize his back. During this time he stayed in the guest room at Bhaktipada's house. Bhaktipada often served him food and made sure that he was adequately cared for. Ironically, within months their roles were reversed after a disgruntled community member wielding a metal rod struck Bhaktipada violently on the head. Dasa was one of several devotees who accompanied Bhaktipada to the local hospital after the incident.

[Name of temple president] came running over. He got me and some-body else and said, "I am going to get his truck and back it up, grab him, and put him in the back." So two others and myself, one grabbed his shoulders, another his legs. We opened the truck up and set him in the back. We were all sitting in the back. [Name of temple president] was in the front and off we went. Going up the road. . . . He was dri-ving on the other side of the road, passing people, honking, going crazy. As we were driving, Bhaktipada kept coming in and out of some form of consciousness. It was actually kind of sentimental, but he kept say-ing, "Prabhupada, Prabhupada." "Krishna, Krishna." When you're in that state, you're not making that stuff up. . . . We were chanting to him. Telling him to lie still. "Hare Krishna. Hare Krishna."

Bhaktipada was hospitalized for about six weeks. When he returned to the community, he was, by all accounts, a very different person. The head trauma had left him mentally unstable and, as time would re-veal, largely incapable of managing New Vrindaban's daily affairs. As Dasa commented, Bhaktipada "was obnoxious and ornery" when he returned to the community at the end of December 1985.

What ended up happening was that he came back and people were try-ing to help the convalescing guru. But he was so obnoxious that nobody would do it. No one lasted more than a day. The summer before, when I had my broken back, I had spent time at his house and he had done a lot of things for me. . . . So from my point of view, he had been so nice to me. I was going to show my gratitude by sticking through his obnox-iousness. So I became the personal secretary, taking care of him from that point on. I looked after him.

Not long after taking over as Bhaktipada's personal secretary, Dasa faced another incident that influenced his life over the next several years. Bhaktipada made sexual advances toward Dasa while he was car-ing for him in January 1986.

He was not even halfway there at that point. But still, "Here is the guru. I am taking care of him." At the time it was more traumatic than it is now. . . . It bothered me a lot. A lot of the therapy I did after I left. When I was in college, I would go and read medical journals. They talk about when people get traumatic blows to the head, one of the things that happens is that they have increased or uncontrollable sexual desires. It's a normal, standard thing for people to have. Once I read this, it was like, a sigh of relief. "OK." Deep breath. It helped give a bigger perspective to the issue. But at the time it was very traumatic. I am his personal servant, his secretary, and he is making sexual advances on me. If I tried to tell anyone else around me, they weren't going to believe me.

After challenging his sexual advances, Dasa promised Bhaktipada, "If nothing ever goes on like this [again], it stays with me. It ends here. It's over. We don't even have to discuss it again." To Dasa's relief, there were no further incidents involving him. But Dasa did see other adolescent boys spending time alone with Bhaktipada in his room. "I'd look in, and there were awkward hands in strange places. Heads on people's laps. Similar setup to what had happened to me."

Bhaktipada's sexual improprieties, combined with the handling of his mother's burial and the abuse he had suffered in the gurukula, left Dasa struggling to break away from New Vrindaban and ISKCON.

At that time each little piece was breaking off. And when he [Bhaktipada] did the sexual encounter, that was like the biggest chunk. The biggest chunk was gone there. So at that point I didn't see him as the infallible, pure devotee. I was just looking at it as some guy who got whacked over the head. So I wasn't seeing him from the same perspective as a lot of people at New Vrindaban.

By December 1987, Dasa was finding it more and more difficult to serve Bhaktipada, and so he asked him for a temporary break from his duties as his personal secretary. Bhaktipada directed him to participate in the Christmas marathon, and Dasa collected funds with a longtime friend and first-generation devotee who had influence in the New Vrindaban community. While they were on the marathon together, Dasa told his friend that Bhaktipada had sexually accosted him. He also spoke of the suspicious incidents he had observed between Bhaktipada and other young men. His friend urged Dasa to speak with their other traveling companion about what had happened, which he did.

In the middle of the marathon, the three devotees returned to New Vrindaban and organized a meeting with some of the more influential members of the community. Dasa was asked to recount what had happened to him and to express his concerns about Bhaktipada's continuing to make sexual advances toward other young men in the community. Those present decided to confront Bhaktipada with the allegations the next morning. But someone at the meeting went directly to Bhaktipada to forewarn him, and the next day Bhaktipada claimed there was no truth to the allegations, that it was all a conspiracy. And as Dasa stated, "All the blind followers bought it."

With his allegations against Bhaktipada out in the open, Dasa found himself in an uncomfortable and even risky situation. Some community members were angry about what they saw as lies being spread about their spiritual master.

> So it became a bigger issue. The whole community knew about it now. Some of the people believed it; some of them didn't. It became a very polarizing thing. The next thing I knew there were people coming to me going, "You know what they do to people who offend the spiritual master. We aren't saying anything is going to happen, but you might want to make yourself scarce."

During the early months of 1988, Dasa left New Vrindaban. He first moved to Pittsburgh where he worked in a restaurant and lived on his own. But he wasn't able to fully escape his past at New Vrindaban. Before leaving the community, federal prosecutors had begun investigating the murder of a former New Vrindaban resident (Rochford and Bailey 2006), and because Dasa had served as Bhaktipada's personal secretary at the time of the murder, they wanted to question him.

> When I left, the federal prosecution was gathering evidence for their case. And a subpoena showed up with my name on it. I was living in Pittsburgh and they showed up at the restaurant, at my place of employment with the subpoena. But they didn't serve it because I wasn't there. So I packed up within the next day or two, because they didn't know where my apartment was. I split town so I wouldn't have to confront that. I had already had people making insinuated threats. I didn't need further threats with testifying. . . . So from the time I left in '88, until several weeks before the trial in 1991, when they finally gave me my subpoena, I had been living with a suitcase packed. For like two years, ready to go out the back door when somebody is knocking on the front door with the legal papers.[6]

Over the next months Dasa lived briefly in Arizona and then in Louisiana before finally moving back to Michigan in 1989 where his family had relocated after leaving New Vrindaban.

From 1989 until 1991 Dasa attended college, first at a community college and then at a major state university, and majored in business administration. During these years in Michigan he had virtually no contact with the movement, the exception being occasional phone conversations with two close friends who remained at New Vrindaban. Like many other college students, Dasa was intent on gaining his piece of the American dream.

> Since moving up to Michigan, except with my family, I was completely isolated from the Hare Krishna. . . . So there was no indication the life I was creating in Michigan had anything to do with the Hare Krishnas. So I created a whole life where I was very motivated. The box you could put me in was like the Yuppie mentality. I am going to get a degree. I am going to be successful. I am going to get the car. All those kinds of things. Upwardly mobile mentality. I developed a whole set of college friends around that.

As a college student Dasa worked a variety of low-paying jobs to pay his rent and other living expenses. For the most part, his transition into college life went smoothly, though there inevitably were difficulties.

> Learning the social interactions was troubling at first. I was speaking a language that people from the outside could not relate to. I think I could understand them better than they could understand me. I would say things and they would say, "Where the heck did that come from?" Expressions like "I'm fried," all the devotee colloquialisms. Words that are very specific to ISKCON. So learning to communicate was a shock, or was difficult. But I overcame that. It helped in my own evolution.

During the school year Dasa occasionally found himself in situations in which teachers or other students made jokes about the Hare Krishna. As he said, "I would just laugh and go along with it." On other occasions, his roommates asked about his past life and Dasa consciously avoided telling them any details of his involvement with the Hare Krishna. He would simply say, "I am from some really boring town in

Michigan, nothing really happened in my life. I had this boring answer down pat. It was so boring that they didn't ask any other questions."

In the summer of 1990, Dasa went on vacation to Los Angeles to visit two longtime friends from his days in the gurukula. By chance, he stumbled on an informal reunion of former gurukula students at the Los Angeles ISKCON community, which reconnected Dasa to his past identity as an ISKCON member, even though much of the conversation centered on the neglect and abuse they had experienced growing up in the gurukula. As he observed, "Just talking to people and stuff is clicking in your head and suddenly, 'OK, I am not so crazy. There are other people who had this stuff happen to them. So it did happen.' You start fitting the pieces together."

Within a few weeks after returning to Michigan from California, Dasa found himself in a situation in which his past life became visible to a number of friends and acquaintances. He had gone to an art fair at the University of Michigan with several student friends. It was a big event, and ISKCON members from the Detroit temple were there doing Hare Nam (public chanting), selling literature, and distributing prasadam. Dasa and his friends found themselves sitting on the grass near the event when the Hare Krishna devotees began singing and chanting in front of them.

> We were just sitting back talking, hanging out and laughing. The devotees were going by back and forth doing Hare Nam. And my friends started laughing at them. Joking. Cracking up. I was starting to get a little uptight. They [the devotees] were going back and forth, back and forth. So they stayed a point of attention for a long period. Not just "ha, ha" and off they went. The devotee who was playing the drum just didn't know what he was doing. It sounded like crap. It was just horrible. So I was sitting there. My friends were getting on my nerves because they were making fun of them, touching a nerve. And this devotee was bothering me even more because he was playing the drum so badly. So I just couldn't stand it any more, so I said, "Guys, watch this." They were all, "What's he going to do? What's he going to do?" I got up and walked over to the guy [devotee] playing the drum. They were all chanting and doing their dancing. I walked up to him and said, "Hey, can I play that?" He was butchering it, and he said, "It might look simple, but it's really a very intricate East Indian instrument that takes

months and years to learn." I just looked at him and said, "Look I went
to gurukula in Vrndavana, India, my name is [name] Dasa. Can I have
the drum please?" . . . He gave me the drum, and I turned around and
looked at all my friends who were going, "All right, you got the drum
off the guy." Suddenly I started playing it, way better than the devotee
did. They were going, "Oh my God." I stood there for the next twenty
minutes playing the drum for them. The kirtan never stopped. Everybody got real ecstatic, jumping up and down.

After he finished, Dasa returned to where his friends were sitting.
"They were shocked. . . . They were just going, "What is all that about?
That's weird." And walked away. I didn't see most of them ever again."
As word spread about the incident with the Hare Krishnas, many of
Dasa's friends began to question their relationship with him. As he said,
"And sure enough, I would say that 50 percent of the people I knew
just didn't want to talk with me again." Not surprisingly, his room-
mates quickly learned about what had happened. For them, reconciling
Dasa's past involvement with the Hare Krishna was possible only be-
cause they knew him well and he didn't conform to their image of a
"cult member."

I remember the guy sharing a room with me going, "You know, I am
glad you didn't tell me up front because I never would have had anything to do with you. But now that I know you, I have to stop and re-
think my prejudices. If you had told us straight away, we would have
never let you move in here." So now it was like wait: "You drink, you
party. Are you still involved in all of that?" I am going yes and no. Yes,
I am involved in that, but no, I am not following the religion. I am the
same person."

Reflecting back, Dasa says that it was the reunion in Los Angeles that
led him to reveal his Hare Krishna past.

I wouldn't have said anything if it hadn't been for the reunion in LA in
1990. . . . There I saw some people who made me feel more comfort-
able with the stuff I was running away from. I just couldn't deal with it.
I was avoiding it. I was denying it. It helped me to be able to say, "I am
OK with this well enough to be able to at least say it out loud now."

In the summer of 1991 another gurukula reunion was held in Los Angeles. This one was widely advertised among members of ISKCON's second generation, and 100 to 150 young people from all over North America came to take part in the event. Nonetheless the authorities at the Los Angeles ISKCON community were far from happy about the reunion and the presence of so many second-generation youths,[7] and the temple president insisted that the reunion be held away from the temple. Accordingly, the events were held at a nearby park. To many adults in the Los Angeles community—leaders and rank-and-file members alike—ISKCON's young people with their long hair, short dresses, and youthful manner appeared to have rejected their Krishna conscious upbringing, which both disgusted and angered some of the older devotees in the community.

The 1991 reunion further helped Dasa to come to terms with his past. Unlike the previous reunion at which the majority of the youths present were from the Los Angeles area, many of those taking part in 1991 had attended gurukula with Dasa, either in India or at New Vrindaban. As Dasa described it, talking with his gurukula friends stirred his memories of what had happened to him during his childhood.

> I remember that was a breakthrough year for me, because I started talking to these other devotee kids. There was a point, from '88 until that time, where I started thinking, "You know I must be just making this stuff up. There is just no way that people could be this way." I had memories. I would think about it and look around at normal society, where there is also abuse, but I thought I must just have this wild imagination to come up with all of this. "I've just got to be nuts to be coming up with all these crazy thoughts." But then when you start sitting down and talking with other people and they go, "Do you remember the time?" and you go, "Oh my God, yeah." There is the validation; "No, I am not crazy. It actually did happen." You start talking to people and ask them, "What do you remember happening?" And so you realize, "OK, so something did happen."

That year, 1991, also was a turning point in another way for Dasa and many other young people present at the reunion. Over several days, intergenerational meetings of a dozen second-generation youths, one longtime male teacher, and the past and present minister of education for ISKCON, were held.[8] Their discussions began after a half-day session at ISKCON's North American Board of Education meetings on the state of the movement's second generation, and they were perhaps the first official opportunity for first- and second-generation devotees to talk openly about the past and their grief and anger about the plight of ISKCON's children.

Out of the meeting between first- and second-generation devotees grew Project Future Hope, the name deriving from ISKCON's founder, Srila Prabhupada, who referred to the children as the movement's "future hope." Project Future Hope was meant to provide support and assistance to ISKCON's second generation—help in locating jobs and apprenticeships and learning new skills. A newsletter was planned in order to keep second-generation youths informed and connected with one another. Start-up funds for the project were committed, and Dasa was asked to become the director. As Dasa noted, "I was enthusiastic, happy about the prospects of dealing with this. Let's really get into it was my attitude." After the reunion, Dasa returned to Michigan to pack up his belongings. Within a month he had moved to Los Angeles.

Along with a team of other second-generation devotees, Dasa began working on the newsletter in 1992. Their efforts were helped when a second-generation devotee, who was producing a newsletter in England for gurukulis, arrived in Los Angeles to lend his expertise. The newsletter ultimately became a magazine entitled *As It Is*. When the first issue of the publication was about to go to press, the temple president of the Los Angeles community called Dasa to his office.

[Name of temple president] starts, "You're not going to publish that magazine." I said, "What are you talking about?" He went on, "You're not going to do it while you're living here in the temple." I said, "Come on, it's no big deal. It's just a gurukuli newsletter." He replied, "The LA temple wants no connection whatsoever with this thing. We want you to move out if you're going to go ahead with it." So I looked him in the eye and said, "You want me out, you take my stuff and throw it on the street. I am not depending on you. I have lived independently; I can do what I need to do. I'm grateful for being allowed to stay here, but I am not dependent on you. If you want me out, then throw my stuff out on the street." He backed off and we published it. Two weeks later he was patting me on the back in front of the temple, after he read it and saw that it was OK. We purposely made the first issue so that it was like fluff. There was nothing in it controversial. After that, the temple president, whose son went through the gurukula, became a strong and vocal supporter.[9]

The funds required to keep the project operating did not materialize. So after the initial funds were exhausted, those working on Project Future Hope found themselves taking jobs and raising money, all the while educating devotees about what had happened in the gurukula. As Dasa explained, when funding was denied by both ISKCON's North American GBC and the newly established ISKCON Foundation, money for their work "came out of our pockets for two years." To Dasa, the refusal of the leadership to provide financial assistance spoke volumes about their commitment to his generation.

> The leadership really didn't want to address anything. They were just hoping we would go away. That was the feeling we were getting then. "If we [the leadership] put it off long enough, eventually they will just get frustrated and go away." Then they wouldn't have to deal with it. That's what they were hoping. . . . Eventually I realized that they [the leaders] weren't going to do anything.

After struggling for two years to bring youth issues to the forefront of ISKCON, Dasa decided he could not continue any longer. "One day I just woke up and said, 'It's not my responsibility. I didn't do this to anyone. I don't have to clean it up. I don't need to be dealing with it.' So that, combined with other reasons, I left."

In January 1994, with his devotee girlfriend (and future wife), Dasa left Los Angeles for Oregon. The two of them stayed with an old friend of Dasa's in Portland for about four months. It was a time of personal reflection about the future direction of his life, as he appeared once again to be finished with ISKCON. But while he was in Portland, Dasa received several phone calls from devotees at New Vrindaban. During his several years of absence, the community had radically changed its theology and religious practice. Under Bhaktipada's direction, New Vrindaban had become an interfaith community blending Hindu, Christian, Buddhist, and Native American traditions (see Doktorski 2003; Rochford and Bailey 2006). But in 1991, Bhaktipada was convicted of racketeering and mail fraud, although the jury failed to reach a verdict on more serious charges of murder (Rochford and Bailey 2006). While Bhaktipada was on house arrest awaiting the outcome of his appeal,

New Vrindaban was reverting back to its original religious orientation and was also looking for new ways to finance the community.

> When I was in Portland, a couple of older devotees from New Vrindaban called and said that the community was in a state of transition; the old system was going out, which meant the interfaith, and they were integrating more traditional Hare Krishna things. But more important to me was they wanted to start a community-based business. . . . It interested me enough, "Here I am. What am I going to do with this [college] degree? I am sitting in Portland whittling away what little funds I had left. I am almost broke. Got to make a living somewhere." So we moved here [New Vrindaban] in May of '94.

Upon returning to New Vrindaban, Dasa received a cautious welcome by members of the community. By now, many of them had come to realize that Bhaktipada had abused his authority as guru and leader of the community. Moreover, rumors continued to circulate about Bhaktipada's illicit sexual activities (Rochford and Bailey 2006).

> Some people came up to me and made statements that I would translate as apologies. They didn't come straight out and say, "I am really sorry." But they would say . . . "Hey look it took me a long time to figure it out." So there were people saying those types of things. And [name of present leader of New Vrindaban] came to me at some point and said, "Now knowing everything that you have been through, it's amazing to me you are even interested in any of this."

Soon after moving back to New Vrindaban, Dasa was asked to become a member of the community's management board. In this position he played a significant role in the transformation of New Vrindaban from a commune to a community of independent householders. To make this change and, at the same time, raise critically needed resources for the community, New Vrindaban began selling parcels of its land to devotees. This change toward privatization was, as Dasa pointed out, "a real struggle. It was difficult to change the mindset from communal to individual ownership." Dasa and his wife bought forty acres from the community, soon after which their son was born.[10]

During the Christmas seasons of 1996 and 1997 Dasa was actively involved in the community business, which was intended to replace

New Vrindaban's long-standing reliance on "picking." From carts stationed in shopping malls during the busy holiday season, devotees sold various products such as specialty foods and candles. But when the financial fortunes of the community business turned sour during the second year, individual devotee entrepreneurs took it over. One of them was Dasa: "One year I made some decent money, and the next I lost a lot of money. It's been a progression . . . going from nothing, a community that is in financial shambles, to starting this business."

After returning to New Vrindaban, a constant source of frustration for Dasa was the inexperience of the first-generation devotees with respect to running a business. Since then, because of this, he has often found it useful to look outside the movement for help and support, and he has gone back to school, taking business and other courses at a local college. Surprisingly, he has found those outside the movement generous with their advice and support.

> There are opportunities, but you have to step outside of this limited [devotee] circle. I have been making those leaps in the last couple of years. And it is not just that you find someone who is knowledgeable, but you also find encouragement, which is something often lacking from devotees.

Dasa's estrangement from the first generation, and increasingly from the New Vrindaban community more generally, also is revealed in where he lives. Although he does live within a short distance from the temple, he bought a piece of land with no devotee neighbors nearby. As he says, "The property we bought is surrounded on all sides by non-devotees. And this was a conscious choice. I made that choice. I have stable neighbors that are friendly, helpful, and they are not intrusive."

Although seeking distance from his lifelong association with devotees and the New Vrindaban community, Dasa continues to be drawn back in ways that he often finds frustrating. In essence, he finds himself both in and between two social worlds, that of ISKCON and that of the conventional society. He feels pushed away by the first generation yet oddly drawn back into the devotee community despite his own reason and judgment, which tell him to do otherwise.

> Slowly but surely the people in the movement, the people in leadership positions more specifically, systematically push you away. I find myself

when I go to those [community] meetings, ignoring the intelligence in me saying, "Get the hell away from this. What the heck are you doing?" No, I want to be involved, I want to make it positive. I want to help change this place [New Vrindaban]. To do this I sometimes find myself ignoring the intelligent part inside me.

But his words beg the question of how Dasa, at the age of thirty, sees his own social identity. When asked whether he still considers himself a devotee, Dasa very quickly responds, "No." But this question makes him think about how those outside the movement "define" what a devotee is. Framed in these terms, he rejects the very idea of being a devotee. "For me, when people ask if I am a Hare Krishna, or am I a devotee, this is the image they think of: the temple guy, driving in the van, talking to himself strangely in the prasadam hall. No I am not that." He then offers another example that reveals his own resistance to the very idea of being a devotee. Once again, his reference point is from the outside looking into the devotee world.

I will give you an example. My mother-in-law goes into town to have her car worked on. The mechanic there figures out that she has an English accent, figures out she is a Hare Krishna. So he says to her, "Are you a pure devotee or are you a fringie?" She thought about it for a minute and said, "Well I guess I would have to be a fringie. Because I am not a pure devotee." For her this means she is not like Prabhupada. For the mechanic, his response was, "Good. I don't like those pure devotees because they never smile or laugh." And when she came back and told me that story it was like, "What more can you say?" That's why when people ask me if I am a devotee, no. I am not that image of what a devotee is.

Despite his rejection of being a "devotee" as part of his self-identity, Dasa continues to believe in God, although his concept of God clearly differs from the one he learned growing up.

D: In a way all the experiences have shaped who I am now. Just generically speaking.
EBR: But what parts do you hold on to? [pause] Do you believe in God?
D: Yes.
EBR: That God is Krishna?

D: Yes. I think the term I found the other day was a *deist*. I believe there are higher powers that can take on various forms and personalities. I also think there are intelligent processes behind what is going on.

In reflecting back over the past ten years of his life, Dasa sees how the philosophy of Krishna Consciousness has moved back and forth from the center to the periphery of his thinking.

At different points in my life, Krishna Consciousness has had more or less significance. There were times, in '88 through '91, where I didn't speak a word of it. I just didn't say anything to anybody. So obviously it was low on the priority list. Other things were being absorbed. But even still inside myself. . . . Even though I was gone for three and a half years, I would still wake up in the morning, no matter how hard I tried to run or get away from it, thinking of Krishna.

After leaving school and becoming involved in Project Future Hope, Krishna Consciousness again took on a greater and more direct role in Dasa's life.

Probably around the time I went to LA, when I was beginning to come to terms with some of that stuff, it did take on a bigger significance. I was pulling out the Bhagavad Gita, which I hadn't done since I was forced to in school. I sat down and started reading through the whole thing. And going, "That's what that means." Now I have a frame of reference in my own life, so that when he [Krishna] says, "Don't be attached or don't do this. Watch out for that. This could happen to you." I would say, "This is someone who is really smart, who put down some intelligent words here. I could learn something by reading this."

Yet in 1998, Dasa again found himself withdrawing from the New Vrindaban community and religious involvement, with Krishna Consciousness moving to the periphery of his life. As he explained, "It has taken a back seat to another stage of growth in my life, family responsibilities and business." Yet while work and his family have become more central, his son helps keep him involved in Krishna Consciousness and in the New Vrindaban community. Like many parents who move away from their religious involvements during adolescence, only to return when they have their own children, Dasa has maintained his connection to Krishna Consciousness for the sake of his four-year-old son. Dasa's wife often takes their son to the temple so that he can play with other devotee children, and the family also attends the weekly Sunday feast and worship service at the temple. Moreover because his wife's parents, whom Dasa labels "orthodox," live next door, his son has learned a considerable amount about Krishna and the philosophy of Krishna Consciousness. Also, despite Dasa's tendency to overlook his own role in his son's religious socialization, he clearly has been influential. Dasa provided two revealing examples.

> Just the other day we took out a trunk. We have been going through our stuff and cleaning things out before the winter comes in. There was a trunk and there was an *arti*[11] tray in it. He pulled it out and he was really into it. And he asked me, "What's this for?" I said, "You put an incense stick in there, and you offer it to the deity or a picture of Krishna." He pulled out the next one and asked, "What's this one for?" "Oh, that is for the gee lamp." He didn't know what a gee lamp was, so I explained, "You remember the fire when we go to the temple?" So he found one of those little candles and stuck it in [the lamp] and put it on the tray. Then he says, "What's this for?" "It's where the flower goes." So he goes outside and runs around for a while, and it's hard now because there aren't flowers around, but he came back with something. And he put it on the tray. So he set up this whole tray. He even got this little conch shell. He went and filled it with water. So you realize he is curious. There is no reason not to teach him.

As Dasa's observation suggests, this ongoing socialization has influenced his son's view of the world, although in this instance he uses it to thwart his mother.

> We will be driving down the road and [his mother] will say, "Sit down. Be good in the car. Don't kick the back of the seat." And he will go, "You're not in charge." And she'll go, "Yes I am." He'll say, "No you're not. Krishna is in charge."

Yet when it comes to schooling his son, Dasa has no intention of educating him at an ISKCON school. In the fall of 2000, his son entered the public elementary school near the New Vrindaban community. As Dasa observed, "There aren't any devotee schools that I would send him to at this point. They are too unstable. Weak curriculum. There is nothing substantial there. As far as the ABCs, 123s go, the public school is just fine." Moreover, he wants his son to "connect with both societies" (ISKCON and the mainstream culture) and to avoid the isolation that he and his generation faced in the gurukula. As part of this, he wants his son to receive formal training in the philosophy and rituals of Krishna Consciousness. He wishes that the New Vrindaban community would close its day school and instead provide an afterschool and weekend program for religious training. As Dasa stated, "The public schools do an adequate or better job than most of these devotee schools ever could. But what is missing is the religious aspect. There is a need to infuse Krishna in their learning."

In the summer of 2000, Dasa and his family moved from New Vrindaban to Los Angeles where Dasa began graduate school at a major university in pursuit of his master's degree in business administration (MBA). Two years later he received his degree and began working as the vice president for a devotee-owned jewelry business based in Los Angeles. The company produces high-end jewelry, which has been very popular in the Japanese market. The owner of the company is a lifelong friend of Dasa's who attended gurukula with him at New Vrindaban and in India. The jewelry is produced at New Vrindaban in a building that during the late 1970s and 1980s served as a warehouse for heavy equipment. The business employs twenty-five to thirty people at the New Vrindaban location, half of whom are devotees. As Dasa says, New Vrindaban and the devotees are "an inerasable part of my history." Yet he remains largely separate from ISKCON, finding little reason to go to the Los Angeles temple except on rare occasions to meet with friends. "I have relationships with people with varying degrees of involvement in ISKCON, but I have no involvement or relationship with the institution." He does, however, attend the ISKCON-sponsored Rathayatra festival each summer at Venice Beach on the Westside of Los Angeles.

Before leaving for California, Dasa and his wife divorced, although she and their son continue to live in Los Angeles. Dasa has since begun a serious relationship with a woman with no previous ties to ISKCON or the Krishna devotees. He and his former wife are cooperatively raising their son. To the surprise of both, their son retains a strong interest in Krishna Consciousness. Recently he asked, through his devotee grandmother, for deities to be set up at home. As Dasa commented, "He wants more involvement in spiritual activities. So we have been trying to figure out what to do; trying to find someone around the temple area that has a Sunday school program going. Unfortunately, no one seems interested in doing these sorts of things." His son also stays spiritually connected by returning each summer to spend a month with his devotee grandparents, who continue to live at New Vrindaban. Largely because of his son, Dasa remains committed to generational issues and is developing plans for a one-week summer camp at New Vrindaban for pre-teen devotee children. As he pointed out, "My involvement is now going to head in that direction. I am still involved in gurukuli issues, but they have had their day as far as my generation goes. My friends and myself are very family oriented, and we need to create something for our children. And I want to do that."

Although it is not representative of all young people who grew up during ISKCON's formative years, Dasa's life story nonetheless illustrates a number of issues that I will discuss in the remainder of the book. Among the most important was the ISKCON leaders' antifamily stance. Because they were committed to expanding the movement through preaching and book distribution, they denigrated family life in an effort to protect these goals. Tragically this resulted in the neglect and abuse of children and women. As we will see in the next chapter, however, family life nonetheless grew and ISKCON's communal structure disintegrated, forcing parents and children out of ISKCON's communities. ISKCON thereafter became a congregational movement, one that had been forever changed.

2

Family, Culture, and Change

The only way that the Supreme Lord can be worshipped is through the functioning system of *varnashram* [culture]. Because it facilitates, [it] gives the maximum opportunity for success in the practice of *sadhana-bhakti*.

—Prabhupada disciple, November 1992

We have the Absolute truth but we lack a culture to support it. . . . And without culture, we find ourselves facing so many different problems as a society. How to educate our kids? Where to earn a living? How to live peacefully in Krishna Consciousness. So many things.

—Prabhupada disciple, May 1992

Movement culture is an area of study that has been largely neglected by investigators of new religions (Rochford 2007), a surprising oversight for a number of reasons. First, some scholars (Dawson 1998:159; Robbins and Bromley 1992) argue that the principal significance of new religious movements is cultural, that they are laboratories of social experimentation and cultural innovation. Second, as prophetic movements, new religions challenge the legitimacy of the existing social order and its cultural underpinnings (Bromley 1997, 2004). Third, given their antistructural tendencies, new religious groups are inclined toward radical forms of social organization grounded in oppositional religious cultures (Lofland 1987; Rochford 2007; Stark 1996; Wilson 1990). The evidence suggests that religious movements in fact produce more elaborate and robust cultures than do their political counterparts (Lofland 1987:105).

ISKCON's development in North America has entailed continuing conflict over the nature of its religious culture. At the heart of the controversy has been incorporating family life into its communities while preserving the movement's goal of transforming American society through preaching and conversion. Because it was unable to create a movement culture inclusive of families, ISKCON profoundly changed during the 1980s and 1990s. But before discussing this, I will briefly consider the place of marriage and family life in other alternative religious communities.

Marriage and Family in Religious Communities

Marriage and family life have always been central to the fate of communal societies, both religious and secular. Kanter's (1972) investigation of nineteenth-century American communes found that marital and familial ties often conflicted with a community's need to build and sustain its members' commitment and loyalty. That is, only by renouncing couple and family relationships could intimacy become a collective good serving the interests of the community as a whole. As Kanter makes clear, utopian communities, both past and present, face the delicate task of building relational structures that "do not compete with the community for emotional fulfillment" (1972:91). To do otherwise is to put the communal enterprise at risk (also see Coser 1974:136–49; Zablocki 1980: 146–88).

Yet previous research has demonstrated that religious communities, especially those favoring a more disciplined way of life, are more stable and exist over longer periods than do their secular counterparts (Berger 1981:129; Foster 1991; Hall 1988; Kanter 1972; Zablocki 1971). Two of the most successful American religious societies, the Shakers and the Oneida, eschewed the nuclear family, although for somewhat different reasons and by means that represented opposite extremes (Foster 1991). Under the leadership of Mother Ann Lee, the Shakers practiced strict celibacy, which allowed women to escape the domestic demands of child rearing, thus freeing them to devote all their energies to the needs of the Shaker community. It also afforded women the possibility of greater equality with Shaker men (Foster 1991:31). By contrast, the Oneida community, founded by John Humphrey Noyes, favored group marriage, or what came to be called "complex marriage." As the *Handbook of the Oneida Community* noted in 1875, "Two people should not 'worship and idolize each other. . . . The heart should be free to love all the true and worthy, [without] selfish love'" (quoted in Carden 1969:49).

Other religious groups devised still other ways to control marital relations. The early Mormon practice of polygamy simultaneously limited the exclusive ties between marriage partners and created an elaborate network of interconnected kinship ties that served the interests of group solidarity (Foster 1991:205). The Amana communities reduced the individual's spiritual status and community ranking following marriage (Barthel 1984:55). In fact, their marriage ceremony itself included a text that read, "To be married is good, but to be unmarried is better" (Kanter 1972:88).

With respect to family life, successful utopian communities of the past restricted parents' involvement and emotional attachments with their children (Kanter 1972:90). Instead, children were viewed as communal property, and child rearing became the responsibility of the community as a whole and not of just the biological parents. At Oneida, for example, young children were separated from their parents and placed in the communal "Children's House," reminiscent of Dasa's separation from his parents at a young age. Until the age of twelve they attended school, worked part time, and received religious training. Parents had only limited involvement in their children's day-to-day lives and were subject to group sanction for becoming emotionally attached to them (Carden 1969:64–65).

Although we know that marriage and family life affect the fate of communal societies, empirically and theoretically we know much less about the circumstances under which these societies gain or perhaps lose control over these exclusive relationships. My discussion traces the history of marital and familial relationships in the North American ISKCON, demonstrating how changes in the structure of the family during the 1980s initiated a process of internal secularization defined by outward-expanding congregationalism and its accompanying decommunalization. My description and analysis emphasize how cycles of economic growth and decline influenced ISKCON's ability to control family relations.

Marriage, Family, and Social Control during ISKCON's Early Years

Until the early 1980s, ISKCON's leadership exercised considerable control over the lives of its members. Accordingly, to practice Krishna Consciousness and be an ISKCON member required cutting ties with the outside secular culture and living a disciplined, communal way of life (Rochford 1985). Despite these personal sacrifices, devotees willingly committed themselves to the requirements set forth by their guru, Srila Prabhupada. Perhaps in no other way was this more evident than in marriage and family life.

Sexual Politics and Marriage

In 1965 and 1966 when Prabhupada attracted his first followers on the Lower East Side of New York City, he was surprised when a number of young women expressed interest in joining his spiritual movement. Within the first year, he had initiated his first female disciple (Goswami, Satsvarupa 1980:184), and by the time of his death in 1977, Prabhupada had initiated approximately fifteen hundred women into his Krishna Consciousness movement (Prabhupada Disciple Database 2006).

Right from the beginning, the question arose as to how to deal with the presence of both unmarried men and women in ISKCON. The spiritual ideal was for single men and women to be strictly segregated, with little or no contact between them. But Prabhupada realized that this was a difficult proposition in America, where "boys and girls are accustomed to mix[ing] freely with one another" (Prabhupada 1992:865). The problem intensified in 1967 when ISKCON opened a temple in the Haight-Ashbury section of San Francisco and began recruiting large numbers of youths who took up residence in the temple complex (Rochford 1985:158–59).

In 1967, one of Prabhupada's first woman disciples raised the possibility of creating a separate women's ashram to house the growing number of unmarried women joining the movement. In response to her suggestion, Prabhupada pointed to the inherent dangers of allowing men and women to freely associate with each other.

> In the scriptures it is said that the woman is just like fire and the man is like a butter pot. The butter melts in the pot while in contact with the fire. . . . In spiritual life attraction of man and woman . . . hampers very much, therefore some sort of restrictions are necessary to check this hampering problem. (Prabhupada 1992:851)

Creating separate living quarters for men and women provided one barrier to male-female interaction. But this was only a partial solution, given that men and women still were housed within the temple complex and thus close to each other. On those occasions when men and women found it necessary to interact, their exchanges were formal and ritualistically structured. A male devotee was required to address a woman as "Mother," and a woman devotee was expected to treat a man as if he were her son.

Limiting contact between members of the opposite sex often required rather extreme strategies. Consider the account of one woman who reminisced about her early days as a devotee in the early 1970s. The occasion was a meeting of ISKCON's North American Board of Education in 1992.

> I remember when I lived in Boston, I had to try and avoid all association from all the men. . . . Just one simple example. I wasn't allowed, *ever,* to look up from the floor if there was a man around. (laughter) In fact we [women] lived on the fourth floor. If there was a man going up the stairs and I was going down, I had to go all the way back up to the fourth floor. I couldn't be anywhere near the stairs if there was a man on the stairs. And if a man walked near me, I'd put my face in a corner until they walked past. I'd face the wall and go like this (covering her face with her sari), in the corner (laughter). [Man:] Having lived as a *brahmacari* [celibate male] in the same temple at that time, I would say you're not at all exaggerating (her emphasis).[1]

Given that the movement's membership was composed of young people in their late teens and early twenties, a life of celibacy was a difficult goal for many, and Prabhupada recognized that many of his male disciples would be unable to live the celibate life of a brahmacari. Accordingly, during his first year in America, Prabhupada received the first of what would prove to be many requests for permission to marry. While reminding his disciples that married life and the entanglements it entailed made it "difficult to make any progress in Krsna[2] Consciousness" (Prabhupada 1992:852), he nevertheless allowed marriage between his disciples. As he told one of his young male disciples in 1969,

> So far as your occasionally getting agitation from *maya* [the material energy], the answer is simple; one must either strictly control the senses, or else he must get himself married. If one is strong enough in Krsna Consciousness, then there is no reason to become *grhastha* [house-

holder], but if one is still disturbed by sex desire, then marriage is the only other possibility. (Prabhupada 1992:857)

Quite apart from the fact that the majority of his male disciples proved incapable of subduing their sexual urges in brahmacari life, in accordance with ISKCON philosophy, the presence of large numbers of women made the expansion of family life inevitable. As Prabhupada explained in a 1975 letter to one of his disciples,

> Of course, it is better to remain unmarried, celibate. But so many women are coming; we cannot reject them. If someone comes to Krsna it is our duty to give them protection. . . . So the problem is there, the women must have a husband to give protection. (Prabhupada 1992:869)

In accordance with the Vedic scripture, Prabhupada recognized that for his women disciples, marriage and family life represented the basis of their spiritual and material fulfillment. Unlike men, for whom celibate brahmacari life represented the spiritual ideal, for women, it was thought that "their natural propensity" was to "desire good husbands, a good home, [and] children" (Prabhupada 1992:854). In many respects, marriage represented two very different social realities for the men and women in ISKCON. For women, marriage was seen as an aid to their spiritual progress in Krishna Consciousness. By contrast, for men, marriage represented a sign of weakness and "spiritual fall-down." Only men incapable of controlling their senses found reason to marry. If a male devotee was committed to going back to Godhead, he remained celibate, dedicating his life to spiritual activities. Because of the widespread acceptance of this philosophy, marriage meant a loss of status for men but had the opposite effect for women.

In most cases, ISKCON marriages were arranged, which often meant that devotees entering into marriage had only minimal contact with their spouse before the marriage ceremony. The responsibility for locating suitable marriage partners generally fell on temple presidents and other ISKCON authorities,[3] and frequently these decisions were guided more by community needs and economic considerations than by concerns for marital compatibility. For example, if a man or woman raised significant sums of money doing sankirtan, a marriage partner would be chosen with an eye toward causing minimal disruption to his or hers financially lucrative service. A temple president might even have refused to arrange a marriage for a woman successful at sankirtan, especially if this meant she would be required to relocate in order to be with her husband. Whatever else went into arranged marriages, questions of romantic love were not a consideration.

Although the Vedic literature provides a somewhat mixed message, Prabhupada taught that householders could gain spiritual realization in their present lifetime. After all, he himself had been a family man for much of his life. Moreover, Bhaktivinoda Thakura, the father of his own spiritual master, preached that in the present age Krishna Consciousness was best cultivated in the role of a householder (Prabhupada 1992:861). Prabhupada considered householders celibate if they limited their sexual activity to begetting Krishna-conscious children and then only if they adhered to strict rules regulating sexual intercourse. Sex was permitted each month only when the woman was most fertile and could only take place after both husband and wife chanted fifty rounds of the Hare Krishna mantra on their beads, a process taking five or more hours. To use sex to serve Krishna and the spiritual master was a sacred act, and to have sexual relations to gratify the senses was sinful. As Prabhupada explained in a 1976 lecture,

> In this way you will find, according to [the] Vedic system, [that] sex life is practically denied. But because we are now in the conditioned state, it is very difficult to completely deny sex life. There is [the] regulative principle . . . no sex life. If you can remain without sex life, *brahmacari*, it is very good. But if you cannot, then get yourself married, live with wife, but have sex only for progeny. Not for sense enjoyment. Therefore even [if] one is married, if he's sticking to one wife and wife sticking to one man, that is real married life, then the husband is also called *brahmacari*. Even though he is *grhastha*. And wife is called chaste. (quoted in Devi Dasi, Urmila 1992:6)

Given the prevailing understanding of marriage and the controls placed on married life, there was little basis for "dyadic withdrawal" (Slater 1963) by married ISKCON members. This was all the more true given that male and female householders alike were engaged in full-time sankirtan or some other work in the ISKCON community. Indeed, it appears that householders were more willing to put their marriages at risk than to fail to meet their obligations to Prabhupada and his movement. As one temple president recounted,

It was a hard-core pressure. I know one of the primary reasons I'm not married anymore is because I was a temple president. And it was expected of me that I would give everything I had. There was no question of vacation. There was no question of taking time off for myself. No question. I can give you an example. We had an apartment down here [in the community]. We put a bakery in the front because we had a cooking business. It was a duplex. So the apartment in the back, it had absolutely no water power 80 percent of the time. At any time all your water would go off. So no one wanted to live in the apartment, obviously. So I moved my wife and two young children into this apartment. With no waterpower! You know, my wife's there washing her hair. The water shuts off. I'm not around of course. . . . This is what happened. These were the sacrifices. She finally got to the point where she said, "That's it. You quit as temple president and get a job and you take care of me and the family, or that's it." And so then I was forced to make a choice.[4] (interview 1990)

Children and Family Life

In 1968, only two years after founding his movement, Prabhupada began making plans to establish a gurukula (Krishna conscious school). Because Prabhupada saw the school system in America as doing little more than indoctrinating "children in sense gratification and mental speculation," he called the schools "slaughterhouses" (Goswami, Jagadisa 1984:1). Instead, the ultimate goal of the gurukula would be to train students in spiritual life so that they could escape the cycle of birth and death. Although academic subjects would be taught in the gurukula, its primary purpose would be to teach children sense control and practices of renunciation.

> The students are taught to use their senses in Krsna's service. They learn that their senses are meant not for personal enjoyment, but for Krsna's enjoyment—their enjoyment will come from pleasing Krsna. By learning to engage their senses in the service of the Lord, the students experience the highest standard of happiness. (Goswami, Jagadisa 1984:2)

By being obedient and self-controlled, a young devotee could act on behalf of his or her guru and thereby achieve spiritual success (Goswami, Jagadisa 1984:34–37).

Because the primary goal of the gurukula was to provide training in sense control, the movement chose to remove children from the care of their parents at the age of four or five. Given the naturally strong ties between parent and child, Prabhupada recognized that there would be little hope for a child to learn self-control from the family context. As one parent and former gurukula teacher explained, "It's understood that the parent is lenient and easily influenced by the child because of the ropes of affection. So this is why it is best if a gurukula teacher is instructing them" (interview 1990). Children attended ashram-based gurukulas year-round, with occasional vacations to visit with parents. Although the number varied widely in some locations, typically in North America they lived in ashrams of six to eight children of similar age and sex. An adult teacher also lived in the ashram, supervising the children and tending to their daily care.

Although all ISKCON children were expected to attend the gurukula at least until the age of fifteen, some parents resisted. When this happened, they faced both formal and informal sanctions to conform and, in some cases, expulsion from the community for failing to send their child to the gurukula. As one longtime teacher recounted, "I remember in New York the temple president told one woman, 'You don't send your kid to the gurukula, you don't live in the temple'" (interview 1990). In other cases, the sanctions were less severe, but the pressure to send a child to the gurukula nonetheless remained. As one devotee woman who removed her daughter from the gurukula in 1982 commented:

> We did try the ashram for a week, but she was very upset and unhappy. So you see that and think you want your child to be happy. And even though there were various devotees around us saying this and that, because I am a social person I was worried about what everyone was thinking. And even my spiritual master was saying, giving hints, "Why isn't she here [in the gurukula]?" . . . And believe me, it would've been easier to just send my child out to the gurukula. Much easier. But intuitively, I just thought it's not right. I just can't do that. (interview 1990)

Other parents who wanted their children to live at home and attend the gurukula during the day met with similar resistance. As a teacher of many years explained, Prabhupada rejected this idea when it was proposed to him in 1975.

Prabhupada made this point strongly, even though we forget. Gurukula means residing. Jagadisa [ISKCON's minister of education] asked him: "What if a parent wants to keep a child outside and bring them just during the day?" Prabhupada said: "I've already told you, gurukula means residing. We have room for children, not for parents." (interview 1991)

Another explicit purpose and function of the gurukula was to free parents from the responsibilities of child rearing. With their children in the gurukula, ISKCON authorities required parents to commit all their energies to the needs of the movement. In the words of one Prabhupada disciple and parent,

> Of course, one of the main things that Prabhupada wanted to achieve was to free the parents from the encumbrance of the children. Because without children and that responsibility, parents would be able to do more book selling and more preaching, and to devote full-time to institutional engagements. (interview 1990)

Under the traditional ashram-based gurukula system, ISKCON effectively controlled family life. For all intents and purposes, children and parents lived separate lives. Being free from day-to-day family obligations, parents could spend all their time advancing the success of Prabhupada's movement.

The Growth of the Grhastha Ashram

Perhaps no development in ISKCON's North American history was more consequential than the expansion of married and family life. ISKCON's early years were defined by the brahmacari and brahmacarini (celibate women) ashrams, with the majority of its members being single renunciates. Slowly at first and then more quickly, the number of marriages began to swell. In time, so too did the number of children.

In 1980, ISKCON had about an equal proportion of unmarried renunciates and householders (see table 2.1). Only about one-quarter of those surveyed had children. Conversely, by 1991/1992 two-thirds of those surveyed were married; and one in five was divorced, separated, or widowed. Only 15 percent had never been married. Family life also expanded, with a substantial majority having one or more children.[5]

TABLE 2.1

Marital and Family Status of ISKCON *Members, 1980 and 1991/1992*

	1980		1991/1992	
I. Marital Status				
Never married	53%	(113)	15%	(34)
Married	39%	(83)	53%	(124)
Divorced and remarried[a]	—		12%	(28)
Divorced	4%	(8)	13%	(30)
Separated	3%	(6)	5%	(12)
Widowed	2%	(4)	1%	(3)
Total	101%	(214)	(99%)	(231)
II. Family				
a. Children				
No	73%	(156)	30%	(70)
Yes	27%	(58)	70%	(162)
Total	(100%)	(214)	(100%)	(232)

[a] The 1980 questionnaire had no category for "divorced and remarried," so ISKCON members with this martial status would have indicated "married." But it is unlikely that more than a small percentage of respondents fell into this category, given the relative youth of ISKCON 's membership, and the movement itself, in 1980.

As these patterns make clear, by the 1990s ISKCON in North America had become a householders' movement, with very few of its longtime male members having managed to realize the spiritual ideal of remaining celibate monks. Moreover, during the 1980s ISKCON had not been able to attract many young unmarried recruits to its ranks.[6]

The grhastha ashram expanded during a period when ISKCON's communities were facing deepening economic decline and instability. This combination of events provided the impetus for the growth and ultimate ascendancy of the nuclear family as the foundation of ISKCON's social organization in North America.

Economic Decline and the Ascendancy of the Nuclear Family

Two interrelated changes took place during the early and mid-1980s that contributed to both the emergence of the nuclear family and the householders' growing independence from ISKCON. The first was the dramatic downturn in ISKCON's economic fortunes, which forced most ISKCON householders to secure employment outside the movement's communities. The second was the collapse of ISKCON's traditional ashram-based gurukula system, leaving parents responsible for raising their children.

Economic Change and Shifting Patterns of Employment

During the late 1960s and early 1970s, ISKCON's communities were supported financially by donations received by devotees distributing incense and the movement's *Back to Godhead* magazine on the streets of America's cities (Rochford 1985:173). Then in 1971 and 1972, the economics of sankirtan changed dramatically as ISKCON members began distributing Prabhupada's commentaries on the Vedic literatures in public locations, first in parking lots and shopping malls and then in major American airports. The book distribution expanded yearly through 1976 and provided large sums of money to help bankroll ISKCON's worldwide expansion. One conservative estimate is that ISKCON's communities in North America grossed more than $13 million between 1974 and 1978 on hard-back books alone (see Rochford 1985:171–89).

By 1980, however, ISKCON's book distribution had fallen to less than one-quarter of its North American peak (Rochford 1985:175), and the corresponding loss of sankirtan revenues had a devastating effect on ISKCON's communities. Although ISKCON's leaders undertook a number of alternative strategies to forestall the movement's economic demise (selling record albums, artwork, candles, and food in public locations), these were successful only in the short run and were highly controversial both inside and outside ISKCON (Rochford 1985:191–211).

With declining financial resources available to its communities, ISKCON faced a significant turning point in its North American history. No longer able to financially maintain its communal lifestyle through literature distribution and other forms of public solicitation and without alternative means of economic support, ISKCON's members had little choice but to seek outside employment.[7] This was especially true for devotees with families to support. As one longtime member of ISKCON explained,

> What happened is that people got married and they just always assumed they would go on living in the temple. I mean I did. We were married in '77. So we thought like that. Life was gonna go on as it always had. It would be a little different. Not much. So eventually a lot of people got married and hung onto the temples and that got very expensive to maintain. Suddenly householders wanted to retire from book distribution. They wanted a job in the temple. Yet you can only employ so

many people that way. In the end, we had temples overloaded with expensive householders. The brahmacaris began to say "Hey. Why should I collect [money on sankirtan] to support them?" (interview 1990)

As the revenues from book distribution plummeted, the occupational structure of ISKCON changed accordingly (see table 2.2). In 1980 nearly all ISKCON's members worked in movement-owned businesses or within their local devotee community. One-fourth worked as sankirtan devotees, and almost none were self-employed or worked in nondevotee work settings. Also noteworthy is that all ISKCON members surveyed in 1980 worked in some capacity, reflecting the fact that during this period those devotees maintained by the temple were obligated to perform community service. Because they were not married and/or free of family obligations, they also were available for work.

By 1991/1992, ISKCON's pattern of employment was strikingly different. A little more than one-third of those surveyed worked outside ISKCON in a nondevotee business or were self-employed. Somewhat more were employed in work settings with other devotees, such as in an ISKCON business, an ISKCON community, or a devotee-owned business. One-fourth were not gainfully employed at the time of the survey.

TABLE 2.2

Types of Employment for ISKCON Members in 1980 and 1991/1992

	1980		1991/1992	
ISKCON business[a]	23%	(48)	8%	(18)
Local ISKCON community[b]	72%	(149)	19%	(43)
ISKCON business and local community	0%	(0)	5%	(11)
Outside ISKCON for a devotee-owned business[c]	2%	(5)	7%	(17)
Self-employed[d]	0%	(0)	14%	(31)
Outside ISKCON for a non-devotee-owned business[e]	2%	(5)	22%	(51)
Unemployed	0%	(0)	25%	(58)
Total	(99%)	(207)	(100%)	(229)

[a] Includes working for ISKCON's Bhaktivedanta Book Trust, ISKCON restaurants, record production company, gift store, natural food company, and ISKCON administration.

[b] Includes teaching in an ISKCON school, book distribution, temple administration, deity worship, general maintenance work, cooking, office work, and farming.

[c] Includes working at a devotee-owned travel agency, art gallery, T-shirt business, and day-lily company.

[d] Includes growing and selling vegetables, photographer, tennis instructor, house painting, lawyer, astrologer, investor, and artist.

[e] Includes teacher, sales work, taxi driver, university researcher, computer programmer, engineer, social worker, physician, real estate agent, military service, dishwasher, secretary, carpenter, and housecleaning.

Nearly all of the latter were women with family responsibilities, the majority (72%) of whom did regular volunteer work in their local ISKCON community.[8]

The Demise of the Ashram-Based Gurukula

The downward turn in ISKCON's economic fortunes had a number of direct and indirect effects on the demise of the movement's traditional gurukula system. By 1986, all of ISKCON's remaining ashram-based gurukulas in North America had closed. Since these schools were subsidized by ISKCON's North American Governing Body Commission (GBC) and by communities sending students to the schools, ISKCON's eroding economic base directly contributed to their demise. As a former ashram teacher in ISKCON's central California gurukula observed,

> I remember while we were still in Three Rivers, they would give out fifteen dollars a week to the devotees teaching there, for expenses. We didn't have to pay for our maintenance, where we lived. We'd get $15 a week in addition. That had to take care of all the gas, things you needed to get in town. Usually we didn't need too much extra. But there were telephone bills, which were pretty costly if you had to make a toll call. And then when you got your break time [for school vacations] to go down to San Diego to visit friends or relatives. Everything had to come out of that $15 a week. And somehow or other we'd always put $5 aside, or $10. But then there came a time when they [authorities running the school] couldn't even give the $15 a week. And then it was like, "What do you do?" You don't even have gas to get into town. It got to the point where it was impossible. (interview 1990)

As long as householders were going out on sankirtan, the ashram-based gurukula was a practical necessity for ISKCON. But as sankirtan revenues fell and householders were forced into the outside labor market, the economic incentives associated with the traditional gurukula system disappeared as well. As one ISKCON teacher who witnessed the demise of the ashram-gurukula system put it,

> Also their [the leadership's] main motive, which was to free up parents, didn't exist anymore. There's no sankirtan. The parents are all out there

working [in the conventional society]. . . . Why should the GBC and the leadership put money and time and manpower into something which they see as having no direct value to the organization? None. The parents are living outside, doing something outside. If the school closes, parents will just end up teaching their kids at home or sending them to karmie [non-ISKCON] schools. (interview 1990)

Other factors also contributed to the demise of the gurukula in North America. Over time, for example, a growing number of parents began to question the quality of the academic education their children were receiving in the gurukula. Indeed, the importance of a strong education for their children took on special significance to parents when most of them were forced to find employment outside ISKCON and realized that if ISKCON could not give them opportunities for paid employment and/or financial support, their children would face a similar fate. Another factor I have mentioned and will consider in more detail later was the growing realization that some of the movement's children were being abused in the gurukula. In sum, economics played an important, if not decisive, role in the closing of ISKCON's ashram-based gurukulas.

In the face of economic decline, ISKCON's system of education was more or less transformed by the end of the 1980s. Although three ashram-based schools reopened in North America in the late 1980s, in 1994 they collectively served only about forty elementary and high school age students,[9] and by 2006, only one of the three ashram-based schools had survived, and it was a combined boarding and day school for adolescent girls.

Today, ISKCON's educational system in North America is made up mainly of day schools, with the majority of ISKCON's children in North America attending state-supported schools. According to the 1996 North American Centennial Survey, 47 percent of the 181 full-time and congregational members with school-age children reported that one or more of their children was attending a public primary or secondary school; 27 percent attended an ISKCON or devotee day school; and 14 percent were homeschooled.

Decommunalization, Congregation Building, and Transformation

The emergence of the nuclear family changed the very structure of ISK-CON as a religious organization, as devotee families became self-supporting and increasingly independent of ISKCON and its control. ISKCON could no longer assert totalistic claims over the lives and identity of householders and their children, in large part because ISKCON's leaders lost their ability to control their members through financial dependence (Das, Ravindra Svarupa 2000b:37). Freed from ISKCON control, householders formed social enclaves between the larger culture and their local ISKCON community, which resulted in the disintegration of ISKCON's traditional communal structure. Having lost control over family life and, with it, the majority of the movement's membership, ISKCON faced organizational change and transformation. Its unconventional structure and lifestyle gave way under the weight of growing congregationalism as householders took up residence in the suburbs of Krishna conscious social life.

During ISKCON's beginning years, the community served as the movement's primary unit of social organization. Like other communally based new religions, ISKCON sought to combine all aspects of daily life in coordinated, centralized, and physically and socially bounded communities. Philosophically and practically, ISKCON's members understood that their association with other devotees was vital to their spiritual progress. To wander outside the confines of the devotee community thus represented a potential threat to any ISKCON member seeking spiritual realization in Krishna Consciousness.[10]

ISKCON's communal structure offered members the opportunity to live and work in a reality-affirming enclave composed of other devotees. As noted previously, in 1980 ISKCON members worked almost exclusively with other devotees. Work represented "devotional service," an offering to Krishna and his devotees. Funds collected on sankirtan became communal property and were used to support the community as a whole and to promote Prabhupada's preaching mission. As Kanter (1972:2) suggested, the "sharing of resources and finances" is the key arrangement distinguishing communes from other forms of social organization.

As the 1980s progressed, the economic strategies of ISKCON's membership necessarily became more diverse and individualistic. Few devotees continued to believe that outside employment was a sign of spiritual weakness. Only 5 percent of the ISKCON members surveyed in 1991/ 1992 agreed with the statement that "working at a job outside of ISK- CON is *maya.*" In addition to this changing attitude toward outside em- ployment was a new understanding of individual versus communal re- sources. No longer did the money earned by ISKCON members go toward meeting community needs. Instead, householders managed their own fi- nancial resources to meet the needs of their families. Although Prabhu- pada emphasized that householders were responsible for giving 50 per- cent of their income to support ISKCON (1992:860), few have been able, or perhaps willing, to make such a sacrifice. In large part, this reflects the fact that ISKCON families have little discretionary income to contribute. The median income category for ISKCON members in 1991/1992 was be- tween $6,000 and $15,000. Furthermore, their unwillingness to contrib- ute also reflected the often bitter feelings that many held toward the leadership. As one householder commented angrily,

> They [the leaders] forced us out to find jobs and live on our own; to raise our families with little money and after being separated from our children for so long. After so much service [work on behalf of the move- ment]. Now they turn around and criticize us because we did what they told us to do. That somehow we are materialistic because we live out- side. How can I have respect for them? (interview 1993)

But ISKCON's communal structure was undermined in even more di- rect ways. Two-thirds of the devotees surveyed in 1991/1992 lived in non-ISKCON-owned dwellings. Of those, nearly six in ten (58%) lived at least a mile from their local ISKCON community. Moreover, the majority (61%) reported that they wanted to maintain their household indepen- dently of ISKCON. One reason was that many devotees no longer trusted ISKCON to tend to the needs of its membership. Sixty percent agreed with the statement from the survey that "I have lost trust in ISKCON's ability to look after the material and economic needs of people like me." Other reasons can be found in the words of three householders living in ISKCON's northern Florida community in 1993:

> I don't like living in too close proximity to devotees. I need my space! I have personal projects I wish to oversee, and it's easier to do that with a little distance between me and the temple.

I don't want to be under the thumb of any temple president.

I value my own newly found independence. Therefore, I would not choose to live on an ISKCON property.

As householders began to create independent lives for themselves and their families, their relationships to ISKCON and their pattern of religious practice and involvement changed accordingly.

Family Life, Commitment, and Involvement

The 1996 North American Centennial Survey allows a closer assessment of the ways that family life has influenced ISKCON's patterns of organizational and religious commitment and involvement. The survey's findings compared parents and nonparents who were full-time or congregational ISKCON members (see appendix 2, table A.1).[11] As one might expect, overall full-time members were both more committed to and involved in ISKCON and Krishna Consciousness than was the greater congregational community. Although these relatively higher rates of commitment and involvement exemplify their full-time status, they also speak to ISKCON's ability to exert greater institutional control over core members than over members of its congregation.

Full-time members with and without children shared similar commitments to ISKCON and their Krishna conscious beliefs, including their commitment to preaching Krishna Consciousness. They also observed similar private religious practices, including chanting their daily japa, reading Prabhupada's books, and adhering to the movement's regulative principles. Noteworthy differences on the basis of family status were related to questions of organizational involvement, collective religious practice, and the authority accorded to ISKCON's leadership.

Full-time members with children were considerably less involved in the movement's collective religious activities. Although about equally likely to engage in volunteer work in their local ISKCON community, nonparents spent considerably more time volunteering than did those with families. Together, these two findings point to the ways that family life limited the availability of core adherents to be more active in their local ISKCON community. Rather than being a negative influence on commitment, as Kanter (1972) suggested, family obligations instead directly limited collective forms of involvement. With children to get off to school and one or more adults preparing for work, parents found it difficult, or perhaps even impossible, to attend morning temple programs. Other family obligations likewise made it difficult to commit longer periods of time to performing community service.

A significant difference also was found in the authority attributed to ISKCON's leadership. Devotees with children, and thus householders, expressed far less support for ISKCON's gurus and the guru institution, as well as for the movement's governing authority, the GBC, whether they were full-time or congregational members. Given this low level of support, householders favored expanding democratic forms of governance within the movement. Such outcomes highlight the ways that householders collectively believed that the leadership remained largely uncommitted to families and their needs.

The Centennial Survey revealed only one major difference among congregational members regarding family status. Parents observed considerably higher levels of private religious practice than nonparents did, in large part because they were more likely to conduct daily worship services in their households. The overall lack of differences points to the ways in which membership is more segmental and less intense for congregational members. Moreover, involvement in ISKCON and its religious practice are more readily integrated into their lives, regardless of family obligations. By contrast, because full-time members commit their lives to ISKCON and Krishna Consciousness, family life demands trade-offs and compromises that reduce their level of involvement.

Considered more closely, the Centennial Survey showed a significant change in ISKCON's religious culture resulting from the demise of communalism, the ascendancy of the nuclear family, and ISKCON's transformation into a congregationally based movement. Bryan Wilson (1976) contends that religion functions within the context of community. Secularization, he argues, represents the decline of community (Wilson 1976:265–66). When community no longer serves as a meaningful basis of social organization, religion succumbs to privatization, with its more public and collective elements fading into the background and leaving the residual, individual religiosity as the essence of religious life. Group ritual and participation simply lose meaning and relevance in the absence of a functioning community of believers (Wilson 1982:160). The household as the center of Krishna conscious religious life displaced ISKCON's temples, once the very symbol of the movement's religious world. Moreover, as ISKCON's communities disintegrated and lost their "sacred" meaning and significance, traditional structures of authority were no longer able to control the actions of individual believers.

Conclusion

During ISKCON's early years when its members were young and unmarried and when substantial revenues were flowing into its communities, the movement was able to create an exclusive religious world in a communal context. But in 1980 when sankirtan revenues plummeted, ISKCON was left without economic alternatives to sustain its oppositional religious culture. Declining resources in combination with an unprecedented increase in family life left ISKCON with a cultural crisis. Without the internal institutions to sustain a domestic culture, ISKCON could no longer meet the changing needs of its membership. As a result, large numbers of householders were forced out of ISKCON's communities, and the organization declined thereafter.[12]

In important respects, ISKCON's founder, Srila Prabhupada, foresaw the changes described here. During the years just before his death in 1977, Prabhupada spent more time on the question of cultural development within his movement. He was concerned that ISKCON had failed to develop a social and cultural system that would allow his disciples to live peacefully in a spiritual life. The seriousness of Prabhupada's apprehension is indicated by a comment that he reportedly made to a disciple, that 50 percent of his mission remained unfinished because ISKCON had failed to establish a varnashram culture (Dasa, Murali Vadaka 1992). The following exchange reported during a morning class in 1992 in the Dallas ISKCON temple echoes this message:

> Toward the end of Prabhupada's stay [before his death], he at one point turned to the devotees with him and said, "So I am going to die. There is no lamentation [on my part]." Then a silence. Finally, Prabhupada spoke up and said, "Actually I have one lamentation." Bramananda asked, "What is that Prabhupada, that you haven't finished the Bhagavatam?" Prabhupada responded, "No, that I have not established varnashram" (Dasa, Murali Vadaka 1992).

Beginning in 1974, during a series of morning walks with his closest disciples in Vrndavana, India, Prabhupada detailed his vision for ISK-CON's cultural development as derived from the Vedic model of var-nashram, which he described in 1975:

> The idea that I am giving, you can start anywhere, any part of the world. It doesn't matter. Locally you produce your own food. You get your own cloth. Have sufficient milk, vegetables. Then what more do you want? And chant Hare Krsna. This is Vedic civilization: plain living, high thinking. (Mauritius, October 5, 1975)

As he explained on one of his Vrndavana walks in 1974, the failure to establish varnashram culture invited the possibility of social chaos:

> First of all *varna* [occupational and social divisions]. And *asrama,* then, when the *varna* is perfectly in order, then *asrama* [living arrangements]. *Asrama* is specifically meant for spiritual advancement, and *varna* is general division [within society]. It must be there in human society, or they're on the animals [platform]. If *varna* is not there, then this is a society of animal.[13] (Prabhupada 1974)

Between 1974 and 1977 Prabhupada repeatedly returned to the question of varnashram. One indication of this is suggested by a study by one of the movement's foremost authorities on varnashram. Of the 167 times that Prabhupada mentioned the word varnashram in his recorded conversations, 17 percent were before his well-known "Varnashram Conversations," in 1974. Over the next three and a half years leading up to his death, Prabhupada mentioned the concept of varnashram on the remaining 83 percent of the recorded occasions (Dasa, Murali Vadaka 1992).

There is every reason to believe that Prabhupada's preoccupation with varnashram grew out of the ongoing difficulty that many, if not most, of his disciples were experiencing in spiritual life.

> If you examine Prabhupada's instructions at the end of his life . . . it's obvious he sees that his devotees who he initially expected, or hoped, would come to the Brahmin Vaisnava platform, had failed. That they couldn't maintain that standard. . . . Prabhupada recognized that we needed help. And that help was varnashram. Prabhupada realized that.

He saw his devotees suffering from contact with the material energy. That they had an inability to develop a spiritual taste, and therefore were falling again and again into material activities. (Dasa, Murali Vadaka 1992)

As we have seen in this chapter, during the 1980s and 1990s, Prabhupada's disciples and the disciples of his guru successors became increasingly entangled in the outside culture. As Prabhupada predicted, the absence of an internal religious culture left both ISKCON and its members vulnerable to the corrosive effects of mainstream American culture. It also meant that ISKCON's religious culture was reshaped to fit the needs of an increasingly congregational membership. As we will see in the next two chapters, ISKCON's failure to develop a domestic culture during the 1970s and 1980s had its most immediate and consequential effects on the movement's second generation. The leadership's resistance to marriage and family life played a tragic role in the abuse of ISKCON's children.

3

Child Abuse

All these boys must be taken care of very nicely. They are the future hope.

—Prabhupada letter, July 1974

These kids were growing up and seriously leaving [ISKCON]. Not a little bit leaving. Not leaving and being favorable, still chanting and living outside. Nothing like that. They were leaving. And suddenly it was like "What happened?" And then it started to be revealed that the kids were molested.

—Longtime ISKCON teacher, interview 1990

Religion and child abuse, "'perfect together' . . . and mutually attractive," so concluded Donald Capps in his 1992 presidential address to members of the Society for the Scientific Study of Religion. Mutually attractive even though religion has often vigorously defended the rights of children, including condemning child abuse and neglect (Capps 1992; Costin, Karger, and Stoesz 1996:47). Yet research on child abuse suggests that religious beliefs can foster, encourage, and justify the abuse of children (Capps 1992; Ellison and Sherkat 1993; Greven 1990; Jenkins 1996). Moreover, church structures may provide opportunities for clergy to abuse (Krebs 1998; Shupe 1995).

Tragically, some of ISKCON's children were physically, psychologically, and sexually abused by people responsible for their care and well-being in the movement's ashram-based gurukulas from 1971 until the mid-1980s. I develop a sociologically informed framework to understand how and why this child abuse and neglect took place, based on a variety of organizational factors that fostered, and indeed created, opportunities for child abuse in ISKCON's schools.

Child Abuse in ISKCON's *Schools*

ISKCON's first formal gurukula was established in Dallas in 1971 and remained the only school of its type in the movement until 1976, when state authorities forced it to close. At the time of its closing, the school had approximately one hundred students, the majority of whom were between the ages of four and eight. In 1975, with the impending demise of the Dallas school, gurukulas opened in Los Angeles and at New Vrindaban, and between 1975 and 1978, eleven ISKCON schools opened in North America. In 1976, the Bhaktivedanta Swami International Gurukula began accepting adolescent boys as students in Vrndavana, India.[1] As ISKCON became a global movement in the late 1970s and early 1980s, gurukulas were also started in France, Australia, South Africa, England, and Sweden, and in 1980 and 1981, regional schools opened in Lake Huntington, New York, and central California (Bhaktivedanta Village), respectively (Dasa, Manu 1998).

Reports by second-generation youths, parents, and educators alike suggest that some of the children who attended the gurukula suffered physical, psychological, and sexual abuse. But it is not clear just how many children were directly abused or saw their friends and classmates being abused. Lacking reliable quantitative findings, it therefore is extremely difficult to determine precisely the exact incidence of child abuse in ISKCON's gurukulas. Over the years several estimates have been offered, ranging from 20 percent of all students who attended an ashram-gurukula suffering some form of abuse to as many as 75 percent of the boys enrolled at the Vrndavana, India, gurukula being sexually molested during the late 1970s and early 1980s. The only quantitative study of the prevalence of child abuse in the gurukulas was a 1998 survey conducted by ISKCON's youth ministry. This nonrandom survey of 115 former gurukula students aged fifteen to thirty-four found that 25 percent had been sexually abused for more than one year; 29 percent reported that they experienced sexual abuse for a period of between one month and one year. With respect to physical abuse, 31 percent indicated that they had been repeatedly hit by a teacher or someone two or more years older, to the point of leaving marks on their body (Wolf 2004:322).[2]

As of January 2002, ISKCON's Association for the Protection of Vaishnava Children (APVC), which was formed in response to the growing awareness of child abuse claims, had received allegations of child mistreatment—including child abuse—against more than three hundred people. The alleged perpetrators often had several victims, and each victim suffered multiple incidents of abuse. Sixty percent of the abuse reports made to the APVC were from before 1992, when "there were clusters of allegations connected with an ISKCON school [gurukulas]" (Wolf 2004:323). Moreover, more than 80 percent of these cases were accusations of sexual abuse (Wolf 2004:323).

Whatever the actual incidence of child abuse, it is clear that abuse directly and indirectly influenced the lives of many children. Yet child abuse did not occur uniformly across gurukulas or even within the same school. As one longtime teacher concluded, child abuse "wasn't all pervasive. It wasn't in all gurukulas. It didn't affect all children. But it was in enough schools and affected enough children and it went on for enough time" (interview 1990).

Abuse and neglect in the gurukula took a variety of forms, and the following statements from young adults and former gurukula students indicate the kinds of abuse that occurred:

> I remember dark closets filled with flying dates (large 3 inch, flying cockroaches) and such, while beatings and "no *prasadam*" [spiritually blessed food] for dinner became everyday affairs. (Devi Dasi, K. 1990:1)

> Seattle was hell because I was only six years old, my mom lived in Hawaii, and I had always been a very shy mommy's girl. The movement was in its earlier stages, and the devotees were fanatical—beyond fanatical. I mean, they would give us a bowl of hot milk at night, so I would, of course, pee in my bed. Then as punishment they would spank me very hard and make me wear the contaminated panties on my head. In general, at that time, because I was so young, I was so spaced out and confused. I would cry . . . for my mom, but that wasn't allowed, so I would say I was crying in devotional ecstasy. I really regret Seattle because I had a dire need for my mother's warmth and reassurance at that time in my life. (Second Generation Survey 1992)

> The teacher used to say, "Oh, you don't know when you are going to die. You could die in your sleep." And one day I was really bad and one of my teachers said, "Who knows you might die tonight. Krishna might be punishing you. He might be taking away your life." . . . And from that night on I used to pray every night, "Krishna please don't kill me. I promise I will be a good girl tomorrow. Please let me get fixed up

enough so I can go back to Godhead. Don't take me in my sleep." And for years I had insomnia. I was too afraid to go back to sleep.[3] (interview 1991)

Two young men recounted their days as students in the Vrndavana, India, gurukula during the early 1980s:

> *Jiva*: I wasn't afraid of being sexually molested. I don't think I was afraid of being mentally abused either. I was definitely afraid of being physically abused. . . . Sexual molestation, all of us, man, we'd just take it, you know . . . that's what we all felt. We didn't even consider it abuse back then.
> *Sesa*: Yeah, that was just normal. . . . The ironic thing about that, though, is probably the mental thing [abuse] was probably the longest lasting.
> *Jiva*: There was no way to escape that. (group interview 1993)

As word of child abuse in the gurukula came to the attention of the ISKCON authorities, they made some efforts to intervene, but their intervention sometimes resulted in new strategies of coercive abuse. Most significant was enlisting older boys in the gurukulas in Vrndavana and elsewhere to physically abuse those younger students whom their teachers deemed to be troublesome and unruly.

> *Subal*: The other thing was that older boys acting in the capacity of monitors were used to abuse the younger students. Some started to realize that "Hey, teachers can't be beating kids." They did it in a new way.
> *EBR*: With the monitors.
> *Subal*: Yeah. Which was the older boys beating the younger boys, and I was one of the older ones . . . and they [the teachers] would call me in on occasion and I would just have to knock the living shit [out of a younger student]. . . . I'd be sitting there going "Man, I love you. I don't want to be doing this." . . . [I]t's like, what are you gonna do? "If I don't do it to you, they're gonna do it to me."
> *Sesa*: That's another kind of mental abuse. (group interview 1993)

Although some of ISKCON's children were themselves abused, others vicariously experienced the terror of abuse as they watched their friends and classmates being mistreated by teachers and others responsible for their care.

If the teachers treated one of our friends bad, then we all felt bad. I remember there was one teacher that used to grab one of us by the ears and bang us against the wall. And we all stood there and watched and felt really bad. . . . She [the teacher] was doing it to all of us. (interview 1992)

Maybe what [name of ashram teacher] was doing to [name of student] was hurting others [students] more than him. For [name of student], it was an everyday thing. I was standing right next to [him] and I was crying. I was freaked out. I was afraid I was gonna be next because I knew he was gettin' it for no reason. If he could get it for no reason so could I. (group interview 1993)

In the school in Vrndavana, India, abusive treatment became so commonplace that students tried to routinize their mistreatment as a protective strategy.

It was like boot camp, but it wasn't temporary. You became part of a unit. Boot camp was a full-time thing for us. They're just constantly knocking you down, knocking you down . . . lower, lower, lower. There were points where it was like, there was no more lower. What are they gonna do? Beat me again? Go ahead. (laughter). Big deal! (group interview 1993)

Beyond the specific cases of abuse by adults in the gurukula[4] was the general environment of neglect. Without parents present, many children felt abandoned or, as Dasa described it, "We were just unwanted." Many young people described the atmosphere in the gurukula as one lacking love and compassion. They felt invisible, abandoned, and unworthy of love and affection from both their parents and their adult caregivers.[5]

Accounting for Child Abuse

A number of factors in ISKCON's gurukulas during the 1970s and 1980s combined to create a context conducive to child abuse. The first is somewhat different from the others because it defines the broader milieu in which parents and children lived in ISKCON's communities.

Attitudes toward Marriage, Family Life, and Children

The ISKCON scholar and leader Ravindra Svarupa Das argued that marriage and family life were viewed favorably during ISKCON's early days. As he stated, "When I joined ISKCON [in 1971] it was assumed that everyone would become married, and indeed devotees were urged to do so" (1994:9). But this view changed after Prabhupada became increasingly discouraged by his disciples' marital problems and turned over the "troublesome business of marriage" to the renunciate leaders under him. The result, as we have seen, was that in ISKCON, married life was fundamentally transformed in both meaning and value.

By the mid-1970s, the changed atmosphere surrounding marriage and family life turned contentious as renunciate leaders began a preaching campaign against householder life and women. As Ravindra Svarupa Das pointed out, this brought with it conflict and factionalism in ISKCON.

> Some of these *sannyasis* embarked on preaching campaigns against householders and even more so against women, whose life in the movement at this time became extremely trying. Feelings grew so heated that in 1976, a clash between householder temple presidents in North America and a powerful association of peripatetic *sannyasis* and *brahmacaries* escalated into a conflict so major that Srila Prabhupada called it a "fratricidal war." (1994:9)

Even with the rapid expansion of marriage and family life, antihouseholder attitudes changed little organizationally, and householder life remained a "dark well" spiritually. Many parents who accepted the leadership's ideas about marriage and family tried to counteract their lowly status by placing their commitment to ISKCON and Krishna Consciousness above their family obligations, which became a huge burden for both parents and their children. One second-generation woman recalled just how difficult this proved to be for her own mother:

> But sometimes I would look at her and I could see her being torn apart inside. I could see how she yearned to be a mother once again; sewing by the fire, cooking our dinners, and helping us with our hard days at school, and at the same time trying her hardest to please the Guru and

the community by showing her detachment to her family. (Devi Dasi, K. 1990:14)

As householder life was more and more disparaged, children were defined and redefined in ways that undermined their status and ultimately the care they received in the gurukula. Until the early 1980s, children born in ISKCON were commonly portrayed as being spiritually pure, as their souls were believed to have progressed spiritually to the point that they had had the good fortune of being born into a devotee family. But by the mid-1980s this view had changed, with some leaders complaining that ISKCON's children were turning out to be little more than "karmies" (nonreligious outsiders) and therefore that the gurukula had failed in its mission to produce spiritually advanced children. The leadership used both frameworks to justify dismissing the gurukula, the children, and their responsibility toward both. As two ISKCON teachers explained,

> They [the leadership] put a lot of energy into making new devotees from outside the community. But you didn't have to put any energy into making children into devotees, or so they thought. . . . And I think there was a lot of misconception about how Prabhupada thought the children [were] conceived. They thought that if the children were conceived properly, then it was a cinch. And that makes no sense at all. I compare it to going through a store and buying good seeds and then you don't plant them, you don't water them, you just throw them around. . . . So many things that we assumed, that we never sat down and analyzed. We just took it for granted; that the children were born into the movement, and particularly if they were conceived properly by chanting five hours of Hare Krishna. Does that make sense? It never made sense to me. I always assumed that we would train the children, that we could never take their Krishna Consciousness, or their character, or anything for granted. (interview 1990)

And everyone just thought that you send them away to the gurukula and when they came back, they were going to be like Pralad Maharaja [a spiritually realized devotee of Krishna]. They were going to be chanting japa. They were going to be shaved up. They were going to be distributing books. They were going to be nice little chaste wives, rolling chapattis. (interview 1997)

By the mid-1980s, as the children were growing into teenagers, the second generation and the gurukula began to be viewed differently. To the surprise of many leaders and parents alike, the children raised in the gurukula were less than pure spiritually. Few were inclined toward a life of renunciation and full-time ISKCON involvement. As a result, some leaders openly challenged the need for the gurukula altogether.

> But they [the leaders] did not go back and become introspective and say, "Well, we should have been taking care of these things. Let's get it together now. We made a mistake, whether an honest mistake or not. Let's now provide an excellent education for the children. Let's re-build the community's faith in ISKCON." They didn't do that. They took (laugh) the opposite track. Instead of saying, "The kids are going to turn out good no matter what," now they were saying, "Things are go-ing to turn out bad no matter what you do." The leaders' position was, "No, we did everything right. We did what Prabhupada said. We had ashrams. We had these nice schools. These wonderful schools. And eve-rything went bad anyway. So why should we put a lot of energy into it [the gurukula]. We're just kidding ourselves. Right." (ISKCON teacher, interview 1990)

But these two very different frameworks for constructing ISKCON's children served the same purpose functionally. In the first instance, the leaders saw no reason to invest resources in the gurukula because it could not fail, given the children's elevated spiritual status. The second framework, precisely because it emphasized failure rather than success, likewise rejected the need to maintain a viable system of education. Yet as we will see, the gurukula did serve a crucial function for ISKCON, one that ultimately had little to do with educating and socializing ISKCON's next generation.

Sankirtan and the Gurukula

Although ISKCON's sannyasi leadership believed that a loss in stand-ing would discourage marriage, the solid majority of ISKCON's member-ship married and most had children. The growth of marriage and family represented a significant threat to sankirtan and thereby to ISKCON it-self, as sankirtan served ISKCON's mission in two respects. First, it rep-resented the principal means by which the movement proselytized its

Krishna conscious beliefs. In fact, Prabhupada continually emphasized that book distribution represented the means to spread Krishna Consciousness in America and worldwide. Second, and of equal importance, sankirtan supported ISKCON's communities financially. Without a workforce of dedicated sankirtan devotees, ISKCON's missionary goals and financial stability would have been jeopardized. The solution rested with the gurukula because it relieved parents of the burdens of child care, thus affording them the opportunity to work full-time sankirtan. Put differently, the gurukula allowed ISKCON's leaders to reclaim householders for sankirtan, a move that only grew in importance by the late 1970s as ISKCON's North American communities faced deepening economic decline. As one parent said, "We got the children, the bothersome children—from the leaders' perspective—we got them out of the way by putting them in the gurukula. Now the adults could do some work. Go out on sankirtan" (interview 1990).

Because the leadership was concerned primarily with distributing Prabhupada's books and raising funds, the gurukula communalized child care, thus freeing parents to work on behalf of ISKCON and its mission. Not surprisingly, many of the young people who attended the gurukula during this period saw ISKCON's schools in precisely these terms.

> I did feel that my mom used the gurukula as a convenience for not keeping me around. My mother later told me [the] authorities strongly encouraged her to put us there so we would not hinder her sankirtan service. (Second Generation Survey 1992)

The 1992 Second Generation Survey made this point more forcefully. Of the eighty-seven youths surveyed, nearly two-thirds (63%) agreed, and one-quarter (26%) agreed strongly with the statement "The ashram gurukula primarily served the interests of parents and ISKCON, rather than the spiritual and academic needs of children."

Parents were freed for sankirtan by enrolling their children in the gurukula as early as age three or four, although the majority entered at age five. Some ISKCON communities communalized children even earlier, establishing day-care centers for infants and toddlers. One such location was ISKCON's New Vrindaban community: "Bhaktipada was very successful because he had a nursery from day one. For those kids born at New Vrindaban, he took the kids and communalized them.

They got so much work out of the people in that community" (interview 1990).

A second-generation woman who grew up at New Vrindaban recalled what happened after her younger brother was born:

> Soon after Kapila was born . . . the Guru of the farm asked her [mother] to go travel and preach in airports, she sadly said "yes." Kapila was only three months old when she left him to be brought up by some other lady who lived on the farm. For months she cried at night wondering if he was okay and yet her body could hardly stand any more emotional work after standing nearly twelve hours that day . . . collecting donations from strangers. (Devi Dasi, K. 1990:14)

The leadership's motivation in providing child care at New Vrindaban is suggested in a saying used in the community to refer to expectant mothers: "Dump the load and hit the road." To "hit the road" meant returning to full-time sankirtan. Even though the approach of leaders in other ISKCON communities was clearly more subtle and more humane, they were no less anxious for mothers to return to full-time sankirtan or other work on behalf of the community, for women were among the most productive sankirtan workers in the movement.

Sankirtan was the foundation of ISKCON's religious world, and the movement's sannyasi elite made sure that it was protected against the presumed deleterious effects associated with the expansion of marriage and family life. While initially established to educate ISKCON's children, the gurukula ultimately served the interests of ISKCON's missionary goals and the need to raise money to support the movement's communal way of life. One teacher from this era underscored the primary interest of ISKCON's sannyasi leadership:

> And you had to have a vision for the future to even understand why you were doing this [the gurukula]. For the teachers this might have been there but for the administration of ISKCON, what it means is that you are paying for a day-care center. . . . You are talking about sannyasis who are thinking like, "Get these kids out of here. And look how much money I am having to pay to get these kids out of here. And look at how many devotees have to be there [in the gurukula] to get these kids out of the way." That was the whole psyche surrounding how the school was put together. (interview 1997)

The importance that ISKCON's leadership placed on sankirtan meant that the gurukula's significance rested on its child-care function rather than as an educational institution. Moreover, as parents were pressured to engage in sankirtan, many could not commit time to the needs of their children. Although children and family life threatened ISKCON's purpose as a missionary movement, each also threatened the financial base on which the leadership's authority rested.

Lack of Institutional Support for Gurukula

Given the leadership's view of gurukula and its purposes, it failed to provide the support necessary to maintain a strong educational institution. Throughout its existence, the gurukula operated with insufficient staffing, funding, and oversight. In failing to provide the necessary resources and management, the gurukula became an institution defined by neglect, isolation, and marginalization. Accordingly, the gurukula also became an institution in which ISKCON's children were subject to abuse.

From the gurukula's first days in Dallas, it was short of trained and qualified staff to serve as academic and ashram teachers. American culture has a saying, "Those who can't do otherwise, teach." During the 1970s and 1980s, ISKCON had its equivalent: "Those who can't do sankirtan, work in the gurukula." As a gurukula teacher of some twenty years commented, "The gurukula was the dumping ground as far as getting staff went. When devotees couldn't do other things like going on sankirtan, they were sent to work in the gurukula." The result was that besides a few professionally trained academic teachers, ISKCON's schools were staffed by devotees untrained and generally not prepared to take on the demands of working with children. Moreover, because there was little or no status attached to working in the gurukula, many devotees had little or no desire to be there. Success at sankirtan brought individual recognition within the devotee community, whereas working with children brought invisibility and a loss of status.[6] As one ISKCON parent stated,

> I was concerned that the teachers were often selected based on their inability to do sankirtan, rather than because they loved children and education. As far as I could see, there were no mandatory classes in childhood development for teachers or staff either. How could anyone

expect those in charge to know what was normal or abnormal behaviors and how it should be dealt with? (Anonymous a 1996)

As a former gurukula teacher and headmaster emphasized, it was assumed that any devotee with a steadfast spiritual practice was qualified to work in the gurukula. But, he added, few were able to stand up to the everyday demands of working with children.

> There were very few qualified or experienced teachers in the early Gurukula at Dallas. . . . At that time in ISKCON in general there was a hubris about individual qualification. It was thought that a devotee who was chanting his rounds was empowered to do anything and that he did not need any special training. The task of dealing with a hundred children or so from morning to night on a tough schedule through *mangal arati* [early morning religious ceremony] to bedtime was too much for most of them. (Brzezinski 1997)

As these remarks make clear, working in the gurukula was stressful, especially for an untrained person with little interest in children and for a single ashram teacher responsible for the care of twenty or more children. It was these conditions that contributed directly to acts of child abuse by teachers. As one teacher from this era observed, "There may have been some [teachers involved in abusing children] who were actually diabolical. But in most cases it was a lack of expertise, lack of training, lack of assistance, lack of knowing who to go to." And as the former headmaster of one school explained,

> Therefore, we have someone like [name of ashram teacher] who is put into a situation in which he does not belong. It is so stressful. So therefore a kid gets out of line—what to speak of his other transgressions— and he pushes him hard and the kid falls on the floor and breaks his arm. And that's what happened. (interview 1997)

While finding people capable of working in the gurukula was an ongoing problem, retaining them was another. Many second-generation youths talked about having as many as fifteen, twenty, or even more ashram teachers during their time in the gurukula. Eight in ten (82%) of the second-generation youths surveyed in 1992 agreed that "the major reason for the demise of the ashram-based gurukulas was the lack of qualified teachers." The former headmaster just quoted offered a reason:

> At one point they sent all the kids from [region of the country] to our school in Lake Huntington. So now we have this big regional school. Then at one point [guru from that region] decides that he needs the ashram teacher [for the oldest boys] to do some other service. . . . So I call him [guru] and say, "Listen there is no one but me. I am the headmaster. I'm already doing this and that. Now I am going to have to do the ashram. There is nobody here that can do it." He just said, "Well you are just going to have to get somebody. Good-bye." Pull the man out, so now we have sixteen older boys who don't have a teacher. What to do? (interview 1997)

The effect of an ever-changing complement of gurukula teachers and staff meant that the children were unable to build and sustain meaningful and perhaps loving relationships with their adult caregivers, which only increased the likelihood that they might be neglected and/or abused.[7]

The question of "what to do" only intensified as ISKCON's communities in North America declined economically. In the late 1970s the dramatic drop in sankirtan revenues had a devastating impact on the gurukula. As the headmaster of one school explained, "Even at the peak of our movement's resources. . . the gurukula was getting barely anything. Anything. And so as soon as there was less to go around, it barely got anything at all" (interview 1997). He then described the financial difficulties of the Lake Huntington gurukula just before its closing in 1986:

> More difficult was our financial situation. And what happened. When New York was broken up, Lake Huntington, Long Island, New Jersey, and Manhattan, each of these areas was assigned a certain number of collectors, . . . sankirtan devotees. Four months after the breakup I was shifted from Long Island to Lake Huntington and I took over the project. Within a few months I became the headmaster. We had eight sankirtan devotees. We were struggling but were making it. But the zone was collapsing [financially]. So the new GBC man . . . came in and took all the sankirtan devotees and centralized it. The plan was to just give money to the different temples in the zone. We lost our eight sankirtan devotees, and we were promised $8,000 a month, which we got for one

month. They reduced and reduced the amount until we got $2,100 to pay the mortgage. When we asked what to do, they said take more students [thereby getting more tuition]. And that's what we did. Until finally it dawned on us that we were killing our teachers and cheating our students. We can't run a school like this. That was the environment we were actually functioning in. (interview 1997)

A final issue pertains to the gurukula's apparent lack of oversight by the ISKCON leaders. While it is true that ISKCON had a minister of education responsible for providing guidance and leadership for its schools, the gurukula nonetheless failed to gain the attention and supervision it required. And without them, the likelihood of child neglect and abuse grew. As one teacher described it, the leadership simply placed too little importance on the gurukula.

I have come to the conclusion that they [the leadership] aren't going to do anything at all, not anything. They should have done something twenty years ago, or fifteen years ago. They had plenty of opportunity. They had money. They had manpower. They had Srila Prabhupada right there behind them. Why didn't they take it? I can tell you why they didn't do it. They didn't think it was important. Obviously. (interview 1990)

One indication of the leaders' disinterest can be seen in the way that ISKCON's renunciate leaders responded when parents complained about the mistreatment of children in the gurukula. As a second-generation youth recounted,

When I was 5 and 1/2 years old, I'd been in gurukula (Dallas) since its [inception] (about 3 years). My dad had come to Dallas (against the wishes of his temple authority, who only cared about my dad's money-making ability on sankirtan) after discovering bruises all over my body on a Rathayatra [festival] visit. After much discussion with the school authority, he found that he could not get them to change the policy of daily beatings. He removed me from the school. Very disillusioned, he nearly left ISKCON. On hearing that Prabhupad[a][8] would be in L.A. [Los Angeles], we went there. When Prabhupada saw me he asked why I was not in the gurukula. My father told him that he'd removed me because of the daily beatings. Prabhupada told him that I belonged in gurukula and that if my dad had a problem with the treatment he should work to resolve it. . . . [Prabhupada] did nothing to resolve the situation. Instead of going himself or sending one of his top people to resolve the problems he sent my dad, who had never had any power. Needless to say, when my dad returned to Dallas nobody listened to him. If a problem arose at some temple or other, Prabhupada was more than willing to go or send someone effective to handle the situation, but for the kids he sent my dad, who was effective at getting people to give him money.[9] (Anonymous b 1996)

After Prabhupada's death, the response of some of the newly appointed gurus was much the same.

Kutila [woman gurukula teacher] was furious when she saw the cuts and beating marks and she ran to tell Bhaktipada [guru leader of New Vrindaban] who coolly said, "Don't complain, do something about it, if you think you can do any better."[10] (Devi Dasi, K. 1990:1)

Initially, the leadership's disinterest in the gurukula stemmed from an overriding concern with maintaining and indeed expanding sankirtan. Yet with Prabhupada's death in 1977, ISKCON faced years of succession problems that preoccupied ISKCON as a whole (Rochford 1985:221–55, 1998b). As ISKCON's newly appointed gurus struggled to establish their own religious and political authority and attract disciples, householders and their children lost further relevance organizationally.

Exclusion of Parents from the Gurukula

One potential safeguard against child abuse rested with the parents' involvement and oversight of the gurukula. If children were being abused and neglected, one might expect that their parents would intervene. Yet in most instances this did not happen, and when it did, the parents' concerns were often ignored or dismissed, as we saw in the previous section. The fact was that parents were often actively discouraged from any involvement in the gurukula and the day-to-day lives of their children, as was apparent in Dasa's experiences at New Vrindaban.

The idea that parents represented a threat to their children's spiritual lives was widely promoted throughout ISKCON and was accepted by many devotee parents. Embracing the "ideological work" (Berger 1981) of the leadership, many parents maintained minimal contact with their children, and in some cases, they essentially abandoned their children to the gurukula. Teachers, too, considered parents to be threats to their children's spiritual well-being. In the words of one teacher,

> There is a problem with parents. The experience that we have had in gurukula is that much of the training that you are trying to give the child is lost when the child is with the parents. Because the parent is not maintaining the same standards or doesn't have the same abilities, whatever it is. . . . And you knew as a teacher that when you sent a kid home for three and a half weeks [for vacation], you knew you were going to get a basket case when they came back. (interview 1997)

As this teacher also suggested, this way of thinking influenced strongly how those working in the gurukula treated parents: "And so maybe unfortunately, in retrospect, the wrong attitude was conveyed about parents. The parents are a problem; keep the parents away, all of that" (interview 1997).

The larger consequence of these ideas was the virtual exclusion of parents from the gurukula, as their involvement with their children was largely unwelcome. Moreover, when children did return to their parents' home community for school vacations, these visits very often gave parent and child only a little time to spend together. As one mother and teacher explained,

> You have to remember that parents didn't have houses. They didn't have their own place. We never had a house. . . . So when you say a kid went home, that's a euphemism. He went to the temple. His mother had service that she was doing all along. His father had service that he was doing all along. And now all of a sudden this kid is there. So now what does he do? He hangs around the temple. He gets stepped on by people as they are coming up the stairs [into the temple]. . . . And he wants his mother's attention when she is cooking for the deities. The fact is no one took care of the kids. . . . The kid did whatever he did. And the parents just kept on doing whatever it was they were doing. (interview 1997)

A second-generation devotee similarly remembers her vacations from school and the burden these visits placed on her and other family members:

When I got older, I started to spend my vacations with my Mata [mother]. But vacation time for me was not vacation time for her. For Kapila [her brother] and I, she would get a motel room every night but her service to the temple still came first. Only after she had chanted all of her rounds without interruption and she had collected at least three hundred dollars did Kapila and I get to do anything. We usually would sit for six hours in the cold van parked outside a shopping mall and wait for her. Finally she would finish, and even though her back was aching and her shoulders were heavy from carrying a ninety pound bag of books all day, she somehow would find the energy to sneak us into a nearby pool and then take us to ice cream. But most of the time we didn't see how tired she really was and so, whining and complaining about how little attention we got, we sometimes drove her to tears. (Devi Dasi, K. 1990:12)

Even more extreme than the North American schools, the gurukulas in India took excessive measures to isolate children from their parents. In the Vrndavana gurukula, the school administrators monitored and sometimes censured letters written by students to their parents. When a student attempted to write his parents about the negligent and abusive conditions at his school, he was reprimanded and told to rewrite his letter.

Jiva: I used to write letters to my mom, during the rough times, saying, "Get me out of here." And he [school administrator] read them and would tear 'em up and make me write new ones.
Subal: He did that to me too. (group interview 1993)

In other cases, students in the Vrndavana gurukula did not write their parents about the conditions at their school because they assumed their letters would be read by the administration or, as in the following case, they feared their parents would reject allegations of abuse. According to one mother,

My son complains bitterly about what went on in Vrndavana. Of course I have asked him a million times why he didn't tell me what was going on because I used to go and visit him every year. And he wouldn't say anything to me. He would just give me his shopping list. When I asked him in retrospect, why didn't you tell me, he just said, "Because

you wouldn't believe me." . . . He assumed I wouldn't believe him. And
he assumed his letters would be censured. And so he never wrote anything that would cause him to be censured.[11] (interview 1997)

In still other instances, the school administrators in Vrndavana tried
to hide the abuse, as Dasa found during his time at the school.

He [the headmaster] knowingly covered up. . . . There are two or three
incidents that I can think of where I was beaten or something happened
to me. He would take me into his room and he'd lock me in there for
like a day with him and he was like constantly preaching to me, and so
finally I just went, "OK! I won't say anything to anybody. It didn't happen!" And he would let me out of the room.[12] (interview 1993)

In the final analysis, it seems clear that the gurukula became an institution unto itself, in Goffman's (1961) terms, a "total institution."
Within the gurukula, children remained largely separate from the day-
to-day lives of their parents and very often from ISKCON community life
more generally. Instead of an institution meant to train and educate, the
gurukula became the functional equivalent of an orphanage. As one
teacher from this period remarked, "The whole scenario set up an orphanage . . . even though you have kids with parents. Because we didn't
allow the parents to become part of their children's lives" (interview
1997).[13]

Avoiding Child Abuse: Resources and Victimization

Although a number of factors and processes contributed to the child
abuse in ISKCON's schools, others allowed some young people to escape
it, even though in some cases their classmates were targeted but they
were spared. Perhaps the most obvious variable in whether or not a
child was abused was the school itself. To a significant degree, the gurukula a student attended directly determined whether he or she became a
target of abuse, as some gurukulas experienced far less child abuse
while others were defined by neglect and abuse. The schools in India,
where abuse and neglect were reportedly commonplace, provide the
most vivid example. Since only adolescent boys attended these schools,
they faced far more abuse than did their female counterparts. In the

United States, child abuse also was common in several of ISKCON's schools (Dallas, Seattle, New Vrindaban), whereas it was considerably less common in others (Bhaktivedanta Village, California, and New Talavan, Mississippi). Child abuse also was far less prevalent in Europe and Australia than in either India or North America.

How can we explain these differences? First, some gurukulas had more stable staffs, with respect to academic and ashram teachers as well as administrators. Often the teachers in these schools were more devoted to working in the gurukula and willing to establish enduring and caring relationships with the children. Two former gurukula students suggest why they especially liked a particular school:

> It was M[other] Kutila who changed our lives and who let us know that someone could love us; that devotees *did* love one another. I swear for the first week I thought I was a princess. We were never hit any more, we had all new clothes, our own bags, filled with our own soap, brushes and hot water showers. It was then that I knew I had a mother and father, they were Kutila and Kuladri [her husband]. (author's emphasis; Devi Dasi, K. 1990:1)

> One of the high points of my life in gurukula was because the teacher [name], took us in as his sons (original Vedic standard) and treated us like adults. We had incredible camaraderie as well as growth—including fitness, mental strength, creativity, and Krishna Consciousness. (Second Generation Survey 1992)

A second factor that was important to limiting the possibility of abuse was the level of parental involvement in the gurukula. Although both the leadership and the gurukula staff opposed parents' involvement, some parents nonetheless found ways to participate in their children's upbringing. In some cases, this was made easier when parents lived in the same community as their children's gurukula. In other instances, parents wrote letters, made phone calls, and regularly visited their children.

The sad irony is that parents who accepted the ideological justifications offered by the leadership and chose to remain "detached" and minimally involved in their children's lives effectively left them vulnerable to neglect and abuse. Simply put, children without involved parents more readily became victims for abusers. As two second-generation devotees concluded, "Usually, if our parents showed an interest in us, by sending us mail and gifts, visiting us, and maintaining a tight bond, the abusive teachers would view that child as a liability to them" (Hickey, Charnell, et al. 1997).

To ensure regular involvement with their children, some parents, particularly mothers, chose to work in the gurukula as teachers. As the headmaster of one school pointed out, "Practically every [female] teacher had their children in the school. And that was an important factor [limiting the potential for abuse] that those parents' eyes were there. It was important." As this implies, the presence of parents working in the gurukula served to protect many children against abuse, not simply their own children. Because mothers were much more likely than fathers to have a position in the gurukula and because mothers were able to maintain relationships with their daughters, more girls than boys were protected against abuse. As one woman teacher recounted,

> With my daughters, it was a little different because I had some ability and determination to keep my daughters with me. So I was a teacher, and I taught my daughters, or at least I knew where my daughters were being taught. But with my son it wasn't allowed. He had to be removed from my presence. (interview 1997)

A child also was protected against abuse if he or she had a male parent who was an ISKCON leader or was otherwise recognized as influential in the movement. These children presented substantial risks to an abuser, and so they were targeted less often. Even in India, children with influential fathers normally escaped abuse. One mother whose son spent years at a gurukula in India reported, "My son tells me that he didn't get abused. And it's funny, isn't it, in light of his [activism over the abuse issue]? But this is because of who his father was [a member of the GBC]"[14] (interview 1997).

Even those children whose parents remained largely uninvolved in their lives had one means of creating a protective shield against abuse. Again, India was the context. Reports indicate that adolescent boys in the gurukula were less likely to be abused if they were initiated by one of ISKCON's gurus. In effect, initiation by a guru created an interested and powerful ally who could expose or punish an abuser. In the absence of involved and/or influential parents, initiation thus served as a means of creating an interested party.

Conclusion

Before the widespread allegations of child abuse, ISKCON represented what Shupe (1995) refers to as a "trusted hierarchy." Religious groups and organizations are distinct from their secular counterparts precisely because "those occupying lower statuses in religious organizations trust or believe in the good intentions, nonselfish motives, benevolence, and spiritual insights/wisdom of those in the upper echelons (and often are encouraged or admonished to do so)" (Shupe 1995:29). Indeed, parents often socialize their children to respect the religious authority of church leaders, thus perpetuating the religious organization's very basis of trust. It was this unquestioned trust in the leadership and in ISKCON as a whole that led parents to assume that their children were being properly educated and cared for in the gurukula. As we have seen, however, this assumption helped create opportunities for abuse and exploitation (for other examples, see Krebs 1998; Shupe 1995).

As one might expect, child abuse affects far more people than those directly victimized. As Pullen observed, "Religious congregations can collectively share psychological, emotional, and spiritual trauma when faced with the reality that their most vulnerable members have been sexually violated by individuals the community invested with authority" (1998:68). Among members of a support group formed in response to clerical sexual abuse of children in California, Pullen found members referring to their own "spiritual abuse." Although not directly abused themselves, they nonetheless indicated "that their trust and faith in the credibility and integrity of their religious leaders had been shattered" (1998:68–69). Nason-Clark (1998) found much the same response among female congregants in the aftermath of child sexual abuse by church officials in Canada. In organizational terms, child abuse by clergy and other religious officials precipitates a crisis of trust among rank-and-file members. Seligman argued that the "existence of trust is an essential component of all enduring social relationships" (1997:13) and is indeed necessary for the continuation of any social order.

The betrayal of trust represented by child abuse has challenged, if not undermined, the commitment to ISKCON of many first- and second-generation members alike. Child abuse stands as a powerful symbol of the failure of ISKCON's leadership and the form of social organization (communalism) that supported its political and spiritual authority. As trust gave way to anger and doubt, householders became less willing to commit their lives to ISKCON than they had in the past. Needless to say, many second-generation devotees also rejected their ISKCON collective identity. In failing to maintain a safe and healthy environment for the movement's most vulnerable members, ISKCON faced discreditation from within and a corresponding loss of legitimacy in the eyes of many longtime members. Many abandoned ISKCON, and others joined a growing congregation of independent householders and their families living on the margins of ISKCON's North American communities.[15]

Besides the internal dissent threatening ISKCON was a federal lawsuit filed on June 12, 2000, in the U.S. District Court in Dallas, Texas. The suit filed on behalf of forty-four young men and women alleged that during the 1970s and 1980s they had been subject to "sexual, emotional, mental, and physical abuse and exploitation" while they were students in ISKCON's gurukulas (Children of ISKCON et al. vs. the International Society for Krishna Consciousness et al. 2000). The plaintiffs, living in the United States, Canada, and England, sought a total of $400 million: $200 million in actual damages and $200 million in punitive damages. The defendants in this case were ISKCON as the lead defendant; sixteen specific ISKCON communities, businesses, and organizations; the executors of Prabhupada's estate; and eighteen members or former members of ISKCON's Governing Body Commission who were serving on the GBC during the period of the alleged abuse. The defendants also were charged with federal racketeering and violations of the Racketeer Influenced and Corrupt Organizations Act (RICO). In a press release, Windle Turley, the lawyer for the plaintiffs, stated, "This lawsuit describes the most unthinkable abuse and maltreatment of little children which we have seen. It includes rape, sexual abuse, physical torture and emotional terror of children as young as three years of age" (Law Offices of Windle Turley 2000).

The federal case was dismissed after the Dallas U.S. district court judge ruled in September 2001 that the plaintiffs' attempt to invoke the RICO Act as part of their case lacked legal merit (Dasa, Anuttama 2001). Subsequently lawyers for the plaintiffs filed a lawsuit in a Texas state court in October 2001 (Children of ISKCON et al. vs. the International Society for Krishna Consciousness et al. 2001). The suit sought $400 million in damages for the plaintiffs. By 2002 the number of plaintiffs in the case had grown to ninety-two (Dasa, Anuttama 2005). Finally, after several ISKCON communities named in the lawsuit filed for Chapter 11 bankruptcy protection, the case was resolved in May 2005 by U.S. bankruptcy courts in West Virginia and California (Dasa, Anuttama 2005). Leading up to the final settlement, an additional 450 claimants were added after, at the request of the bankruptcy court, the ISKCON authorities agreed to seek out all former students claiming abuse in its schools (Dasa, Anuttama 2005). A total of 535 former gurukula students will receive compensation, ranging between $2,500 and $50,000, from the $9.5 million settlement (Dasa, Anuttama 2005).[16]

But whether or not they had been abused, ISKCON's young people faced serious identity challenges as they transferred from the movement's ashram-gurukulas into American public schools during the 1980s. It is to these issues that we turn in the next chapter.

4

Public Schooling and Identity

I spent three years in a public high school and now I'm attending college. It's really tough to do the spiritual thing in these circumstances. 'Cause you go to school and you can't ignore it, what everyone else is doing. They're doing different things than you're used to and it's hard not to worry about being accepted. This is what happens when gurukula kids go to the nondevotee schools. When the Krishna Consciousness part of their life is not affecting them more than the other part, in consciousness. They're not burned out on Krishna Consciousness. They're just not interested. It no longer makes any sense to them. It makes no sense in that place [public high school].
—Words of one second-generation devotee, 1992

Richard Niebuhr (1929) noted long ago that the process of educating the young plays a determinative role in the development of religious communities, especially sectarian ones. In being attentive to the educational requirements of children, the fundamental character of the religious enterprise changes in the direction of secularization. The result is that "as generation succeeds generation, the isolation of the community from the world becomes more difficult" (Niebuhr 1929:19–20).

Although educating and socializing those born into the faith does represent a pivotal moment in the career of any religious movement, it is by no means certain that accommodation with the mainstream culture will be the result, as Niebuhr suggested (Wilson 1987:41; 1990: 108). Rather, effective socialization distinguishes successful religious movements from those that fail (see Stark 1987:24–25; 1996:144). In general, religious communities succeed in securing the commitment of their young by socializing them into the values and lifestyle of the group while at the same time limiting or neutralizing the countervailing influences of the conventional culture (Kraybill 1977). Moreover as Stark

(1987:25) noted, enduring religious communities and movements give their young useful and significant things to do, thereby building group commitment and loyalty.[1]

Traditionally, the ashram-based gurukula served as the institution responsible for enculturating ISKCON's youngest members, that is, transferring the movement's spiritual and material culture to the next generation. To do this the gurukula was structured to maximize boundary maintenance, thereby limiting the possibility of cross-cultural exchange between young devotees and the surrounding conventional culture. The gurukula was thus expressly structured to limit acculturation, the "intercultural transfer of values and behaviors between groups" (Kraybill 1977:2). Given that the traditional gurukula system has largely disintegrated over the past two decades, with the majority of ISKCON's young people being educated outside the movement, we may ask what effect this has had on ISKCON's second generation and on ISKCON as a whole. The following discusses how ISKCON youths who attended ashram-gurukulas during the 1970s and 1980s negotiated the public high school experience and its consequences for their identity.[2]

The Public High School Experience and the Negotiation of Identity

For adolescents raised in an alternative religious community, the public high school is a "reality disrupting," and even potentially "reality transforming" social environment (Berger and Luckmann 1967:159). Such a setting, to use Berger and Luckmann's apt phrase, represents a "'laboratory' of transformation" (1967:157). As this term implies, the public school setting is socially and ideologically antagonistic to the socioreligious world of persons raised in unconventional religious groups like ISKCON. According to one ISKCON mother whose daughter attended a Catholic high school,

> Association, Prabhupada said, is 95 percent. You put these kids in with a bunch of rotten apples, like in the public school, this is what you get, a rotten apple. . . . Kids are taking drugs, they're having sex, they're taking intoxication, they're stealing. It's the norm for a kid to have a boyfriend at thirteen. What do you expect to happen? (interview 1990)

Although logical sociologically, this view effectively reduces social actors to little more than passive objects shaped by the structure, goals, and activities associated with institutional life. Such a perspective obscures the ways that individuals remain active agents in making choices and constructing their own identities (Burke and Reitzes 1991:244). It also risks wrongly portraying unconventional religious beliefs as inherently fragile and readily subject to disconfirmation (see Snow and Machalek 1982).

Donald Kraybill's (1977) investigation of Mennonite public high school students is informative in this regard. Compared with those of young people enrolled in Mennonite high schools, the religious commitments of those attending a public high school were no different. Kraybill concluded (1977:35), "The public high school environment does *not* erode attitudes toward religious orthodoxy" (my emphasis). Kraybill's study suggests the need to look more closely at the specific social processes that work for and against assimilation and at changes in religious identity. Given these considerations, the question of how, and if, a public school environment affects the identity of Hare Krishna youths must remain an empirical one.

Interaction, Identity, and Consciousness

A person's identity makes reference to where he or she is located in social life and establishes what and where a person is socially (Stone 1981:188). A person has identity to the extent that "he is situated, that is cast, in the shape of a social object by acknowledgment of his participation or membership in social relations" (Stone 1981:188). A social movement collective identity is a status that is attached to an individual as a consequence of his or her participation in the movement's activities (Friedman and McAdam 1992:169). As these definitions suggest, social identity—whether individual or collective—is shaped by ongoing interaction and identification with others. Role transitions and related shifts in identity thus depend on the relative significance of both existing and emergent social networks in people's everyday lives (Silver 1996:2).[3]

Given these considerations, it seems reasonable to hypothesize that ISKCON youths who are able to establish close relational ties with conventional high school students will undergo a change in identity, becoming more assimilated into mainstream American culture. This may even involve a process of "deconversion" (Jacobs 1984, 1987) as their Krishna conscious worldview loses salience in everyday affairs. Conversely, those who eschew ties with non-ISKCON students in favor of devotee relationships are unlikely to change their collective identity.

The 1992 Second Generation Survey allows to determine how ISK-CON youths negotiated the public high school environment and its consequences. Of the eighty-seven ISKCON youths who took part in the survey, fifty-three at some point attended a public high school and thus are the focus here.[4] As table 4.1 shows, a substantial majority of the ISKCON students did establish meaningful social ties with their nondevotee classmates. Moreover, these relationships appear to have formed at the expense of ties with other devotee youths and their religious involvement and beliefs.

Approximately three-quarters of the ISKCON youths who attended a public high school developed close friendships with nondevotees, visited the homes of these friends, and dated nondevotees during their high school years. Of equal significance is that only a small minority (15%) associated primarily with other devotee students while they were in school. Less dramatically, somewhat fewer than half (42%) admitted withdrawing more generally from their relationships with devotee young people. Thus, although most interacted with and established friendships with nondevotee students, roughly an equal proportion did

TABLE 4.1
ISKCON Youths' Negotiations in Public High School Setting

Negotiated Involvements	Percentage
I. Social Relationships	
Spent time visiting homes of nondevotee friends	75% (40)
Developed close friendships with nondevotee students	77% (41)
Dated nondevotees	72% (38)
Associated mostly with other devotee students when in school	15% (8)
Became less involved with other devotee youths	42% (22)
II. Involvement in School/Youth Culture	
Involved in popular "kids' culture"	60% (32)
Involved in school sports	53% (28)
III. Religious Involvement and Commitment	
Became less interested in attending temple activities	53% (28)
Experimented with breaking some regulative principles	74% (39)
Began to question my Krishna conscious beliefs	51% (27)

TABLE 4.2
Selected Measures of Nondevotee Friendship Patterns for ISKCON *Youths*

	Involved in Popular "Kids' Culture"	Became Less Involved with Devotee Youth My Age	Less Interested in Attending Temple Activities	Breaking Some Regulative Principles	Questioned Krishna Conscious Beliefs
Have close nondevotee friends	73% (30)***	44% (18)	56% (23)	83% (34)**	56% (23)
Have no close nondevotee friends	17% (2)	33% (4)	42% (5)	42% (5)	33% (4)

** $p < .01$; *** $p < .001$.

and did not withdraw from interpersonal relationships that kept them tied to the world of ISKCON and Krishna Consciousness.

As the findings further reveal, many ISKCON young people participated in their classmates' social worlds, a majority in various aspects of contemporary "kids' culture"—listening to popular music, drinking alcohol, smoking marijuana, and generally keeping up with trends in the conventional youth subculture. Half played high school sports, several distinguishing themselves as star athletes.

With respect to their religious involvement, more than half those enrolled in public schools became less interested in attending religious activities at their local ISKCON temple. A similar number began questioning their Krishna conscious beliefs. Particularly striking is that three-quarters admitted to breaking one or more of the movement's regulative principles, behavioral standards that define ISKCON's religious way of life.

If we compare ISKCON youths who did and did not become involved in nondevotee friendships, we gain a more precise picture of the influence of nondevotee attachments, although only twelve of the fifty-three ISKCON youths rejected such ties. As table 4.2 shows, those young people who established nondevotee friendships were much more likely to become involved in aspects of conventional youth culture and were more likely as well to violate some of the movement's regulative principles. Although the differences are not as noteworthy, ISKCON students with nondevotee friendships more often withdrew from relationships with other devotee youths, became less interested in attending temple services and activities, and were more likely to question their Krishna conscious beliefs. Consider the statement of one young woman who attended a public high school:

I was into partying, going out. I was curious and so I got into it. When I was fifteen, I experimented with drinking, going to parties. I had my first boyfriend, all of that. I felt that I had to be part of the whole scene, or I wouldn't be accepted. If I went around "Hare Krishna, Hare Krishna," you know, who would be my friend?

Given the significance of nondevotee friendships, it is important to consider some of the ways that these ties were forged. As suggested by the woman just quoted, dating was one means by which devotee young people formed relational ties with their nondevotee counterparts. This was especially true for the women devotees surveyed, as 82 percent of them dated nondevotee classmates, compared with 55 percent of their male counterparts.[5] Sports played a significant role in the integration of both men and women into nondevotee friendship networks, with only two of the twenty-eight youths who played sports failing to establish close friendship ties with their nondevotee classmates. The role of sports in establishing friendships is indicated in the comments of a second-generation male devotee who attended a public high school in West Virginia:

The most difficult thing for me was to fit in [at the local high school] because of the way I acted and dressed—it just wasn't "up to par." I wasn't really "cool" like the other dudes. I was a mess until I played football and did well, which created many friends.

Identity Work and Identity Change

The foregoing findings suggest that most ISKCON youths did, in fact, become integrated socially into the public high school culture, establishing close nondevotee friendships and becoming involved in popular adolescent culture. But even though they are revealing, these findings leave us with little understanding of what actually transpired when devotee youths encountered the social world of the public high school. How and why, for example, did some become socially integrated into nondevotee networks while others escaped, or perhaps resisted, such involvement? Moreover, how did the differing levels of involvement and integration into the nondevotee world influence these youths' ISKCON identity? To answer these questions, we must further explore the relations between

ISKCON youths and their nondevotee student counterparts. In particular, we must determine how being a Hare Krishna itself shaped the identity negotiations taking place in the public high school. Two issues are particularly relevant.

First, devotee young people became public high school students with little practical knowledge of the social world they were about to enter. Not only was this environment antagonistic to what they believed and who they were, they also were not familiar with the particulars of this environment. Second, devotee young people entered the public high school with a highly stigmatized personal identity. To be a Hare Krishna was (and is) viewed by others as "deviant," "strange," "dangerous," or, in the words of Goffman (1963:5), "not quite human." This was all the more true during the 1980s, when anticult sentiment was particularly virulent in North America, and it was during this period that most of the ISKCON youths considered here were attending high school or approaching high school age. Because of the dual challenge posed by having "stigma potential" (Schneider and Conrad 1993) while simultaneously having little working knowledge of the conventional world, ISKCON young people found themselves preoccupied with the problem of social acceptance and undertook strategies to deal with it (see Goffman 1963:8–9).

Commonsense Knowledge and the Problem of Social Acceptance

The problem of gaining social acceptance and avoiding victimization was a troublesome proposition for ISKCON young people in ways that rarely confront others with stigma potential. Having been raised apart from the dominant culture within a totalistic community, ISKCON youths lacked even the most basic knowledge about what their nondevotee classmates claimed as the "common culture." As Garfinkel suggested (1967:76), such an understanding is a prerequisite for group participation and claims to group membership. As one particularly astute devotee youth commented about his transition into the public high school: "I had large gaps in my culture-specific knowledge. I had no skills." The following statements point to the content that defined these "gaps."

> I couldn't relate to these kids. I wasn't seeing anything the same way. From age eleven, when we thought of men, we thought of marriage.

Nothing was lighthearted and funny. I had to *learn* to laugh, how to have a sense of humor. As a girl we were taught to be chaste—therefore we never learned to ride even a bicycle, and so when I was put into PE class, it was one of the most embarrassing moments for me. I didn't know what third base was or what to do when the ball came to me. (her emphasis)

I think the most difficult thing was that I didn't know how to deal with these people [nondevotee students]. . . . I didn't know anything about the way people grew up. I never saw any [of the] TV shows they were talking about, etc.

This may seem strange, but the names of the students were confusing at first because they weren't Indian, and I had never heard them before.

Sister 1: We [she and her sister] didn't even know what "the finger" was. And we got into fights because we didn't know who Michael Jackson was. We were so lost.

Sister 2: It was so hard. So hard for us to deal with karmies [nondevotees]. (interview 1992)

For many, the "dis-ease" they felt in the public high school environ-ment caused confusion and even a sense of "anomic terror" (Berger and Luckmann 1967:103).

I was scared. I didn't know how to deal with my fellow classmates. I was very uptight. I thought I was so different from them because we had been raised to believe they were bad people. Mainly I was terrified that everyone knew how I was raised.

I did not fit in at all! It was a major change. In the ashram we were kept so segregated from the nondevotees and never taught much [about] the outside world. When we were, it was always negative. I was very afraid and felt totally out of place. I felt everyone noticed how strange and dif-ferent I was.

To deal with the structural strain associated with attempting to cope with an unfamiliar and even hostile world, ISKCON youths undertook what amounted to a "secret apprenticeship" (Garfinkel 1967:147). Such a strategy allows actors to simultaneously mask incompetencies while permitting the "environment to furnish . . . the answer to its own questions" (Garfinkel 1967:147). ISKCON's young people mentioned two interrelated roles—being shy and being a loner—that allowed them to stand back in an apprenticeship role, although they tended to view each as a personality trait rather than strategies allowing for social adaptation.

A number of the second-generation devotees observed that in the school environment they and their devotee peers were often shy and withdrawn.

> At first I was shy. A lot of the devotee kids are shy but I was extremely shy. . . . You have to understand we didn't know how to relate. This was all new to us.

> I was shy and extremely self-conscious. I found that going to school with these "strangers" made me very uncomfortable. Dealing with girls was difficult and the most embarrassing aspect. . . . But I adjusted after a while and learned how to relate to this new "species" of human.

> When I first entered public school, I was very shy. I had a lot of catching up to do with the latest trends, and cliques were something new to me.

Some youths were loners in the public high school environment, remaining largely uninvolved with their nondevotee classmates. But as the following statement demonstrates, the loner role had strategic value:

> Even though I was around them [the other students], I kept myself pretty isolated. I felt very alone. I wanted to be open about myself, but it was too risky. I just didn't want to have the pressure on. I didn't know anything about these kids. I wanted to stay on the side[lines]. That way I could check them out.

Assuming the role of loner or being shy allowed devotee young people to gain a marginal degree of acceptance in the adolescent world of the high school without their devotee status becoming a public issue. Not only could they learn the ropes of adolescent culture from within these roles, but they also could create a social distance between themselves and the very culture they were trying to understand. Although for most, this strategy appears to have been temporary, for others being shy or a loner formed the basis of a stable social role that allowed them to escape integration into student friendship networks. One devotee youth stated:

> I didn't want to get too close to them because I know that when you hang out with party animals, you become one yourself. So I believe in association, that if I associate with devotees, I will become a devotee. So I chose to stay on my own.

Stigma and the Problem of Social Acceptance

In his classic work on the topic, Goffman (1963:3) defined stigma as "an attribute that is deeply discrediting." An individual who is stigmatized, be it on the basis of "abominations of the body," "blemishes of character," or the "tribal stigma of race, nation or religion, possesses a trait that can obtrude itself upon attention and turn those of us whom he meets away from him, breaking the claim that his other attributes have on us. He possesses a stigma, an undesired differentness from what we had anticipated" (Goffman 1963:4–5).

Despite being unaware of much of American adolescent culture, devotee youths attend non-ISKCON schools fully aware of their movement's public reputation as a deviant "cult." They are cognizant as well that as "outsiders" (Becker 1963) they may be shunned or harassed. As one devotee youth commented, "When I first went to public school I was afraid the kids wouldn't like me because of the devotees' reputation." And in fact, some ISKCON youths did face stigmatization and rejection at the hands of nondevotee students and teachers.

> The transition was very hard. I wasn't use to being ridiculed for who I was. I fought because that was all I could do.

> The embarrassment when the nondevotees made fun of me was real hard to take. Some of the teachers' insolence toward us also. Just trying to become another person at school was so difficult. Every time something went wrong, we devotee students were always accused of doing it.

Because of the stigma attached to being a Hare Krishna, most young people were intensely self-conscious as they anticipated the transition to the local public high school. Indeed, because of the ever present potential for rejection and harassment, many studiously avoided mentioning their ties to ISKCON or Krishna Consciousness.

> I felt a bit nervous about saying, "I am a Hare Krishna," because they [nondevotee students] would call me bad names. The bad names will start coming right away. People will make fun of us.

> *Devotee Woman 1*: I mean if people were to find out what your religion was they're like "Oh my God!" So it's better not to tell them what your religion is so they can get to know you as a person.

> *Devotee Woman 2*: Like you can't say, "Hi, I'm Sally and I'm a Hare Krishna." Because you will never make friends. We had to keep it—not a secret but (pause).

> *Devotee Woman 1*: There are such stereotypes about us. I must admit for a while I was embarrassed to admit that I was a Hare Krishna. (interview 1992)

The Second Generation Survey also supports the concerns expressed in the foregoing comments. Fifty-three percent of those who attended a public high school agreed that when they began school, they were at least "somewhat embarrassed at being a devotee." While not embarrassed by their devotee identity, others nonetheless tried to avoid being stigmatized and hid their Krishna identity from their classmates. Overall, when entering the public high school, six in ten (61%) admitted "try[ing] to avoid revealing the fact that I was a devotee."

As these findings suggest, interactions between devotee youths and their classmates required identity work, at least during their initial transition into the public school environment. The interactional challenge was one of information control, or managing self-presentation to avoid revealing their collective identity as Hare Krishnas. As discreditable persons, ISKCON students continually concealed "creditable facts" (Goffman 1963:42), as they were committed to not be different. Being "ordinary" allowed for the possibility of gaining acceptance. One devotee woman who attended a public high school in Denver explained:

> It was kind of odd because I felt like an oddball. . . . And of course I never, never, told anyone that I was a Hare Krishna. . . . The thing was I didn't go around with my head covered or anything like that. I was just into the whole scene there. They really didn't know anything—that

I was different from a normal student, any other student coming to school. (interview 1992)

To avoid conveying information that might reveal their actual identity, devotee young people used a number of interactional strategies to gain acceptance as conventional students.[6] In turn, these strategies facilitated the integration of ISKCON youths into conventional networks and the social world of their nondevotee peers.[7]

Stigma and Self-Presentation

In the process of interaction, the demands of social life routinely require people to convey information about themselves. On the one hand, this allows actors to make claims about who they are, and on the other hand, it provides others with the "raw materials" to construct "working" identities for those who are otherwise unfamiliar. Such signs, of course, can communicate status or prestige as well as to draw attention to the deviant or debasing qualities of a person's identity. Goffman (1963:43–44) refers to the latter as "stigma symbols," and they constitute the focus of "stigma management," or passing. Essentially, a discreditable person engages in identity work to neutralize or hide from public view any discrediting information about himself or herself. By so doing, this person preserves the basis of social acceptance.

To avoid revealing their actual social identity, ISKCON young people used a variety of self-presentation strategies to make invisible their identity as Hare Krishna members. These strategies were specifically crafted with an eye toward gaining acceptance from their classmates.[8]

Dress: In his research on appearance and the self, Stone (1981:202) concluded "that the self is established, maintained, and altered in social transactions as much by the communications of appearance as by discourse." Through our appearance we mobilize specific self-definitions in the minds of those with whom we interact. It is in this sense that our appearance serves as a public announcement of our identity (Stone 1981:193). As one second-generation ISKCON woman put it,

Wearing a sari helps me stay pious and remember Krsna. . . . It helps remind me and others that I'm a devotee of Krsna, in the same way a policeman's uniform helps him remember his service and reminds citizens he's an agent of the law. (Devi Dasi, Madireksana 1994:41)

Almost without exception, devotee young people attended their local public high school dressed in clothing like that worn by their nondevotee classmates. Such an appearance was a statement of their "ordinary" student status. Until this point, most had spent their lives attired in traditional religious garb: a dhoti for men and a sari for women.

Only in one instance did a second-generation youth report going to school wearing clothing that openly acknowledged her Hare Krishna identity. The young woman in question did so only at the insistence of her stepfather, whose motives are clear from her comments.

We went to junior high—public. But my stepfather wouldn't let my brother and me wear normal clothes—made [name of brother] keep his *shika* [clump of hair on back of head], me wear a long dress. But worst of all, we were not allowed to associate with other kids our age because he was afraid of our contamination by nondevotees. So in other words, [we had] no friends.

In Goffman's terms, this young woman's stepfather explicitly wanted her and her brother to face discreditation at the hands of their nondevotee classmates. By so doing, he was trying to forestall any possibility that they would become friendly with nondevotee students, thereby avoiding potential threats to their devotional way of life. Such actions by parents, however, appear to have been rare.[9]

Name changes: The devotional names of ISKCON youths represented a significant threat to their efforts to be accepted as conventional students. When they entered public high school, they routinely Anglicized their devotee names (for example, Caitanya became Chris) or, if they had one, reverted to their legal Christian name. The following exchange illustrates the implications of using a devotee name and the resulting pressures to seek an acceptable alternative:

Man 1: Feeling different, being teased about my name made for a difficult adjustment to the public high I went to.

Man 2: Everyone had difficulty with my spiritual name. Eventually I took a Christian name. It just made things a lot easier for me. (interview 1992)

Very often, the use of Christian and Anglicized names moved beyond the boundaries of the school environment as devotee youths referred to one another by these names even in the ISKCON community. On many occasions and in different ISKCON communities, I observed teenagers referring to one another using Christian names or obviously Anglicized devotee names. The act of changing their names to conventional ones represented a fundamental symbolic break from the world of ISKCON.[10]

Vegetarianism: Diet was one element in the lives of devotee youths that worried them most as they made the transition into public education. Given a lifetime of strict vegetarianism, eating meat was not an option.[11] Even though American attitudes toward vegetarianism have become increasingly favorable, many saw this aspect of their lifestyle as making them particularly vulnerable to the curiosity of other students.

> Being a vegetarian . . . was one of the things I tried to keep hidden. I excluded myself from social actions with other students and would not eat near anyone else.

> I was vegetarian. The kids thought my bread, lettuce, tomato, and cheese sandwich was weird and wouldn't taste it.

> Explaining why I didn't eat meat was the most difficult. It was like you weren't human if you didn't eat it.

As the following comment by one ISKCON youth suggests, being a vegetarian occasionally did raise suspicions and identity challenges:

> Even people who asked me: "You're a vegetarian. You do this. You do that. Are you a Hare Krishna by any chance?" "No. Are you kidding?" Just a flat-out lie.

Association with other ISKCON youths: The possibility that a discreditable person's identity might be revealed is heightened when he or she associates with others who share the same stigma. As Goffman (1963: 47) observed, "to be 'with'" someone reveals information about social identity because we usually assume that people associate with others like themselves.

Being in the presence of other devotee young people while at school carried two potential risks. Because not all devotee young people were as equally skilled in the techniques of passing and because a few apparently had little or no regard for protecting their ISKCON identity, being with other devotees invited the possibility of public exposure. The devotee might, for example, slip into distinctive ways of speaking and acting that appeared "out of character" to nondevotees. For these and other reasons, the vast majority consciously avoided other devotee young people when in school, favoring contacts with nondevotee students (see table 4.1).[12]

> *EBR:* Were there other devotee kids at the [Los Angeles] high school where you went?
> *D:* Oh yeah. Lots of them.
> *EBR:* Did you hang out together? D: No not really. . . . I wasn't really that interested in being with them [devotee kids]. I was just trying to deal with all that was happening [at the high school]. That was enough [for me]. I didn't want other [nondevotee] kids to know who I was anyway.[13] (interview 1992)

Passing, Social Relationships, and Identity

The findings reported in table 4.3 suggest that concerns about stigma and attempts to pass influenced how devotee youths adapted to both the high school environment and ISKCON. The findings indicate that devotee young people who neither were embarrassed nor made special efforts to avoid revealing their ISKCON identity integrated more fully into the high school social milieu. They also were more likely to maintain

TABLE 4.3

Selected Measures of ISKCON Youths' Responses to Stigma

Response to Stigma	Avoided Revealing Devotee Identity	Developed Close Friendships with Nondevotee Students	Involved in Popular "Kids' Culture"	Became Less Involved with Devotee Youth My Age	Less Interested in Attending Temple Activities	Breaking Some Regulative Principles	Questioned Krishna Conscious Beliefs
a. Embarrassed at Being a Devotee							
Yes	89% (25)***	64% (18)	50% (14)	50% (14)	75% (21)***	71% (20)	57% (16)
No	28% (7)	92% (23)*	72% (18)@	32% (8)	28% (7)	76% (19)	44% (11)
b. Sought to Avoid Revealing ISKCON Identity							
Yes	—	72% (23)	59% (19)	53% (17)*	69% (22)***	69% (22)	56% (18)
No	—	86% (18)	62% (13)	24% (5)	29% (6)	81% (17)	43% (9)

@ $p < .10$; * $p < .05$; *** $p < .001$.

relationships with other devotee youths and retain their Krishna conscious beliefs and practices.

A large majority of youths who felt embarrassment at being an ISKCON devotee tried to avoid revealing their Krishna identity in high school. These adolescents were also less likely to establish close friendships with nondevotee peers, although nearly two-thirds did so despite these feelings. In addition, those embarrassed by their ISKCON identity were less involved in popular "kid's culture" and were far less interested in taking part in temple activities. These youths were only somewhat more likely to reduce their involvements with other devotee young people or question their Krishna conscious beliefs, compared with devotee youths who were not embarrassed by their ISKCON identity. In fact, the majority of both groups of youths broke one or more of the regulative principles.

Attempts to avoid revealing an ISKCON identity did not discourage the development of nondevotee friendships, which suggests that ISKCON youths' efforts to pass and gain social acceptance were largely successful. Avoidance was associated with being less involved with other devotee young people and less interested in taking part in temple activities.

Collectively, the findings in table 4.3 raise a more fundamental question about identity and self-presentation. If ISKCON youths engaged in passing strictly as a strategic device to avoid revealing their Krishna identity, we might reasonably expect that their ISKCON ties and involvements would remain more or less stable. To avoid their devotee peers and to lose interest in attending community activities at the temple, however, imply something far more significant. As pointed out previously, individual identity and collective identity are grounded in social relations. To the extent that ISKCON youths responded to their potential for stigma by withdrawing from devotee relationships and community life in favor of ties with nondevotee classmates, the social basis for their identity changed.

Table 4.4 compares the collective identity of ISKCON youths who did and did not attend public high schools at the time of the Second Generation Survey. Only those ISKCON youths who completed high school were included in the analysis.[14] Youths who attended a public high school were much less likely to embrace an ISKCON collective identity as either a core or a congregational member. Moreover, one-fourth of those who attended a public high school rejected both ISKCON and Krishna Consciousness as a meaningful part of their identity. But a more significant

TABLE 4.4

Collective Identity of ISKCON Youths According to Public High School Attendance[a]

	Collective Identity			
	Active Core/ Congregational ISKCON Member	Little/No ISKCON Involvement but Devotee	No Longer ISKCON Member or Devotee	Total
Attended public high school	10% (4)	67% (28)	24% (10)	101% (42)
Did not attend public high school	33% (7)	57% (12)	10% (2)	100% (21)

[a] Significant at < .05.

finding is that relatively few of either group actively identified with ISK-CON. In fact, the majority of second-generation youths from both groups had little or no involvement in ISKCON, although most continued to define themselves as Krishna devotees (believers and followers of Krishna Consciousness).

These findings suggest that the transition associated with attending a public high school did influence the ISKCON collective identity of second-generation youths but had far less effect on their identity as Krishna devotees. ISKCON youths may have traded their ISKCON collective identity in order to gain social acceptance from their nondevotee peers, but most held on to their religious identity even if they became less involved in the practices and lifestyle of Krishna Consciousness. Thus, few can be said to have undergone deconversion. Rather, the majority found ways to socially and cognitively bridge their Krishna beliefs with the mainstream American culture.

Conclusion

New religions require cultural and institutional development in order to secure the commitment of those born within them, and the findings presented in this chapter underscore that need. Lacking an internal system of secondary education, ISKCON parents faced the uncomfortable decision of sending their children to schools outside the movement, thereby setting off a complex set of negotiations resulting in identity challenges and change for the second-generation youths. Significantly for ISKCON, young people found themselves exchanging their ISKCON collective identity in the interest of gaining social acceptance from their nondevotee classmates. The result was that second-generation youths became less involved in ISKCON and less identified with its purposes and goals.

The findings point to still other consequences associated with ISKCON's lack of cultural innovation. A majority of the young people who avoided a public high school education still remained largely uninvolved in the movement and rejected any identification as an ISKCON member, suggesting the presence of yet other sources of estrangement for ISKCON's second generation.

Young people growing up in ISKCON ultimately have little basis for making a life for themselves within ISKCON's North American communities. Opportunities for employment and/or other meaningful activities that could help integrate ISKCON's young people are sorely lacking. In a presentation to ISKCON teachers, parents, and second-generation youths in 1994, the chair of ISKCON's North American Board of Education made this very point. In his talk, appropriately entitled "All Dressed Up with No Place to Go," he argued that even those ISKCON young people who had been educated entirely within the movement's school system lacked any real hope of making a life for themselves within ISKCON. The future remains bleak for all of ISKCON's second generation, given the sheer lack of paid work opportunities in the movement's communities (Dasa, Murali Vadaka 1994). Unable to find secure lives in ISKCON, young people are following in the footsteps of their parents' generation, seeking life options outside the movement's ranks.

Without a culture supporting family life, ISKCON's development during the 1990s continued to move toward greater accommodation with the larger culture. As first- and second-generation devotees alike continued to "make peace with the world" in an effort to create a life for themselves and their families, their ISKCON collective identity lost relevance to and meaning in their everyday lives. Without committed followers, ISKCON faced an uncertain future as it moved toward the new millennium.

Although children suffered from mistreatment and institutional shortcomings that directly influenced their lives and commitments to ISKCON, women too faced their own struggles within ISKCON's traditionalist religious culture, which we will consider in the next two chapters.

5

Women's Voices

Spiritual life begins with the realization that one is not the material body but an eternal spiritual soul. The designations "male" and "female" refer only to the material body. So ultimately they have nothing to do with the soul, or self.
—Devi Dasi, Sitarani, "What's the Role of Women in Krsna Consciousness?" 1982

The abuses and neglect of women and children must be corrected immediately, as our sexist and inhumane behavior reflects badly on Srila Prabhupada and taints the movement in the eyes of the world.
—Dasi, Rukmini, presentation to ISKCON's leaders, 2000

The question of women's place in religion is long-standing and controversial (Daly 1985). On the one hand, women fill the churches, do much of the work of maintaining congregations, and are largely responsible for socializing children to religious values and practices. Yet on the other hand, in most of the world's religious traditions, women are excluded from formal religious roles and often condemned as spiritually weak, polluted, and less capable than men of reaching spiritual enlightenment (Puttick 2003:230). Among new religious movements however, we find considerable range in how women are defined and the roles they perform. Whereas some new religions are enclaves of patriarchal power, others represent utopian experiments embracing feminism and matriarchy (Aidala 1985; Jacobs 1984; Palmer 1994, 2003, 2004; Puttick 1996).

Although new religious movements collectively encompass a great variety of gender roles, there has been little research on the process by which women's roles change and the factors that influence that change (Puttick 2003:230). Moreover, scholars have failed to consider how conflicts over gender roles influence the development of new religious organizations. In ISKCON's case, women's issues have remained contentious for many years. Knott (1995) even went so far as to suggest that women's issues are second only to ISKCON's crisis of leadership in threatening the movement's future.[1]

Marginalization and Abuse

Beginning in the mid-1970s, a traditionalist patriarchal framework began to dominate ISKCON. As a consequence, women devotees became targets of public criticism, scorn, neglect, and abusive treatment at the hands of men, signaling a fundamental change in women's identities as Krishna devotees and ISKCON members.

Women's lives changed as the political power of renunciate sannyasis grew organizationally in the early and mid-1970s (Dasi, Visakha, and Dasi, Sudharma 2000; Deadwyler 2004; Devi Dasi, Jyotirmayi 2002). As they ascended to positions of organizational leadership, ISKCON's religious culture changed in ways that profoundly marginalized devotee women. Thereafter, "devotee women were no longer viewed as partners in a spiritual renaissance, rather they were categorized as personifications of the illusory energy Mayadevi, who threatened to cause men to deviate from their noble spiritual quest" (Dasi, Visakha, and Dasi, Sudharma 2000:2). One ISKCON leader reflected on the changes that took place during this period, and the implications for women's lives:

> The population of *sannyasis* increased dramatically. A genuine desire for transcendence often commingled with an urge to acquire prestige, position, and power within ISKCON, propelled most of these young men into rash and improvident heroics. The persistence of desires they could neither acknowledge nor control began to erupt as intolerance and fanaticism. The social climate turned ugly. (Deadwyler 2004:159)

Renunciate leaders believed that women directly threatened ISKCON's preaching mission. As one renowned sannyasi of the 1970s proclaimed, "Whenever you make a woman a devotee, you lose one man" (cited in Goswami, Tamal Krishna 1984). Because women's spiritual fulfillment rested largely on marriage and family life, it was assumed that in time they would marry, thus converting renunciate brahmacaries into householders. Indeed, such concerns became so great in the mid-1970s that some of the movement's sannyasi leadership considered sending all devotee women in North America to Australia (Das, Ravindra Svarupa 2000a:4; Dasi, Sudharma 2000:14).

Over two decades, the patriarchal message preached by ISKCON's renunciate leaders both directly and indirectly shaped gender politics in ISKCON's North American communities. Sannyasis and brahmacaries routinely denigrated devotee women, finding scriptural support for their actions. One woman explained:

> The men thought it was Vedic to spit on the ground to demonstrate their resentment toward women. They got their cue from a stanza in the scriptures that said, "Since I have been engaged in the transcendental loving service of Krishna, realizing ever-new pleasure in Him, whenever I think of sex pleasure, I spit at the thought, and my lips curl with distaste." (Srimad Bhagavatam 4.25.24, purport, cited in Muster 2004: 313)

To counteract the influence of women, ISKCON's male-dominated temple communities instituted a number of changes that fundamentally reshaped women's lives. These included relegating women to the back of the temple during worship services to avoid "distracting" men and discontinuing opportunities for women to give classes, to lead kirtans, and to help manage temple affairs. Women routinely faced disparaging and demeaning public lectures by sannyasis and other men, in which their "intelligence, motives and capabilities" were criticized or dismissed (Dasi, Visakha, and Dasi, Sudharma 2000:2). Women's identities were thereby effectively reconstructed, becoming "unintelligent," "spiritually dangerous" to men, and incapable of little more than household duties and tending to the needs of children (Deadwyler 2004; Judah 1974:86; Whitworth and Shiels 1982:161). According to one devotee woman who lived through this era,

> In the not-so-distant past, the climate has been so intolerable, that daily Bhagavatam classes proclaimed the position of women as a dangerous element in our society to be reckoned with. And we reckoned with them by instituting unspoken laws prohibiting them from certain services,

keeping their participation in temple programs to an absolute minimum, and allowing an atmosphere . . . to create deep inferiority complexes and fear. Most women were embarrassed to be women, and knew they were thoroughly unwelcome in ISKCON. (Devi Dasi, Pranada 2002:1)

Although we do not know how many devotee women were neglected and abused, it is clear that the antiwoman climate resulted in the mistreatment of many. As one woman reported in a 1981 interview,

I've never so much regretted being born in a woman's body since I joined the ISKCON movement. I've never been so much criticized, abused, slandered, misunderstood, or chastised because I have this woman's body. It makes it very difficult to do my service and/or assist others with their service if they are always thinking about these bodily designations instead of the constructive things I could do or say to help them in their service and to help this movement go forward. If you are a single woman [brahmacarini], every man thinks he is an authority and will yell at you if he feels like it. But it's worse when you're married, because you have one authority and you have to surrender to his inflexible, lord-it-over nature whether he is right or wrong and whether he is nice or cruel about how he relates to you.

An influential ISKCON leader linked the abuse suffered by women to the hostile social environment of the movement under the influence of ISKCON's renunciate leadership.

I remember a number of temples which were perfect illustration[s] of the colonial/plantation style of management; they seemed eerily straight out of the pages of Frantz Fanon's "The Wretched of the Earth." Only in these cases, the *sannyasi* and *brahmachari* leaders were the white guys; the women, the n——s [niggers]. In short, there was widespread exploitation and abuse of women—physical abuse, emotional abuse, sexual abuse—and also neglect. (Das, Ravindra Svarupa 2000a:4)

Women's devalued status also significantly reduced the types of organizational roles they could assume. As attitudes turned negative, women found themselves excluded from and forced out of responsible ISKCON positions (Devi Dasi, Jyotirmayi 2002:3). As the head of ISKCON's women's ministry asserted, this was done not because they were incompetent but because they were women.

> In New Vrindaban, I was able to open a bookstore in the basement of the Palace of Gold. From there, with very little support from the management . . . I was able to distribute a sizeable quantity of Srila Prabhupada's books. . . . Unfortunately, like so many previous efforts, it was not to last. I had just completed a Labor Day weekend of book sales that totalled $10,000 when I was once again informed that it was now time to bring in a more qualified [male] individual. I will not dwell here on the demoralizing manner in which the transition took place, but I will say that after my departure from the New Vrindaban book store, the sales immediately decreased to less than a tenth of what they had been when it was under my care. (Dasi, Sudharma 2000:15)

Another example of how women's contributions were often diminished can be seen in the differing understandings of men and women successful at book distribution. The devotee community routinely acknowledged men as being "spiritually advanced" for their achievements in distributing Prabhupada's books. Other ISKCON members greeted successful male distributors with respect and even awe. Although success at book distribution did bring recognition to women, they garnered fewer accolades and status. In the late 1970s, several male book distributors remarked to me that while it was true that women were among the movement's most accomplished book distributors, this was only because they used their feminine charm and sexuality to their advantage (Rochford 1985:146–47).[2]

Given the neglect, abuse, and diminished status accorded to devotee women, many knowingly or unknowingly conformed to the negative stereotypes attributed to them. One woman who joined ISKCON in the late 1960s described the problem:

> Instead of being considered full-fledged devotees, women were considered only as "women" in the most pejorative sense. . . . Women were considered stupid and incapable and became subject to gross mockery. . . . Belittled in such a way, lots of women lost confidence in themselves and in their material and spiritual abilities, accepted being deprived of

their human dignity and played the part that was expected of them, being brainless, ignorant, and unproductive.[3] (Devi Dasi, Jyotirmayi 2002: 3–4)

Findings from the Centennial Survey also show how women's reconstructed identities influenced their lives in the movement.[4] Six in ten (61%) of the 137 female respondents agreed that "as a woman, I sometimes encounter a degree of sexism in our movement that is a barrier to my spiritual advancement," and nearly one-third (31%) of these strongly agreed. In addition, three-quarters (77%) agreed that "many women devotees suffer from low self-esteem largely because they feel mistreated by devotee men," with one-third (37%) strongly agreeing. It is worth noting that two-thirds (68%) of the 129 male respondents likewise agreed that mistreatment by men had negatively influenced the self-esteem of devotee women.

Clearly, devotee women had reason to stand up against abuse and organizational marginalization, but their grievances were subject to differential interpretation across individuals, social groups, and time. How grievances are interpreted and how, in turn, emergent frameworks are diffused and gain acceptance or not are critical to the emergence of collective protest (Snow et al. 1986:465). As Turner (1969) argued, the growth of significant social movements demands a revision of the ways that people look at problematic conditions that affect their lives. Rather than interpreting their lot in life as a matter of misfortune, they come to see injustice at work. Moreover, if people are to collectivize in pursuit of common interests, these sources of injustice must be perceived as mutable and changeable. McAdam (1982:34) refers to this process of reframing problematic conditions from misfortune to injustice as "cognitive liberation." The devotee women recognized this injustice only after a thorough reassessment of their lives as wives, mothers, and ISKCON members.

Redefining Women's Lives

The impulse toward activism emerged only as women began a process of critical reflection that, for many, led to a transformative reinterpretation of their lives and those of their Godsisters. In reconstructing the meaning of their lives in this way, women engaged in what scholars of social movements refer to as "constructing a collective action frame." Collective action frames are "accenting devices" (Snow and Benford 1992:137) that underscore the seriousness and injustice of problematic social conditions, and they also serve a diagnostic function by attributing blame to individuals or structures seen as promoting unjust social conditions (Snow and Benford 1992:137).

Throughout the 1970s and 1980s, both men and women devotees viewed their everyday experiences through a religious lens in which their entire lives were infused with spiritual meaning. For women being neglected and abused, this meant interpreting their lives in terms of "renunciation" and "austerity." Consider the words of one devotee woman who responded in the following manner after learning that one of her Godsisters had been neglected and abused by her husband:

> The life of a woman in Krishna consciousness is not easy; it is one of austerity. We must submit to the authority and wishes of our husbands. Voluntarily accepting these austerities is what makes us glorious and eligible to enter into heaven. . . . Perhaps [name of abused woman] can take solace in the fact that she followed her husband in austere circumstances. Whether his desires are right or wrong is not for us to question, because in our unalloyed service to our husbands we are serving the Supreme Lord. (Dasi, Yasomati-stanya Payi 2004:1)

Although such a response is consistent with ISKCON's religious beliefs, it undercuts the very possibility of devotee women's finding injustice, and not misfortune, at work in their lives. For in equating "neglect" and "mistreatment" with the "austerities" that define a woman's religious quest, there is little basis for feeling unjustly wronged.[5]

The acknowledgment of widespread child abuse in ISKCON dramatically influenced the ways that ISKCON women appraised their lives. Although many women, like the one just quoted, found ways to attribute spiritual meaning to the hardships they faced, few, if any, could accept the abuse suffered by the movement's children in the gurukula. This abuse greatly influenced the views of devotee women, most of whom were mothers. As in other situations in which children are placed at risk (toxic contamination of neighborhoods and communities), mothers are often at the forefront of activism (Brown and Ferguson 1995; Cable 1992; Levine 1982). This clearly was the case for devotee women when they connected their own organizational marginalization to the tragic abuse suffered by ISKCON's young people. As a pro-change activist and leader asserted,

> The widespread disgust with child abuse, and women finally just not taking the nonsense [any longer] have all contributed to the women's voice finally being heard. . . . Admitting to the child abuse—most all of it committed by men, and probably *only allowed to go on because of the de-empowerment of women* [the mothers]—is admitting to the abuse of women and how the devaluation of them contributed to our problems, socially and with the children. Gradually that point is dawning on people. (my emphasis; personal communication 1998)

Aligning the two situations of abuse became a critical mobilization strategy of the pro-change activists. At annual women's conferences attracting audiences of 150 or more women, they repeatedly drew parallels between child abuse and the neglect and abuse of devotee women. Note, for example, how one pro-change leader linked the two situations of abuse at ISKCON's first women's conference held in Los Angeles in 1997:

> As a society, we have finally come to understand and accept the abuses our children have suffered in the gurukula system. I don't believe we have understood the physical abuses women have suffered . . . from inferior living facilities, to lack of equal *prasadam* [food] facilities to physical abuses women have suffered in ISKCON. *It is not less significant than the abuse our children have faced.* (my emphasis; Devi Dasi, Pranada 2002:1)

Pro-change advocates not only tried to reshape the ways that devotee women interpreted their ISKCON lives, but they also highlighted how ISKCON authorities shared significant blame for the misery inflicted on women and children. The leaders' strident antiwoman and antifamily beliefs marginalized women to such a degree that they were unaware of the ongoing child abuse and incapable of intervening on behalf of their children or themselves. From the standpoint of pro-change women, ISKCON's leadership came to represent what Gamson, Fireman, and Rytina (1982) refer to as "unjust authorities." Because the GBC is ISKCON's ultimate governing body, it became a target of women's indignation.

Findings from the Prabhupada Centennial Survey, presented in tables

TABLE 5.1

"Sexism Is a Barrier to My Spiritual Advancement" by Authority of GBC[a]

	Low	Mid-Low	Mid-High	High	Total
Agree strongly	67% (28)	19% (8)	14% (6)	0% (0)	100% (42)
Agree	45% (19)	24% (10)	14% (6)	17% (7)	100% (42)
Disagree	18% (7)	33% (13)	20% (8)	30% (12)	101% (40)
Disagree strongly	8% (1)	15% (2)	8% (1)	69% (9)	100% (13)
Total	40% (55)	24% (33)	15% (21)	20% (28)	99% (137)

[a] Significant at $p < .001$.

TABLE 5.2

"Needs and Problems of Householders Largely Ignored by Leadership" by Authority of the GBC (for women only)[a]

	Low	Mid-Low	Mid-High	High	Total
Agree strongly	53% (29)	24% (13)	16% (9)	7% (4)	100% (55)
Agree	38% (23)	27% (16)	15% (9)	20% (12)	100% (60)
Disagree	17% (4)	9% (2)	17% (4)	57% (13)	100% (23)
Disagree strongly	0% (0)	50% (1)	0% (0)	50% (1)	100% (2)
Total	40% (56)	23% (32)	16% (22)	21% (30)	100% (140)

[a] Significant at $p < .001$.

5.1 and 5.2, reveal how antiwoman and antifamily attitudes in ISKCON's social milieu influenced women's views of the GBC and its authority. Table 5.1 cross-tabulates women's assessments of GBC authority with their responses to the statement "As a woman, I have sometimes encountered a degree of sexism in our movement that is a barrier to my spiritual advancement" (also see appendix 1, figure 1). The findings show a strong relationship between women's experiences of sexism and their views of ISKCON's GBC leadership. Two-thirds (67%) of the women who agreed strongly that sexism had impeded their spiritual advancement expressed minimal support for the GBC. In addition, nearly half (45%) who agreed were equally unsupportive of ISKCON's governing body. Just as noteworthy is the fact that women whose ISKCON experiences did not include sexism, or whose experiences were not interpreted as such—thus disagreeing with the statement—were far more supportive of the GBC's authority.

Table 5.2 considers the GBC's authority in relation to women's responses to the statement "The needs and problems of householders have been largely ignored by ISKCON's leadership." The findings reveal a strong relationship between women's perceptions of the leadership's commitment to family life and their overall assessments of the GBC's authority. Particularly telling is the fact that only one in five (18%) women disagreed with the statement. As table 5.2 indicates, large percentages of those who agreed or agreed strongly with the statement did not strongly support the GBC, whereas the minority of women who disagreed with the statement generally did support the GBC.

The Problem of Framing Injustice

The question of how pro-change women framed their grievances in order to promote collective protest was hardly straightforward but was a difficult undertaking. While gender equality has become normative in American society (Chaves 1997:50–51) and represents a powerful protest frame for women challengers, it proved to be of little direct use to ISKCON's pro-change women. The reason lies largely with the close association between "gender equality" and feminism. From the perspective of ISKCON's traditionalist theology, feminism is symptomatic of the "diseased" secular culture. In rejecting "gender equality," ISKCON thus affirms its general resistance to modernity, as antifeminism is one of the defining features of fundamentalist antimodernism (Chaves 1997:105). For most ISKCON members, including many pro-change women, "feminism" stands for rising rates of divorce, countless abortions, and the general deterioration of the contemporary American family.

The concept of "rights" posed another problem for pro-change women, as the very idea of "rights" is antithetical to ISKCON's religious beliefs, as can be seen in the comments of an ISKCON leader otherwise sympathetic to the plight of devotee women:

> The whole dialogue about rights/entitlements is a flawed and material conception. If you study the Vedic culture (Mahabharata, Ramayana), you will find almost nothing on rights. What you will find is a deep understanding and outline of *duties* . . . duties of fathers, wives, sons, leaders, children, teachers, etc. Obviously ours has been a history of the powerful exploiting the weak, but the solution may not be to fall back on the often-flawed system of modern society. (my emphasis; personal communication 1998)

Given the association of "equality" and "rights" with feminism, pro-change activists had little choice but to search elsewhere for the materials needed to construct a resonant protest frame. Not surprisingly, however, this did not stop their opponents from labeling women activists as feminist in an attempt to derail their efforts to change. One activist, for example, described her early attempt to persuade ISKCON authorities to reconsider the policy that prohibited women from giving class in the temple:

> I put my concerns in writing, finally, in 1984. That letter was sent to all the GBC members and was published in the *Vaisnava Journal*. That letter also sealed my fate, as I stood alone for my Godsisters, as a black sheep of my family. I was told that I was a demon destroying Prabhupada's movement, and I received the most controversial label: Pranada is a women's libber. . . . And what was my great sin to receive such rejection? I suggested women should give Bhagavatam classes and were authorized to do so by Srila Prabhupada. (Devi Dasi, Pranada 2002:1)

Time and again, women activists faced charges that their "real" agenda was to advance a destructive feminist agenda. Sensitive to such charges, they often explicitly distanced themselves from any association with feminism. Such distancing can be seen in the words of two women who spoke to ISKCON's leadership about women's issues at the 2000 GBC meetings in India. One woman prefaced her remarks by saying,

> There was a rumour going around that we ladies were in Mayapura to present some feminist agenda. The idea was that, under the influence of the modern women's rights movement . . . we would plead with the GBC to change the philosophy of or adjust Srila Prabhupada's teachings in order to fit in with the times. You can feel reassured that the ladies here before you are among the most philosophically conservative in our movement. (Dasi, Saudamani 2000:12).

The head of ISKCON's Women's Ministry stated as part of her comments, "You will understand that this is not feminism, but rather a sincere attempt to create an environment conducive to devotional service for Vaisnavis [women devotees]" (Dasi, Sudharma 2000:14).

While "equal rights" could not provide the basis of a legitimate protest frame, ISKCON's religious doctrine proved of limited use as well. This contrasts sharply with other religious groups to which "using doctrine to critique doctrine" (Dillon 1999:164) has been central to the emancipatory projects of women and other aggrieved populations (see Chaves 1997; Dillon 1999). A recent statistical analysis of Prabhupada's commentaries relating to women in the Bhagavad Gita and five books of the Bhagavata Purana (i.e., Srimad Bhagavatam), shows why doctrine was of limited utility to ISKCON's pro-change women. Lorenz's study (2004:122) found that 80 percent of Prabhupada's scriptural commentaries referring to women were "negative" in substance. Prabhupada routinely referred to women as less intelligent, lusty, inferior, and dangerous to the spiritual advancement of men. Given these qualities, Prabhupada emphasized that restrictions should be placed on women, that they should be grouped with other socially inferior classes (low-class sudras), and, because women are alluring sex objects, that men should scrupulously avoid them. For example, Prabhupada writes, "Women are generally not very intelligent"; "Women in general should not be trusted"; and "Girls should be completely separated from the very beginning. They are very dangerous. . . . They should be taught how to sweep, how to stitch . . . clean, cook, to be faithful to the husband. They should be taught how to become obedient to the husband" (Lorenz 2004:378–79).

Because Prabhupada's followers view him as a pure representative of God, most accept his words as literal truth. In fact, 97 percent of the 363 men and women that responded to the Centennial Survey agreed that "I accept as truth Prabhupada's translations of and commentaries on the Srimad Bhagavatam and other Vedic scriptures." This fact, combined with Prabhupada's largely derogatory scriptural commentaries about women, led Lorenz (2004:384) to conclude that Prabhupada's teachings played a *direct* role in the abuse suffered by ISKCON's women and children.

Despite Prabhupada's largely derogatory characterizations of women, pro-change women did discover some scriptural support to advance their cause. Far more important however, was Prabhupada's personal example in dealings with his earliest women disciples. It was in these encounters between Prabhupada and his early women disciples that pro-change women unearthed the critical ingredients to construct a viable collective action frame. The telling and retelling of "Prabhupada stories" by Prabhupada's earliest female disciples went a long way in reshaping women's understandings of their lives in ISKCON. Not only did these stories portray Prabhupada's respectful attitude and behavior toward his women disciples, but they also indirectly revealed how ISK-

CON's leadership had misinterpreted or otherwise misused their guru's instructions and teachings. In hearing these anecdotal accounts, women came to realize that their rights and interests as women and devotees had been sacrificed to further the religious and political agenda of ISK-CON's renunciate leadership.

Constructing and Diffusing a Protest Frame

Women activists tried to redirect the focus away from Prabhupada's strongly worded scriptural commentaries about women by emphasizing Prabhupada's "social application of Krishna Conscious principles" (Devi Dasi, Jyotirmayi 2002:5). For Prabhupada had acknowledged the significance of teachings in his interactions with his disciples. In 1975, he argued against a GBC opinion that only his books and taped lectures should be taken as definitive of his teachings. Prabhupada reportedly replied, "No, what I say in talks also, many things I say are not in my books" (quoted in Devi Dasi, Jyotirmayi 2002:5).

When Prabhupada came to the United States in 1965, he did the unthinkable from the perspective of his Godbrothers in India: he accepted women as members of his fledgling movement. This included formally initiating them as his disciples. Prabhupada justified these decisions by appealing to the notion of "time, place, and circumstance." As he wrote in the *Caitanya caritamrta,*

> An *acarya* who comes for the service of the Lord cannot be expected to conform to a stereotype, for he must find the ways and means by which Krishna Consciousness may be spread. Sometimes jealous persons criticize the Krishna Consciousness movement because it engages both boys and girls in distribution of love of Godhead. Not knowing that boys and girls in countries like Europe and America mix freely, these fools and rascals criticize the boys and girls in Krishna Consciousness for intermingling. But these rascals should consider that one cannot suddenly change a community's social customs. (chap. 7, purport of verses 32 and 38; quoted in Devi Dasi, Jyotirmayi 2002:1)

By accepting women into his temples and conferring on them the status brahmacarini, Prabhupada extended to them the same rights and duties of his male disciples. As one woman who joined ISKCON in 1968 remarked, "The women devotees had exactly the same spiritual activities, the same tasks, the same possibilities to progress spiritually and they were entitled to the same respect" (Devi Dasi, Jyotirmayi 2002:2). Prabhupada allowed women to accompany and serve him when traveling, to lead kirtans in the temple, to give classes and public lectures, to perform public artis, to stand and sit on one side of the temple rather than being relegated to the back, to write articles in ISKCON magazines and publications, to chant alongside men in the temple, and to assume significant institutional positions in ISKCON. As one of Prabhupada's earliest women disciples described,

> For many years, in different countries and circumstances, I had the good fortune to render personal service to him [Prabhupada]. He trained me, urged me to accept more and more responsibility, and regularly asked me to lead kirtanas, give classes, arrange programmes, manage departments, provide comforts for visiting devotees, meet with leaders, and actively promulgate Krsna consciousness.[6] (Devi Dasi, Yamuna 2000:6)

Yet as we have seen, when Prabhupada began turning over the reins of leadership to a growing number of sannyasis, women's lives changed dramatically. These changes first appeared in North America before spreading to Europe and other portions of the ISKCON world. As one woman who lived in France at the time remembered,

> A note on the temple room door said that women devotees were forbidden to lead *kirtans* or to give class. Then they were forbidden to circumambulate Tulasi [spiritual plant worshipped in the morning] with the men devotees, could not chant *japa* in the temple room, had to stay behind the men in the temple during *kirtans,* classes, Harinama [congregational chanting]. Each of their important responsibilities [was] removed, as well as their rights to offer *aratis* to Prabhupada. (Devi Dasi, Jyotirmayi 2002:2)

These and related changes appear to have been made without Prabhupada's blessing, although few devotees were aware of this until years later. Evidence suggests that on a number of occasions Prabhupada admonished sannyasis and brahmacaries for trying to marginalize or otherwise mistreat his women disciples.

On various occasions, brahmacaries complained to Srila Prabhupada they were [sexually] agitated by the presence of women in the temple, and Srila Prabhupada replied that if they could not restrain their senses, they should go live alone in the forest. [Prabhupada wrote] "Regarding the disturbance made by the women devotees, they are also living beings. They also come to Krishna. . . . If our male members, the brahmacaries and sannyasis, if they become steady in Krishna Consciousness, there is not [a] problem." (Devi Dasi, Jyotirmayi 2002:7)

In 1973 and 1974 when women were no longer allowed to give classes in the temple, a number of them complained to Prabhupada. He wrote to one of his female disciples,

You can also keep giving Bhagavatam class if you like. Women in our movement can also preach very nicely. Actually male and female bodies, these are just outward designations. Lord Caitanya said that whether one is *brahmana* or whatever he may be if he knows the science of Krsna then he is to be accepted as guru. . . . The qualification for leading class is how much one understands about Krsna and surrendering to the process. Not whether one is male or female.[7] (Prabhupada 1992:2585)

Pro-change woman used the anecdotal accounts of senior devotee women to argue that Prabhupada was not sexist in his dealing with his female disciples. Rather, Prabhupada's personal example clearly demonstrated his strong support for them. Because of this, pro-change women insisted that Prabhupada would never have supported the discriminatory and abusive practices of ISKCON's renunciate leadership.

A highly publicized conflict in 1999 between devotee women and renunciate males in Vrndavana, India, demonstrates how pro-change activists successfully used Prabhupada's example to defend women against abuse. The occasion was Kartika (a major festival) that annually attracts large numbers of Western devotees, including many women. On these occasions the ISKCON temple in Vrndavana normally fills to capacity, thus constraining the ability of worshippers to approach the altar to take *darsana* of (to view) the deities. Immediately before the festival, the temple authorities changed the darsana policies, limiting women's access to the altar. This shift in temple etiquette was reportedly made at the request of sannyasis and brahmacaries who had grown weary of women moving forward to view the deities in a space normally reserved for them during the morning arti. Because the temple authorities failed to consult with the women in attendance, few were even aware of the new darsana policies (Das, Abhirama 2000:1). Over several days, renunciate men actively tried to limit women's access to the altar, reportedly lining up shoulder to shoulder the length of the altar to keep the women from viewing the deities. Testimonies by those present suggest that some of the men were "physically abusive," kicking and pushing women near the altar (Das, Abhirama 2000:2). The event elicited numerous responses by men and women on both sides of the issue. Various women aligned with the pro-change movement expressed outrage and invoked Prabhupada's example to demonstrate the injustice of the situation.

> Certain men feel it is not Vedic for women to be in the front [near the altar], and that it is more appropriate to facilitate *sannyasis'* and *brahmacaris' darsana*. Neither local custom nor examples set by Srila Prabhupada obligates ISKCON managers to enforce a rule that women cannot take *darsana* in the front. Temples all over the Indian [sub] continent allow women *darsana* up front. . . . Why do certain ISKCON temples in India insist on this unwritten rule? It has been claimed that Prabhupada did not allow women *darsana* up front. However several senior women disciples [names cited] . . . recollect being in the front [of the temple] in Vrndavana when Prabhupada was present. (Dasi, Pranada 1999:1–2)

Pro-change activists also used Prabhupada's interactions with his female disciples in another important way. These exchanges provided a basis for distilling new meaning from Prabhupada's otherwise unsympathetic scriptural commentaries about women. At issue was whether Prabhupada's philosophical writings about women were meant to include his female disciples. Accounts like the following suggested to advocates of change that he did not:

> One such exchange is what I called the Canakya Pandita episodes. I was present on four occasions when Srila Prabhupada repeated the Canakya adage: "Never trust a woman or a politician." On each occasion Srila Prabhupada looked me in the eye to see my response. On the last occasion, in Bombay in 1973, he quoted the saying, heartily laughing in front of a small group of men. Then he said: "What do you think,

Yamuna?" Immediately I retorted: "Of course it is true, Srila Prabhupada," whereupon he became grave, looked at me with great feeling,
and said, "*But you are not a woman, you are Vaisnava.*" (my emphasis;
Devi Dasi, Yamuna 2000:6)

Another devotee woman recounted,

When Srila Prabhupada first said in class that for a man, association
with a woman is dangerous because she makes him lose control over his
senses, the male devotees started acting very nastily with the women of
that particular temple. The ladies expressed their pain to Prabhupada
who then called in all the men and said: "*I was talking of materialistic
women, not of the women of the movement.* They are angels." (my emphasis; Devi Dasi, Jyotirmayi 2002:7)

In hearing the many accounts underscoring Prabhupada's fondness
and respect for his female disciples, many women throughout ISKCON
realized that neither religious tradition nor Prabhupada himself was
responsible for the plight of ISKCON's women. Instead, Prabhupada's
teachings about women had been misinterpreted and/or misused by a
leadership determined to maintain its control over ISKCON's unconventional religious world. In coming to this conclusion, many began to embrace the pro-change cause. One woman who helped organize ISKCON's
initial Women's Conferences stated:

I think the mobilization of women and their issues has increased because of the educating we have been doing. It was a widespread belief
that the status quo of women in ISKCON was Prabhupada's doing. It has
become increasingly evident that this is not the case. Therefore, changing it and questioning it has become acceptable. Indeed, ten years ago
no one would hear the discussion because it was heretical against Prabhupada. Now I would venture to say that there are a rising number of
people convinced that what happened to women in ISKCON was NOT
what Prabhupada intended. That was a big shift. So education, communication, discussion has done a lot to change the atmosphere among
women devotees. (her emphasis; personal communication 1998)

Not only did education radically shift devotee women's understanding of their ISKCON lives; it also taught them basic tactics of dissent

and gave them the confidence to act on their convictions. A pro-change leader stated at the first Women's Conference in Los Angeles:

> Whatever the cost of our personal social status, let's not remain silent in even one negative Bhagavatam class, in even one negative conversation. Let's use every method of communication to raise consciousness. Let us no longer tolerate psychological abuses or the de-empowerment of [women]. (Devi Dasi, Pranada 2002:3)

Organizational Decline and Women's Labor

Since the early 1970s, men exclusively had held positions of institutional responsibility within ISKCON, but this began to change when the collapse of communalism forced devotee men into the outside labor market to support their families. Stripped of prestige, money, and authority, few devotee men stepped forward to serve in these administrative positions. In the face of mounting labor shortages, ISKCON's communities therefore began turning to women to serve as temple presidents, managers, and local, national, and international administrators.[8] As they did, the women's pro-change agenda began to appeal to growing numbers of men and women throughout the movement.

Two devotee women and Prabhupada disciples offered the following description and analysis concerning the relationship between ISKCON's (literally) manpower shortages and the increasing institutional opportunities afforded to devotee women:

> In most temples there is a severe shortage of manpower and of male devotees willing to take up responsibilities. There are less men overall, and among those present, less are willing now to take up responsible positions. . . . So women are invited to take up responsibilities more and more, because there is nobody else to do the job. If there would be available men, we have no doubt or illusion that they would get a chance first. We are not so naive to think that the men leaders appreciate us so much more than in the past; in a way they became forced by circumstances to engage us and give us more responsibilities. (personal communication 1998)

These two women go on to say that even though some devotee men support women's holding responsible ISKCON positions, "maybe Krishna is tricking them a little bit." That is, organizational circumstances have essentially forced ISKCON's male hierarchy to turn to women's labor to run the temples.

Another devotee woman reflected on the dilemma she faced when she was asked to assume new responsibilities in a local ISKCON temple:

Before leaving [location], I was asked to take up two important posts of responsibilities, to my great astonishment, in the very temple where I had suffered so much, attending *tulasi puja* in the cold outside the temple in the wintertime and never being invited to give a class, which I love to do. When they asked me to take up these posts, I thought they were really desperate and had quite some guts to ask, knowing my feeling on the matter. (personal communication 1998)

In a position of decline and facing substantial shortages of manpower, ISKCON's leaders had little choice but to turn to women to manage temples and assume other critical organizational roles. As a result, traditionalist ideas concerning women became increasingly difficult to sustain, and most were set aside or otherwise reinterpreted to allow women to fill positions in ISKCON's management structure. The Centennial Survey indicates that in 1996 three-quarters of all women and two-thirds of all men agreed that qualified women should have the opportunity to serve in the positions of temple president and GBC representative. Moreover, it appears that gender attitudes are changing more broadly among rank-and-file members. Table 5.3 shows that both men and women reject important elements of ISKCON's traditionally defined gender ideology. Although there are significant differences between the sexes with respect to the strength of their agreement, both generally embrace equality for women. Women and men agree that women should be allowed to chant in the temple with men, have equal access to the deities during worship, and have the same opportunities as men to realize their potential in devotional service (work in ISKCON). In addition, both agree that performance, not gender, should be the criterion for placement in an ISKCON position. Both sexes agreed that women are the spiritual equals of men and that Prabhupada never intended women devotees to be treated as other than equal to devotee men. Finally, there

TABLE 5.3

Select Agree/Disagree Items Regarding Women's Roles in ISKCON *by Gender*

Statement	Women		Men	
	Strongly Agree	Agree	Strongly Agree	Agree
Women and men should be able to chant japa together in the temple.	49% (76)	34% (52)	23% (55)	53% (128)
Men and women should worship on different sides of the temple so that both have equal access to the deities.	49% (72)	35% (51)	31% (74)	51% (120)
Women should have the same opportunities as men to realize their full potential in devotional service.	73% (111)	24% (36)	53% (131)	42% (104)
Performance, not gender, should determine who is placed in a given ISKCON position.	62% (91)	28% (41)	45% (106)	39% (92)
Women are the spiritual equals of men.	66% (100)	29% (44)	49% (120)	45% (110)
Prabhupada never intended for women to be treated as if they were less than equal to men.	61% (90)	28% (41)	39% (91)	45% (107)
Over the past several years I have seen the attitude of devotee men toward women devotees become more accepting.	7% (10)	76% (105)	9% (20)	80% (172)

is strong agreement that over time, male attitudes have become more accepting of devotee women.

Considered as a whole, the findings from the Centennial Survey confirm that ISKCON's traditionalist gender ideology has lost its appeal to wide portions of the movement's membership. Pragmatic organizational needs have made it impossible to sustain traditional ideas that women are "unintelligent," "incapable," and "a threat to men" when they are increasingly called on to assume demanding administrative work on behalf of ISKCON and its communities. The ideals defining the pro-change women's agenda (equal standing with men spiritually and materially, performance being the relevant criterion rather than gender, and so on) are increasingly compatible with ISKCON's need for skilled female labor in the absence of men. In sum, the content of women's resurgent voices has increasingly been incorporated into both ISKCON's organizational and religious cultures.

Political Opportunity and Gender Reform

Scholars of social movements and political protest have often been perplexed about the timing of insurgency. Groups of people suffering from extreme and unjust hardships frequently fail to mobilize in pursuit of their common interests. In other cases, people organize effective protest groups when their grievances appear less severe. The question is, why? One response is that protest activity is more likely when political elites are under siege, internally fragmented, and thereby unable to act collectively to crush or otherwise undermine dissent. In other words, when elites are in disarray, more opportunities are created for staging protest activity and for such challenges to prove successful. As the political scientist Sidney Tarrow explained, political opportunity structures are "dimensions of the political environment that provide incentives for people to undertake collective action by affecting their expectations for success or failure" (1994:85).

Years of scandal and controversy surrounding ISKCON's gurus and GBC leadership clearly have taken their toll on members' perceptions of these institutions (Das, Ravindra Svarupa 2000b; Goswami, Tamal Krishna 1998; Rochford 1998a). As we have seen, in the eyes of many devotee women, the leaders' antiwoman and antifamily stance further eroded the authority of both institutions. As one guru, GBC member, and ISKCON scholar noted,

> And now the GBC has become very, very weak. The principal reason for this has been the fall-down of spiritual masters and the decay of spiritual authority in general. This applies to *sannyasis,* gurus, and the GBC. There has been a big overlap of these three categories, and they are all in disrepute. The renounced order of life has come to be called the denounced order of life—we hear that all the time. People are very dubious about gurus—everyone is wondering when the next one is going to fall. And the GBC seems to be floundering and cannot do anything about it. There is a feeling that we do not know where our vision is going to come from. (Das, Ravindra Svarupa 2000b:38)

The fragility of ISKCON's institutions of authority offered various prochange groups the political opportunity needed to push for change. Perhaps the most significant was the emergence of the *ritvik* movement, discussed in chapter 7, which has challenged the very legitimacy of

ISKCON's guru leadership (Desai et al. 2004; Rochford 1998b). Yet other challenging groups, including women and youths abused in the guru-kula, successfully organized to pressure for change. Fragmented and weak, ISKCON's authorities were forced to negotiate reforms rather than to actively resist. For women this has meant a progressive expansion of their "rights," including greater opportunities to take part in ISKCON's religious and organizational life.

In 1996, the GBC approved the creation of the International Women's Ministry. Bowing to local pressures by pro-change women, some temples in North America began allowing women to serve on the altar, worship with men on different sides of the temple, and chant collectively with men in the temple room. Less frequently, women could be found giving the morning class on Prabhupada's scriptural commentaries and leading congregational chanting in the temple. In a move of considerable symbolic significance, a senior woman was elected to serve as a GBC representative in 1998. Moreover, two women served as temple presidents in the United States in 1998 with several others serving in the same capacity in western Europe (Dasi, Visakha, and Dasi, Sudharama 2000:3). In addition, women held other significant administrative positions at the local, national, and international levels within ISKCON. For instance, one woman was elected as the executive officer for ISKCON in North America in 1995.

In 1998, the then chairman of the GBC openly acknowledged the mistreatment of devotee women in a letter widely circulated throughout the movement:

> We have not offered proper protection and respect to the women in our movement. We have not understood woman's role as mother of society. We have hurt women by insisting they behave according to Vedic standards, yet we have not been able to offer the proper standard of Vedic protection. (Letter from the Executive Committee of the GBC, signed by Harikesa Swami, June 1998)

A number of significant gender reforms were made following the incident in Vrndavana, India, reported earlier. After repeated attempts by the Women's Ministry to have the GBC examine the plight of women in ISKCON, the widespread publicity of this event forced the issue. For the first time, the GBC heard presentations by representatives of the Women's Ministry. In March 2000, seven senior women spoke to members of the GBC about the legacy of neglect and abuse suffered by ISK-CON women. In the aftermath of these presentations, the GBC adopted a number of official resolutions aimed at recognizing "the value of women in ISKCON and ensuring their rights to fully participate in the Society according to their abilities and wishes" (Dasi, Visakha, and Dasi, Sudharma 2000:20). The GBC acknowledged "the mistakes of the past and the need to provide *equal and full opportunity* for devotional service for all devotees in ISKCON, *regardless of gender*" (my emphasis; GBC Resolutions, sec. 501, 2000). The GBC also recognized "that many of the social issues that confront us are exacerbated because the voices of our women, who are the mothers and daughters of our Krsna conscious family, have been hushed and stifled owing to misinterpretation of our Vaisnava philosophy" (GBC Resolutions, sec. 501, 2000). The resolutions mandated that all qualified devotees, regardless of gender, could speak on the Vedic scriptures during regular temple classes. Moreover, all of ISKCON's worldwide temples were required to designate half the temple room area, divided in the center from the altar, for women (GBC Resolution, sec. 618, 2000).[9]

Conclusion

The exploitation and abuse of women is an unfortunate part of religious history, and several contemporary new religions have been linked to their mistreatment and abuse (Chancellor 2000; Downing 2001; Jacobs 1984, 1987; Palmer 1994). Research on the abuse of women in new religions has focused largely on how these experiences produced disillusionment and subsequent defection (Jacobs 1984, 1987). Yet many women who were neglected and abused chose not to leave their religious groups but to stay and fight these injustices. The obvious question is why they have remained, given the seriousness of the hardships they encountered. One answer that emerges from the discussion in this chapter is that women remain because of the strength of their commitment to a charismatic leader. Female disciples of Prabhupada tried to change the lives of devotee women, but they also tried to exonerate their guru from any wrongdoing in their abuse.

Jacobs's research on the process by which women voluntarily separate from religious movements indicates that defection is a two-stage process. Social defection is the demise of group commitment and the disintegration of social bonds, and emotional defection is the rejection of the religious leader and his religious philosophy (Jacobs 1987:297–98). Total deconversion occurs only when an individual's crisis of faith escalates to the degree that the leader's religious authority comes to be perceived as "less than godly" (Jacobs 1987:300). Yet challenges to "unjust" authority are only rarely directed at a charismatic leader. Instead, members tend to direct their disillusionment toward leaders who occupy "the middle level hierarchy" (Jacobs 1987:298), such as ISKCON's GBC. It is these leaders who normally shoulder the responsibility of carrying out the directives and plans of the group's charismatic founder. By targeting these leaders and their abuses of power, members are able to maintain the sanctity of the charismatic bond, even in the face of unspeakable abuse and neglect.

ISKCON's pro-change activists engaged in political struggle to bring about necessary changes in the lives of devotee women. But these very attempts also served to reaffirm the charismatic bond between themselves and their guru, Srila Prabhupada. In demonstrating that Prabhupada was not behind the abusive practices that so radically shaped women's lives in the 1970s and 1980s, women activists preserved Prabhupada's integrity for both themselves and a new generation of women who have committed their lives to Prabhupada and his movement. Perhaps ironically, their activism also helped save a failing organization as the reshaping of gender attitudes allowed women to take responsible positions in the midst of a labor crisis.

Although pro-change women did achieve significant gender reforms, the forces of resistance were gathering strength as well, and the next chapter considers the emergence of male backlash. For just as women had begun to see positive results from their activism, a group of traditionally minded men were organizing to undermine their political gains.

6

Male Backlash

The present Women's Ministry and movement in ISKCON appears
to be influenced by the demoniac feminism of karmi [nondevotee]
society, which has been and is a major factor in the ongoing moral
degeneration of the world.

—Swami, Bhakti Vikasa 1998

The real issue is one of cultural values. Whose values are we going
to cleave to? Lord Krsna's values as taught to us in the eternal
Vedas and which are true in the past, present and future. . . . You
choose: do you want Krsna's eternal spiritual Vedic culture or, the
ephemeral, bacterial culture of modern materialistic society?

—Internet text, January 2000

A male backlash often is created in religious organizations
when women gain cultural and organizational power allowing them to
successfully challenge prevailing gender norms (Nesbitt 1997:113). Such
challenges effectively "confront head-on men's sense of owning the organization" (Cockburn 1991:46). In ISKCON's case, giving women greater
institutional equality also ignited a wider conflict over religious culture
and ISKCON's overall character as a new religious movement. As one
critic commented, "It is significant to understand that a culture expresses
its ontological conclusions by its gender ethics" (Dasa, Jivan Mukta
1999d:2). Growing gender equality also signaled to traditionalists that
ISKCON was rapidly accommodating to mainstream American society,
thus abandoning its goal of building an oppositional religious culture.

GHQ and Traditionalist Backlash

At the end of September 1998, while approximately 150 devotee
women were attending the second annual ISKCON Women's Conference

in northern Florida, a group composed of men and a single woman launched a secret Internet conference on ISKCON's communication system called the General Headquarters, or the GHQ. The mobilization of this group appears to have coincided with the appointment of a woman to ISKCON's GBC in February 1998. A woman active in the Women's Ministry explained:

> I think it is specifically a knee-jerk reaction to Malati being confirmed as a GBC candidate. These men and their vehemence are not new. It's exactly why the women have suffered all these years with philosophical misconceptions, etc. I think that when Malati was confirmed to the GBC, it finally dawned on them how much progress and strength we actually had. They are determined to remove it before our progress becomes more entrenched and it is simply too late to turn back. (personal communication 1998)

A longtime Prabhupada disciple, known for his work as an astrologer, organized the GHQ. The group appears to have been a spin-off from another electronic conference known initially as the Dharma of Women and later renamed the Dharma of Men and Women. The number of active participants in the group was small, seventeen core members plus an unknown number of sympathizers (Dasa, Ardhabuddhi 1998).[1] Initially the group sought to recruit devotee men concerned about the growing influence of feminism in ISKCON. As one GHQ participant noted, "The feminist issue in our movement is a big cancer that needs to be taken seriously" (unknown author, Internet text, December 1999). To eliminate the "cancer of feminism," GHQ members pressured ISKCON's leaders to reverse past decisions granting women greater institutional equality.

The group's objectives, though not uniformly embraced by all members, included the following, as stated by GHQ's organizer:

> (1) No women in leadership positions, this means in GBC, temple presidents, the GBC secretaries, ISKCON officers or spokespersons (such as in ISKCON Communications [public relations] which is heavily dominated by feminists); (2) Terminating the present Women's Ministry; (3) The Grhastra [Householder] Ministry should be an umbrella for the Women's Ministry, no previous officers of the Women's Ministry to hold office in the Grhastra Ministry. This in keeping with no women in

leadership positions; (4) Feminist philosophy to be banned as material-istic, atheistic and mayavada.[2] . . . Any person advocating or propagat-ing feminism in any way, shape, or form to be considered as seriously deviating from Srila Prabhupada's teachings. . . . They must all resign all positions in ISKCON and leave the movement; (5) All ISKCON media such as COM [ISKCON's electronic system], *Hare Krishna World* [news-paper], *ISKCON Communications Journal* [academic publication], etc., censored for feminism; (6) No temple shall host feminist meetings; (7) Women not allowed to give classes or lead kirtanas. (GHQ Conference)

Another goal was later added by a sannyasi GHQ member: "Women (and men) should be trained in traditional role models."

GHQ members considered the values and social standards of West-ern society as fundamentally at odds with Krishna Consciousness. In-deed, contemporary Western values were viewed as "formidable imped-iments" to developing a spiritual life (Dasa, Jivan Mukta 1999d:4). As the latter author also noted, Krishna Consciousness and ISKCON are ex-pressly meant to confront Western culture: "The Krishna consciousness movement is the cultural movement intended to crush Western civiliza-tion by a comprehensive purging of Western atheistic social, political, educational and cultural conventions" (Dasa, Jivan Mukta 1999d:5).

GHQ's supporters believed that those advocating gender reform were feminists[3] determined to transform the movement from the inside by "actively and determinedly assert[ing] economic, social, legal and polit-ical rights for women in ISKCON" (Das, Krishna-kirti 2005:1). They viewed such actions as attempts to align ISKCON's future with that of contemporary Western culture. Accordingly, the conflict over gender equality was ultimately about culture. As one GHQ member acknowl-edged, "Those who espouse the *apasiddhanta*[4] paint it as a gender war. It is not a gender issue but a cultural issue" (Internet text, January 2000).

In place of modern Western society, GHQ members championed Prab-hupada's vision of ISKCON's becoming a traditional varnashram-dharma society. Such a Vedic society would be based heavily on the concept of *dharma,* or duty. By performing one's God-given duty, a devotee is able to achieve the goal of liberation. This requires strictly complying with the prescribed norms and expectations that define social and religious roles. GHQ members believed that ISKCON could never realize Prabhu-pada's vision of varnashram unless devotees fulfilled their duty to guru and to Krishna. For men, this meant strictly following the instructions of ISKCON's founder, Srila Prabhupada, and included providing ";protection" to wives and daughters. By contrast, the prescribed duty for women was to be chaste and submissive wives dedicated to their children and household responsibilities. The dharma of a woman also required that she serve her husband and other men who provided protection (Knott 2004:298).[5] Within this traditional patriarchal framework, gender equality is seen as threatening the complementary roles that define the divine obligations set forth by Krishna for men and women. As Prabhupada stated in a 1971 lecture in Bombay,

> Man is meant for hard working, and woman is meant for homely comfort, love. So both of them, if they are situated in their respective duties under proper training, then this combination of man and woman will help both of them to make progress in spiritual life. (quoted in GHQ 1999:29)

Feminism became a political cause for GHQ members to battle precisely because it challenged the very basis of varnashram-dharma by encouraging women to act contrary to their sacred duty. By failing to carry out their prescribed duties, devotee women placed not only their own spiritual lives in jeopardy but also the family and ISKCON's overall mission of establishing an oppositional religious culture founded on Vedic ideals. In the minds of the GHQ, by choosing "rights" over "duty," devotee feminists knowingly or unknowingly were promoting social chaos and disorder.

> It has become very obvious that in order to establish Varnashram-Dharma, and in order to create a peaceful and organically functioning SOCIETY that motherhood and family must be protected, and separate social duties must be encouraged. . . . So, let's assume that we encourage that the young girls, our daughters, they should all become GBC, TPs [temple presidents], and other leaders of society. Then who will take care of their children? Who will become the mothers of society? (Das, Ameyatma 1998)

Although the GHQ's efforts to re-exclude women from positions of organizational power were based on the desire to realize Prabhupada's vision of varnashram-dharma, such a cultural project effectively left men in positions of control and privilege. A male backlash against women often emerges in just such a religious context, in which men seek to preserve their authority and sense of entitlement as a ruling group (Nesbitt 1997:112–13). Based on scripture, GHQ members thought it only "natural" that authority should reside with men and that women were just as "naturally" obligated to submit to their authority. In this traditionalist framework, male entitlement is seen as the very embodiment of social relationships found in the spiritual world. Peter Berger talked about fathers and paternalism in his treatment of the "cosmization of institutions":

> When this role is legitimated in mimetic terms—the father reiterating "here below" the actions of creation, sovereignty, or love that have their sacred prototypes "up above"—then its representative character becomes vastly enhanced. Representations of human meanings become mimesis of divine mysteries. . . . Paternal authority mimes the authority of the gods, paternal solitude the solitude of the gods. (1969:38)

Thus for GHQ supporters, gender equality represented a fundamental break with the sacred order. Feminist challenges to male authority in the "here below" placed at risk the very foundations of Krishna Consciousness. One GHQ member concluded, GBC decisions enhancing women's rights "effectively upturn . . . the sastric [scriptural] principle of male social dominance" (Dasa, Jivan Mukta 1999c:2)

What shocked GHQ members into action was what they saw as the ISKCON leadership's largely sympathetic support of devotee feminists. Such a stance indicated to the GHQ that the leadership was acting in clear opposition to the movement's religious beliefs as represented by Prabhupada's teachings. A GHQ member stated, "We are concerned that those who should be leading us on this Vedic cultural revolution and revival are instead succumbing to the darkness of Western, immoral, social expressions" (Dasa, Jivan Mukta 1998). The leadership's liberal position on women contrasted with its generally uncompromising position concerning initiations and the guru institution, and this apparent inconsistency suggested to GHQ members that the feminists had won over the leadership, a fact that promised to alter the future of Prabhupada's movement.

Many of the GBC [representatives] have become completely bewildered by their charms and have become dancing dogs. Shyness and chastity are the only safety valves and our pathetic bad excuses for men on the GBC, are betraying us and all future generations by their cowardly and despicable policies. (October 6, 1998, GHQ conference)

Yet the presumed complicity of ISKCON leaders with the feminist agenda was not the only political target of GHQ members. They also repeatedly lodged charges of feminist support against ISKCON Communications, that an undue concern for public relations and public opinion had led devotees working at ISKCON Communications to support gender equality.

Aside from the GBC itself, there is the very powerful ISKCON Communications cabal who in many ways have hijacked ISKCON. They are so concerned with what the public thinks about ISKCON that it cares more for public opinion than [for] the opinion of the Acaryas of the *guru-parampara* and Lord Krsna. Heaven help us if we offend the liberal press by trying to follow the dictates of Lord Krsna. (Avantika 2004)

Mukunda Goswami [previously head of ISKCON Communications] and his followers want us to retrench our philosophy in regard to feminism so as to be in line with the relative values of contemporary, secular, Western culture. This is an egregious error. . . . Consider that we chant Hare Krsna in the street, wear strange clothing, shave our heads, and put yellow "mud" [clay] on our noses all without caring for public opinion. Frankly, they already think we are more than a "little" strange. So why should we care what they think of our values?[6] (GHQ 1999:41)

Strategically, GHQ members tried to pressure the GBC to disband ISK-CON's Women's Ministry or otherwise bring it under the auspices of the male-led Grhastha Ministry. They also sought to halt the emerging trend of women serving in institutional roles traditionally filled by devotee men (GBC representatives, temple presidents). Members of GHQ attempted to reverse the 2000 GBC resolutions granting women opportunities that included teaching morning classes on the scripture, leading temple kirtans, and worshipping nearer the altar. They began by classifying ISKCON leaders on the basis of their presumed support for GHQ's traditionalist ideology. Sixteen leaders and influential devotees were identified as "pro-Vedic" and thus in sympathy with GHQ goals; fifteen were labeled as unsupportive; and sixteen were viewed as potentially supportive, or those whose "loyalty was unknown." Group members tried to rally "pro-Vedic" leaders to their cause while preaching "vigorously" to potential supporters "so they [have to] support us or show their colors." Leaders deemed unsupportive were denounced as the enemy, "the ones who we are contending with in this ideological war for the future of ISKCON and Vedic Dharma" (October 2, 1998, GHQ Conference). One ISKCON leader who initially was considered a GHQ supporter was denounced after he made a public statement supporting the appointment of a woman to the GBC.

> It is men like him that undermine a husband's authority over his wife. Instead of seizing the moment to preach to her [woman GBC member] and show her the path of dharma, how she should follow her prescribed duty, etc. he wimps out and encourages her! Who said this guy is on our side anyway? He is a total embarrassment! (October 6, 1998, GHQ conference)

Although the GHQ's primary strategy was to lobby leaders, the group also aspired to build a grassroots movement within ISKCON to counter the feminist influences. As the organizer of the group stated,

> I don't think getting allies will be very difficult; practically everybody I've mentioned it to was very enthusiastic. The vast silent majority of devotees are fed up and sick of these feminists. But they have felt isolated because of thinking they were alone because of the volume of feminist rhetoric. It is our business then to give them the weapons, which they can then use to fight against feminism. (October 2, 1998, GHQ Conference)

Like other backlash movements, the GHQ appealed to the authority of scripture as "the weapon" to advance their cause. Scripture establishes "an objective intransigence that allows proponents of resistance to refrain from taking personal responsibility for their views" (Nesbitt 1997:113). Those who resist change thus become defenders of the faith. To influence both the leadership and what was thought to be a sympathetic "silent majority," GHQ members researched both Prabhupada's scriptural commentaries and his spoken words to demonstrate "why feminism is very dangerous for Vedic culture" (October 2, 1998, GHQ Conference). Such an effort was specifically meant to demonstrate that giving women independence in the form of institutional responsibilities was fundamentally at odds with Prabhupada's teachings. On this basis, the gender reforms granted by ISKCON's leaders amounted to a grave error in judgment. One devotee with reservations about the GHQ was forced to admit that

> the problem is . . . that the conservatives have Prabhupada on their side. Prabhupada explicitly states that women should not be given any managerial position. It is even in the *Lilamrita* [Prabhupada's biography]. He says umpteen times that the Manusamhita is the authority where women are concerned. He says (patronizingly, I may add) that women are to be contented with ornaments and that will keep them quiet. He may have said other things at other times, but in his books, in the lawbooks that are to stand for 10,000 years, that is what he said. Now what hermeneutical tool will free us from what Prabhupada said? (Internet text 1998)

By using Prabhupada's words to develop their antifeminist agenda, GHQ members sought to lay claim to the theological high ground. By contrast, ISKCON's reformers were seen as relying on the law and the force of the state.

> It should be exposed that the feminists are appealing to a totally non-sastric [nonscriptural] source; the laws of a demoniac society that supports divorce, homosexuality, etc, in the name of "equality" and "rights." . . . What is more frightening is the possibility that our liberated mothers might throw the karmi [nondevotee] law book at us and use the clout of state law to enforce "women's rights" in our temples and communities. (Swami, Bhakti Vikasa 1998:3-4)

Apart from the persuasive power of Prabhupada's teachings within ISKCON, using his words also helped the GHQ solve a strategic problem. GHQ members worried openly that they would be labeled as "women haters," which would limit their appeal to potential supporters while provoking hostile reactions from opponents.

Men generally, instinctively come to the defense of a woman. So if we are seen as "attacking" a woman, then this response is triggered. So somehow we have to present our case without appearing to be "attacking women," let SP [Srila Prabhupada] do the talking. (October 7, 1998, GHQ Conference)

For instance, using Srila Prabhupada's definition of a prostitute, we can (in polite terms) question the status of remarried ISKCON women. This is certain to get the feminazis highly riled, as they are mostly remarried divorcees, but we can coolly again present the Prabhupada quote to them and not allow them to obfuscate the point with their name-calling.[7] (September 24, 1998, GHQ Conference)

Prabhupada's teachings played a central role in the GHQ's attempt to discredit feminism and women leaders while at the same time promoting varnashram religious culture.

Strategies of Discreditation

GHQ members used Prabhupada's teachings, in combination with the Manusamhita,[8] in their attempt to turn back ISKCON's gender reforms. They first argued that women were ultimately unfit to serve in positions of institutional responsibility because their psychophysical nature denied them the attributes necessary for leadership. In place of independence, women required male protection. GHQ's second strategy was using scripture to disparage the character and morality of devotee women holding positions of ISKCON leadership.

Protection and Independence

A fundamental element of ISKCON's traditionalist theology is that men should protect women. As one GHQ member stated, "A woman is always to remain under the dependence of a father, husband, or older son. . . . And women are to be protected by a man" (Das, Ameyatma 1998). According to Prabhupada, freedom and independence are dangerous for women because they lead to sexual exploitation by men. The need to protect women is a consistent theme in Prabhupada's scriptural commentaries about women. Prabhupada stated in the *Bhagavad Gita as It Is,*

> Good population depends on the chastity and faithfulness of its womanhood. As children are very prone to be misled, women are similarly very prone to degradation. Therefore, both children and women require protection by the elder members of the family. (quoted in Devi Dasi, Sridhari 2000:2)

> Now, in the Manu-samhita it is clearly stated that a woman should not be given freedom. That does not mean that women are to be kept as slaves, but they are like children. Children are not given freedom.[9] (quoted in GHQ 1999:29)

From a traditionalist perspective, gender equality in the form of independence threatens the dharma of both women and men because it limits, or negates, the need for male protection. According to a woman supportive of the GHQ,

> The "equal and full opportunity" they are clamoring for is nothing more than the beginning of the end, because when women receive freedom or rights for "equal opportunities," they automatically relinquish their right to be protected. . . . So even if men want to protect women, as long as women demand equality, they automatically forfeit their status for being protected. (Devi Dasi, Sridhari 2000:2)

Because women require protection, GHQ members contended that they should not hold ISKCON leadership positions. As one GHQ member observed, "When women assume independent managerial roles in ISKCON, it compromises their chastity and lessens the motivation for men to properly protect them" (Devi Dasi, Sita 2005:1). Left unprotected, "women leaders become subject to various forms of mistreatment and abuse," as one GHQ member concluded about the GBC's misplaced decision to appoint a woman to the GBC. "It is an unfortunate fact of life, even in our [ISKCON] society, that leaders get all sorts of nasty things said about them—which is another reason women shouldn't take leadership roles. They should be protected from such nastiness" (Swami, Bhakti Vikasa 1998). As one GHQ member concluded about the GBC's misplaced decision to appoint a woman to the GBC, "Women are like children. And in that sense Malati is not fully responsible for her actions. Nevertheless, it is only a fool or an organization with a death wish that elevates these childlike women into positions of social leadership" (October 6, 1998, GHQ conference).

Personal Attacks on Token Women

Women used as tokens to break new ground often face substantial opposition and even open hostility. Challengers may attempt to block or reverse policies that afford women new institutional opportunities, and they may also attack the qualifications and character of token women. Such challenges are usually accompanied by "a mythology that unqualified members of that status group are being promoted," thus further fueling the potential for backlash (Nesbitt 1997:131).

GHQ members directly challenged the qualifications and personal character of women in ISKCON leadership positions. Two women in highly visible institutional positions, ISKCON's newly appointed GBC representative and the head of the Women's Ministry, became both targets and symbols of the GHQ's resistance to gender equality. Both were subject to various forms of character assassination meant to highlight their lack of qualification to serve in positions of leadership. These negative portrayals linked their presumed feminist leanings with what GHQ members defined as immoral behavior.

Women Leaders as Prostitutes and Whores

Even though divorce is commonplace in ISKCON and affects men and women equally, GHQ members found reason to attack ISKCON's most prominent women leaders as divorcees. They also debased other characteristics of each woman in an effort to discredit their credentials for ISKCON leadership. As one sannyasi GHQ member concluded, "Devotees in positions of authority in ISKCON should have morally clean records" (Swami, Bhakti Vikasa 1998).

GHQ members presented Prabhupada's strongly worded scriptural commentaries on divorce and remarriage to deride the qualifications of the director of ISKCON's Women's Ministry:

In the laws of Dharma, in the eyes of Shastra [scripture] and the eyes of Krsna there simply is no such thing as divorce. A woman who leaves one man and sleeps with another—both Prabhupada and the Vedas describe this as prostitution. (Das, Ameyatma 1998)

As Prabhupada wrote in a Srimad Bhagavatam commentary,

> If her husband is fallen, it is recommended that she give up his association. Giving up the association of her husband does not mean, however, that a woman should marry again and thus indulge in prostitution. If a chaste woman unfortunately marries a husband who is fallen, she should live separately from him. (quoted in Dasa, Jivan Mukta 1999a:8)

Yet to GHQ members, women with children who divorced and remarried were guilty of more than being "prostitutes." Their marital history in combination with being mothers also left them open to charges of "child abuse." One influential GHQ member argued that a remarried woman places her children in the position of being unwanted by her new husband, given the latter's interest in fathering his own children. Moreover, because divorced women are likely to criticize their former spouse, children often lose respect for their fathers. Divorced women thus "become the worst enemy of their own children" (Das, Ameyatma 1998).

Using divorce and remarriage as a criterion for denying women positions of leadership, GHQ members pressured for the removal of the woman in charge of ISKCON's Women's Ministry.

> [Name] has remarried, she has daughter[s] from different husbands. This is acceptable for setting example for others to follow by giving her authority to start an authorized ISKCON Ministry? . . . Don't the GBC members have anything but Bull Dung for brains? What were they thinking? (October 6, 1998, GHQ conference)

This GHQ member went on to complain that he had recently seen the women's minister at the grocery store, where she was, "dressed like an old hippie. . . . My wife, to my good fortune, always wears sari. She always covers her head in public. Here was the woman in charge of the Women's Ministry, and I mistook her for a karmi hippie" (October 6, 1998, GHQ conference).

Because the women's minister and some of the ministry's female supporters were remarried and thus considered "prostitutes," GHQ members cynically suggested renaming the Women's Ministry. "A Prostitute Ministry would also be appropriate considering the current state of affairs. Actually, it should be called the Whore Ministry so that the initials can remain the same" (October 6, 1998, GHQ Conference). Another member of the group suggested that ISKCON's International Women's Conference be renamed the International Witches Conference. Along similar lines, one GHQ member offered the following opinion about feminists, including the women's minister: "Mmmmmmmm! I must admit although they appear to be spirit souls like those of us wearing either male or female bodies, in actuality they have no soul" (September 29, 1998, GHQ Conference).[10]

Dismissive derogatory statements also were used against ISKCON's newly appointed GBC representative. A GHQ member stated the following about her rumored past involvement in the sex trade:

> A madam is not only a whore herself, but she employs other young ladies (and/or men) in the sex trade. Even if she has reformed herself, is it appropriate to elevate her to the position of GBC? [11] (cited in GHQ, 1999:22)

Given this leader's background and presumed feminist sympathies, a GHQ member expressed concern about her ability to attract women recruits to her ISKCON center in Columbus, Ohio. From his perspective, ISKCON's new GBC representative was a danger to Prabhupada's movement because of her determination to spread feminism.

> [She] starts her own preaching centre training punk female lib radicals to go out and preach to others of a similar ilk. She doesn't show them what true femininity is because she herself doesn't know. She is a liability to Prabhupada and to our society, and we elevate [her] to a position of leadership. (October 6, 1998, GHQ conference)

Responding to Male Backlash

The GHQ's attack on supporters of gender equality provoked a strong reaction from various quarters of the movement. Pro-change women activists, their supporters, and ISKCON's North American leadership were drawn into the conflict. Men and woman opposed to the GHQ's traditionalist agenda argued that members of the group were using Prabhupada's teachings to reassert control over women's lives. The Vedic conception of a woman's dharma was being used to control and exploit, rather than for religious purposes. In the hands of GHQ members, Prabhupada's teachings had become political tools used for destructive ends.

> The group of "GHQ" men and women who had been hiding behind a veil of "Prabhupada said" and "Vedic culture" and "women's dharma" have had their veil blown off. They in fact are using these terms for another agenda—one of misogyny. (Anonymous 1998)

Another pro-change advocate active in the Women's Ministry turned to U.S. history to frame the GHQ's ultimate intentions:

> The blanket labels applied to the Women's Ministry and others involved in this debate are reminiscent of the McCarthyism prevalent in the U.S. in the 1950s. Then, as now, labels were used to silence people for political reasons. (Devi Dasi, Radha 1998)

Supporters of gender equality were especially outraged by the GHQ's repeated insistence that women were ill prepared to serve in positions of ISKCON leadership because they required male "protection." To the GHQ's critics, a review of ISKCON's history made it clear that "protection" had too often been used to serve the interests of misogynist men determined to exploit devotee women. According to two devotee women highly critical of the GHQ's traditionalist agenda,

> It seems GHQ or men of similar mentality want to have freedom to do whatever they want while they expect a woman to stay in the marriage, regardless of what he does to her. Otherwise they call her unchaste, prostitute, or irreligious. Such philosophies result in abuse where men can have absolute authority, uncontrolled senses including anger and sex, along with total freedom. (Devi Dasi, Prtha 1998)

> To all members and readers of the GHQ conference. . . . Where have you been during the child abuse period? Did you stand and fight to protect the devotees' children (who were abused by leaders of ISKCON) like real Vedic leaders? Where have you been when most of the gurus and lead-

ers sent girls (nicely dressed with make-up) all day long on parking lots and airports, risking their life and virtue, collecting so much money for the big crazy expenditures of the "star leaders?" . . . Do you call this dharma and vedic culture? (Dasi, Syamasundari 1999:1)

Criticism of GHQ also came from ISKCON's North American leaders who denounced the group's vilification of devotee women in the name of religious principles, and the Executive Committee of ISKCON's North American GBC published a strong response to the GHQ:

The North American GBC/Temple President Executive Officers wish to voice our strong disapproval of, and our protest against, the demeaning and ill intended statements made by some members of the GHQ com conference. . . . Multiple statements made by members of this Internet conference ridicule, berate, and vilify women, other minorities, and in- dividual Vaisnava devotees. They document an organized attempt to prevent women from their God-given rights of self expression and ser- vice to Srila Prabhupada. (GBC Executive Committee 1998)

The controversy surrounding the GHQ spilled over into a wider and perhaps more consequential conflict. Because the GHQ's defense of Vedic dharma relied exclusively on Prabhupada's teachings, the debate about gender equality ultimately placed Prabhupada and his scriptural com- mentaries at the center of the debate. The conflict escalated dramatically after some supporters of gender equality challenged Prabhupada's scrip- tural commentaries about women as "sexist." This and a related chal- lenge raised both sensitive and critical questions about Prabhupada's authority and ISKCON's scriptural inheritance.

Prabhupada on Trial

The GHQ's use of Prabhupada's scriptural commentaries in its attempt to turn away feminist influences produced a second round of contro- versy. This time, however, Prabhupada and his teachings became the source of debate and conflict. Some pro-change women, in partner- ship with a number of academically trained ISKCON intellectuals, began to raise questions about Prabhupada's writings on women. This chal- lenge led to a questioning of Prabhupada's authority as a "pure devotee

[who] only repeats Krsna's message as Krsna directs him to do so" (Das, Ameyatma 2000:2). Should Prabhupada's commentaries about women be considered eternal truths or products of his education and upbringing in India? Should Prabhupada's collective teachings be considered infallible, or were they subject to human error? These and related questions grew into what one GHQ supporter called a "wedge of doubt" (Das, Ameyatma 2000:14). One influential ISKCON leader suggested that the conflict over women's rights had placed "Prabhupada on Trial" (COM 2000b:2).[12]

Prabhupada's views of women became a topic of considerable interest on an electronic conference made up of academics and other ISKCON intellectuals. Messages posted on the Vaisnava Advanced Studies (VAST) conference were leaked to one GHQ member who subsequently published them on the Vaisnava News Network (see Dasa, Jivan Mukta 1999a). A sampling of these posts reveals how members of VAST questioned Prabhupada's scriptural commentaries about women. One major point of contention concerned Prabhupada's statements about women being less intelligent than men.[13] As one pro-change advocate and VAST participant noted,

> I also object to the characterization of women as less materially intelligent, based on both psychological research and personal experience. I know that, materially speaking, I am more intelligent than many men in our [ISKCON] society. (quoted in Dasa, Jivan Mukta 1999a:3)

Another member of the conference attempted to explain Prabhupada's controversial views regarding women's intelligence on the basis of Prabhupada's educational training at Scottish Churches College in Calcutta. In doing so, he implied that Prabhupada's misinformed statements about women's intelligence should be altered in future editions of his books.

> A lot of erroneous sciences like phrenology were doing the rounds. Such sciences determined intelligence or culture by brain size, or nasal index (Ripley). Women's skull size was considered evidence of their lesser intelligence. If Prabhupada picked up information from such sources which he later used in preaching, then we have to be prepared to correct it and contextualize it on behalf of our spiritual master. (quoted in Dasa, Jivan Mukta 1999a:3)

Given the derogatory statements about women in Prabhupada's writings, many of VAST's academic members worried openly about using Prabhupada's books in their college courses. One member of the group recounted the reactions of his students after they read one of Prabhupada's texts.

> What are you going to tell your students when they read these things in Prabhupada's books? I had all my students read one of Prabhupada's little books and they hated the sexist statements (and sexist atmosphere in the temple) while appreciating much else. (quoted in Dasa, Jivan Mukta 1999a:6)

The suggestion that some of Prabhupada's commentaries on women were incorrect and that his books should be changed accordingly in future editions brought a strong response from GHQ members. Indeed, the GHQ member responsible for leaking the VAST messages concluded:

> The feminist agenda and ideology is so diametrically opposed to Prabhupada's direct statements, teachings and ISKCON's cultural mandate, that the only way to fully rectify this "problem," as they [VAST members] themselves accurately concluded, is to change his books . . . it is, in fact, the only logical conclusion for those who pursue and propagate what Prabhupada calls a "puffed up concept of womanly life." Why? Because feminist ideology can never be supported on the basis of current editions of Prabhupada's books. (Dasa, Jivan Mukta 1999a:2)

In October 1999 another controversy emerged that had far-reaching implications. A devotee woman who was a participant in another electronic conference (Topical Discussions) posted a series of controversial messages about Prabhupada that created an outcry. The woman in question had worked for a number of years translating and editing Prabhupada's books for ISKCON's Bhaktivedanta Book Trust in Europe, and her reading of Prabhupada's texts had convinced her that his commentaries contained several logical "contradictions." At first, she listed some of what she regarded as contradictions in Prabhupada's writings (see Das, Ameyatma 2000; Dasa, Jivan Mukta 1999b) and then followed this with comments questioning the very "truth" of Prabhupada's scriptural commentaries. As she admitted, her concerns had led her to doubt Prabhupada's authority.

Another thing that bothers me is that Srila Prabhupada is always so sure of himself. He is fully confident in his own judgment. He is fully confident that the world is full of girls, that in certain places all people are rascals, that "Bad things means Western type of civilization," etc. Very strong, super simple black-and white general statements. . . . Srila Prabhupada passes absolute judgments, and he is not even consistent in them. I am ready to believe the source of his certainty is [a] direct link with Krsna's absolute knowledge, *if* it can be proven he was absolutely right each time. Up till then, I will rather suppose Prabhupada's absolute self-confidence was a feature of his own individual character. (her emphasis; quoted in Dasa, Jivan Mukta 1999b:2)

Unlike participants in the VAST electronic conference, Dhyana-Kunda Dasi (1999) argued against changing Prabhupada's books to correct errors and contradictions:

The books should stay as they are. I think that we would do Srila Prabhupada a disservice by removing these sorts of errors from his books. This would only increase the tendency of some readers to see him as a materially infallible oracle. The way the books are now, he looks more human.

A spokesperson for the GHQ responded as follows to this attack on Prabhupada's authority:

There has been an ongoing controversy with regard to what constitutes proper respect for pure devotees like Srila Prabhupada, and what is considered improper, or offensive. This controversy is a most serious concern for many devotees . . . because the authority, respect and honor of our acaryas, specifically Srila Prabhupada's is being questioned. All other controversies we have experienced to date are quite minor in comparison because they never precluded discussion on the basis of Srila Prabhupada's teaching. . . . But when Srila Prabhupada's authority itself is derided, and shastra is minimized then there is no question of a debate. (Das, Ameyatma 2000:2)

The doubts raised about Prabhupada's authority resulted in a number of angry and hostile reactions that soon found their way to ISK-CON's leadership. As one ISKCON leader described it, the virulent tone of the response approached "the ancient, atavistic mob-cry, 'Burn the witches'" (COM 2000a:2). Despite the outcry from GHQ members and other devotees equally concerned about the challenge to Prabhupada's authority, ISKCON's North American leadership made no formal effort to sanction, or otherwise stop, those responsible for defaming Prabhupada.[14] As one prominent GHQ member declared, "These GBC men did not rise to defend Srila Prabhupada, they did not rise to come to the defense of those who were trying to defend Srila Prabhupada" (Das. Ameyatma 2000:9).[15] One GBC member hinted at the reasons why the leadership failed to respond when he declared, "I hereby confess I came to find these reactions, 'in defense of Srila Prabhupada,' equally—no, even more so—troubling and upsetting than that which occasioned them" (COM 2000a). As this statement implies, ISKCON's leaders found themselves in an uncomfortable position, as pursuing a vigorous and public defense of Prabhupada meant aligning themselves with GHQ and its controversial agenda. One GBC member decided, "They are like the John Birch Society, and we didn't want to raise their visibility and status. Plus it was politically safe just to ignore them, and we did" (interview October 2005).

There also is evidence suggesting that at least some of ISKCON's North American leaders tried to quietly disassociate themselves from Prabhupada's controversial writings about women, given the movement's past history of abuse. As one GBC member acknowledged, Prabhupada's statements are "under currently established norms of business, government, and academics, labeled 'sexist,' and regarded as on the same moral level as anti-Semitic or racist utterances" (COM 2000a). Another suggested that the leaders, though "not wanting to talk about Prabhupada's mistakes," also found it important to

> distinguish between what Prabhupada says about the tradition and what he said about contemporary issues. To say that Prabhupada is a pure devotee, which I believe he is, doesn't mean that he is materially omniscient. What Prabhupada said about World War II or women's intelligence, he himself didn't represent as absolute truth. He had a human side; he gave his opinions that go beyond quoting and commenting on the scripture itself. We have to place these opinions in a different box from his commentaries directly addressing matters of scripture. . . . Let's face it, twenty years ago what the GHQ is saying was accepted. It was the way we thought. But there has been a gradual, steady, historical

transformation. There has been a gradual and peaceful shift in ISKCON, in the Prabhupada hermeneutic. Given the extreme sensitivity of some of these issues, I think the GBC is relieved that this shift has occurred. (interview October 2005)

The failure of the leadership to throw its support behind the GHQ on this and other issues thus set the stage for its ultimate failure.

GHQ's Failed Mission and the Demise of Traditionalism

In February 2005, a member of the GHQ petitioned the GBC to reconsider the 2000 resolutions that provided "equal and full opportunity for devotional service for all devotees in ISKCON, regardless of gender" (GBC Resolutions, 2000). The GHQ's objections to the resolutions were many, but the overriding concern was that "equality for women and everything it implies is now established as a core principle in ISKCON, actually not only a core principle but a 'priority,' i.e., the topmost principle" (Dasa, Paradhyeya 2005, quoted in Dasa, Basu Ghosh 2005:3). At a minimum, the supporters of the GHQ-backed initiative wanted to remove the word *equal* from the 2000 GBC resolutions because of its identification with feminism and gender equality (Dasa, Basu Ghosh 2005: 4). One GHQ supporter argued,

> The [2000] resolutions use ambiguous wording such as equal opportunity and equal facilities which are easily interpreted to support adharmic [nondharmic] feminism. . . . The very wording of the GBC resolutions removes women from their natural family role of daughter, wife, and mother and can easily be used to promote artificial, adharmic equality in ISKCON. (Devi Dasi, Sita 2005:1)

In response to the GHQ proposal, the Women's Ministry initiated a petition drive to mobilize its supporters in opposition. As the 2005 GBC meetings in India approached, many expected a major confrontation after one GBC member agreed to sponsor the GHQ proposal for GBC consideration. In the end, however, it never made it to the floor of the GBC for debate and a vote, as GBC deputies, who review proposals before they go to the full GBC body, rejected the GHQ proposal. An official ISK-CON source reported that the 2000 resolutions were affirmed by the GBC and that the "attempt to have these resolutions overturned was itself quickly overturned at this year's meetings and may be *no more than a blip on the radar historically*" (my emphasis, iskcon.com 2005b:1–2).

GHQ supporters not only lost any hope of turning back previous gender reforms. In what was described as "a quiet, but radical move," the GBC gave its formal approval to women serving as initiating ISKCON gurus (iskcon.com 2005a). While acknowledging opposing views on the subject, ISKCON's Sastric Advisory Committee concluded nonetheless that "permanently disallowing women from giving initiation cannot be philosophically supported by either sastra or Srila Prabhupada's statements" (GBC Meetings 2005).

The GBC's abrupt dismissal of the GHQ's petition to reconsider the 2000 women's resolutions, combined with the GBC's decision to grant women the right to serve as initiating gurus, signaled the end of GHQ's campaign to turn back gender equality within ISKCON. Although individual GHQ members continued to advocate traditionalist views about women, the group lost any claims to legitimacy and essentially collapsed following the 2005 GBC meetings.[16]

Conclusion

The politics surrounding women's place in ISKCON clearly point to the ways that the Krishna movement has edged ever closer to American mainstream culture. The GHQ's failed attempt to turn back gender equality only reinforced this shift. Although inequalities continue to exist, as they also do in mainstream societies, ISKCON's organizational policy now fully endorses equal and full opportunities for men and women devotees alike. Such a cultural turn is significant because it signals the ways in which traditionalism no longer serves as the foundation of ISKCON's religious culture. In embracing gender equality, ISKCON's leaders aligned the organization with a defining feature of modern liberal culture (Chaves 1997:51).

The conflict over gender equality, incited by the GHQ's determined effort to assert traditional Vedic conceptions of dharma, opened a Pandora's box that may forever remain open. The debate about women's roles and place in ISKCON led to critical questioning of Prabhupada's scriptural commentaries, as well as to his overall authority as Krishna's pure representative. The fact that the leadership failed to act decisively on Prabhupada's behalf was an acknowledgment that his authority no longer was absolute. Given ISKCON's increasingly pluralistic membership, it was perhaps inevitable that Prabhupada's teachings would be questioned, especially in light of their past misuse resulting in the abuse of devotee women and children. As one ISKCON leader expressed it, "There is irreducible diversity within ISKCON. It is a mistake trying to find the straight line. What is important is whether a devotee fits within the boundaries of Prabhupada's teachings." Yet as these teachings become reframed as guides for thought and action, in place of being "absolute truths," traditionalism will continue its march to the margins of ISKCON. As it does, the goal of creating a viable cultural alternative to mainstream American culture will cease to exist.

While women activists stood and fought against the injustices they faced, other ISKCON members chose to lower their voice and move on, seeing little in the way of a future for themselves and their families within ISKCON. As a result, ISKCON faced an uncertain future in North America.

7

Moving On

"Bloop" is the sound the soul makes when it falls into the material world. But leaving ISKCON does not mean leaving Krishna or Prabhupada.

—Prabhupada disciple, 1996

The days are gone when you can visit temples and understand ISK-CON. If you just have temples on your radar, you are going to miss what is going on.

—ISKCON leader and guru 2005

Researchers of social movements often assume that defection and schism rob a movement of its energy and vitality. Gamson (1975: 101–3) went so far as to argue that factionalism is the major cause of movement failure. Yet this view of failure confuses the conceptual difference between movement organizations and movements. If the fortunes of movements are made equivalent to those of movement organizations, defection, factionalism, and schism readily become signs of decline and failure. If we view social movements as fluid, however, organizational boundaries become less important than the broader contexts in which movements operate (Gusfield 1981:323).

Studies of disengagement from new religions have largely treated defection as an individual experience involving a breakdown in the ideological and cognitive linkage between a convert's values and beliefs and the group's religious doctrines and practices. Defection is thus characterized as a process of "falling from the faith" (Bromley 1988) or as an outcome of dissonance problems leading to "deconversion" (Jacobs 1984, 1987; Skonovd 1983; Wright 1983, 1984). Yet as new religions developed, internal conflict and factionalism emerged, resulting in mass expulsion, group defection, and schism (Balch and Cohig 1985, cited in Wright 1988; Chancellor 2000; Ofshe 1980; Rochford 1989; Rochford and Bailey 2006; Wallis 1976, 1982). Each of these collective forms of disaffiliation places a group's survival at risk, as membership loss is often associated with economic decline (Chancellor 2000; Balch and Cohig 1985, cited in Wright 1988:157; Rochford and Bailey 2006).

Beginning in the early 1980s, Prabhupada's movement moved beyond the organizational boundaries of ISKCON as large numbers of devotees abandoned its North American communities. Because those leaving did so largely for reasons of economic necessity and differences with the leadership, the majority remained part of Prabhupada's movement. Yet the mass exodus out of its communities left ISKCON in a state of decline and facing a precarious future.

Taking Leave of ISKCON

Throughout ISKCON's North American history, individual defection has been commonplace (Rochford, Purvis, and Eastman 1989). Beginning in the late 1970s and early 1980s, however, the pattern changed toward more collective forms of disengagement (Rochford 1989). As we have seen, the collapse of ISKCON's communal structure led the leadership to force large numbers of householders and their families out of ISKCON's communities to find jobs, schooling, and independent living situations. This amounted to a mass expulsion, as householders ultimately had little control over their disengagement. Yet many of those pushed out of ISKCON's temple communities formed new congregations that reshaped ISKCON's social organization as well as its religious culture. Congregational members became less involved in ISKCON as the household displaced the temple as the center of Krishna conscious religious life.

Because they were forced out of ISKCON's communities, many householders remained resentful toward a leadership that they viewed as largely out of touch with devotee families' needs. As one Prabhupada disciple who left ISKCON in 1982 commented, "I have little faith that ISKCON will be able to move ahead fast enough in my lifetime to understand my family's needs what to speak of do anything about them." Another longtime ISKCON member who moved with his family into the congregation in the late 1980s stated,

> But here we have sannyasis who are considered "socially dead" because
> of their position dealing with householders, women, children, educa-

tion, and all these issues that make up a society. And who do you have running it? A bunch of devotees who are socially dead, incapable of understanding, what to speak of dealing with householders and their needs. Yet they are establishing the rules, guiding and planning the [ISK-CON] society. It's ass backwards. (interview 1993)

Some of those pushed out of ISKCON's communities chose to leave ISKCON altogether rather than join the emerging congregation.

Ever since they kicked us out, I have worked hard to establish myself and family materially. It has taken many years to become stable and successful. I can't see how I could uproot and move to where a temple is only to be kicked out again. (Prabhupada disciple, Centennial Survey 1996)

My wife and I were discarded by ISKCON. Our spiritual and material success has been without ISKCON. And finally ISKCON's help is not needed any longer. But our success is much attributed to Lord Krishna's influence. (Prabhupada disciple, Centennial Survey 1996)

Apart from the householders' being expelled from ISKCON was a broader crisis of authority that led to the defection of large numbers of devotees from the organization. Repeated scandals and abuses of power involving the gurus and their GBC supporters raised fundamental questions about the legitimacy of Prabhupada's successors.[1] As guru controversies arose in quick succession beginning in 1980 (Rochford 1985: 221–55; 1998a), devotees began leaving ISKCON in ever larger numbers to avoid what one described as "the nonsense that went on after Srila Prabhupada's passing." Dasa and his family were among the many who left New Vrindaban in the wake of Bhaktipada's sexual indiscretions and abuses of power during the 1980s. Initially, those defecting were Prabhupada disciples disenfranchised by the new gurus' claims of spiritual authority equal to Prabhupada's. By the mid-1980s, disciples of the new gurus also began defecting as a majority of the latter betrayed their sacred vows and voluntarily or involuntarily left ISKCON (Rochford 1985:227–45, 1998a; Rochford and Bailey 2006). In 2005, only two of the eleven original gurus succeeding Prabhupada remained as initiating gurus.[2] Moreover, after the guru system was reformed in 1986, a substantial number of the gurus appointed thereafter also fell from their positions. Of the 104 ISKCON gurus appointed between 1977 and 2004, 34 were relieved of their positions, and an additional 14 were sanctioned by the GBC for misbehavior (*Back to Prabhupada* 2005c:10). Including the Prabhupada disciples, as many as two-thirds of ISKCON's membership became "spiritual orphans," having lost their gurus (Collins 2004:218).

The Centennial Survey permits us to determine how leadership issues entered into decisions to defect from ISKCON. I compared eighty-two congregational members and eighty-seven former ISKCON members[3] in regard to the authority that each group attributes to the GBC and the gurus (see appendix 2, table A.2).[4] The former ISKCON members expressed much less support for ISKCON's GBC and guru leadership, and more than half (56%) indicated that their "lack of trust in the GBC" represented a "major influence" limiting their willingness to remain active in ISKCON. Only 19 percent of the congregational members indicated the same. Half (48%) the former members responded that their "lack of respect for ISKCON's current gurus" strongly influenced their willingness to remain involved, whereas only 17 percent of the congregational members were similarly influenced.[5]

When asked on the Centennial Survey why they discontinued their ISKCON membership, former members uniformly pointed to the failures of the leadership. As two former ISKCON members explained,

> I have left ISKCON but not Krishna Consciousness. My practices are minimal but my beliefs are in the philosophy. I believe that the GBC are the least mature and advanced and that the devotee population is progressing faster than the leadership. The leaders are self-motivated, stuck, and holding back progress. I love devotees but have no real use for official ISKCON. This may sound radical, but I would like to see official ISKCON disbanded and let Krsna Consciousness grow from a grass-roots movement. (Prabhupada disciple, Centennial Survey 1996)

> I left because I became disgusted with the constant oppression of women, the mistreatment of children, and the constant corruption and mismanagement. I was not able to express my full personality because of the oppression. Not given the opportunity to show or use my abilities—constantly having to see and hear mistreatment being committed against myself and other female devotees and tolerating those offenses in the name of humility (or that might have been cowardice or stupid-

ity). Following the order of my spiritual master out of fear of being ostracized for speaking out. So I thought it better to live on the outside looking in, and not get so deeply involved and disturbed with what was going on in the name of Krishna Consciousness. (Disciple of one of Prabhupada's successors, Centennial Survey 1996)

An ISKCON sannyasi and guru similarly acknowledged in a 1987 letter to the GBC that the leadership was responsible for driving substantial numbers of devotees out of ISKCON:

> The GBC, both indirectly by impure acts and directly by confrontation and force, has driven large numbers of Srila Prabhupada's disciples out of their service, out of their homes, and out of ISKCON. . . . By allowing, advocating, taking part in, perpetuating, and defending these and other forms of contamination and decay, the members of the GBC have brought the ultimate managing authority of the entire International Society for Krishna Consciousness to a state of disrepute and pollution. (Swami, Jayadvaita 1987; quoted in *Back to Prabhupada* 2005d:2)

Clearly, the leadership's actions played a decisive role in large portions of ISKCON's membership defecting from the organization during the 1980s. Their legacy of abuse, mismanagement, and spiritual corruption convinced many that ISKCON no longer represented a legitimate vehicle for realizing Prabhupada's teachings. On this basis, disillusioned ISKCON members began searching beyond the "sacred fortress" of ISKCON's temples (Squarcini 2000:256) for new contexts in which they could renew their commitments to Prabhupada and Krishna.

Ties That Bind: Prabhupada and Krishna

In virtually every case, those former ISKCON members who responded to the Centennial Survey affirmed their unwavering commitment to Prabhupada. It was on this basis that they remained part of Prabhupada's movement, if not of ISKCON. Only one former ISKCON member disagreed with the statement "I accept as truth Prabhupada's translations of and commentaries on the Srimad Bhagavatam and other Vedic scriptures." Among the Prabhupada disciples, two-thirds (62%) indicated that they remained strongly committed "to fulfilling the orders of my spiritual master." Whether a Prabhupada disciple or not, however, most who left ISKCON remained firmly committed to Prabhupada and Krishna. In comparison to congregational members, former ISKCON devotees were equally committed to Krishna Consciousness, to preaching Prabhupada's teachings, and to the truth of Prabhupada's scriptural commentaries. Moreover, they were equally involved in private religious practices and just as likely to adhere to the movement's regulative principles as congregational members were (see table A.2).

As one devotee woman who left ISKCON in 1987 pointed out, Prabhupada continues to have a major influence in her life:

> I think that Srila Prabhupada has had the best possible influence on all of our lives since the appearance of Lord Chaitanya. Even on a very insincere part-time devotee like myself. Prabhupada has taught me to see that Krsna is always there, even in the most difficult and darkest times. That there is always a solution and that Krsna takes care of me even though I really don't deserve his attention or care. (Disciple of one of Prabhupada's successors, Centennial Survey 1996)

A Prabhupada disciple who left ISKCON in 1984 described the importance of Prabhupada in his life:

> I consider Srila Prabhupada the source of my inspiration for spiritual life. I regularly read his books. Sometimes I understand and deeply appreciate his ideas, and sometimes I disagree. But I keep hearing from him anyway. Srila Prabhupada lifted me from a fallen, filthy hippie lifestyle and placed me in direct service to the Supreme Lord, turning me into a gentleman. He turned my simple but sincere devotion toward a God I couldn't see into an ocean of understanding about my position as an eternal soul. I must admit that the greatest happiness, peace, and pleasure I have ever experienced have always been in the service of the Lord. I pray that in all my millions of births I must take, I may always be fortunate enough to place my head at the feet of my eternal spiritual master Srila Prabhupada. (Centennial Survey 1996)

Although most of those moving on from ISKCON did so with their faith in Prabhupada and Krishna Consciousness intact, collectively they pursued a variety of paths to advance those commitments. Most moved into independent living situations in which they practiced Krishna Consciousness in their households with little or no ISKCON involvement. Others sought institutional alternatives to ISKCON, becoming followers of religious leaders associated with the Gaudiya Math, the organization founded by Prabhupada's spiritual master in India. A determined minority joined together to form an insurgent organization, the ISKCON Revival Movement, to restore what they considered the "true" ISKCON. Other devotees relocated to self-governing householder communities to distance themselves from ISKCON's leadership.

Going It Alone

Defection from ISKCON involved a complex reshaping of individual identity. Not only did those leaving look to maintain their commitments to Prabhupada and Krishna Consciousness, but they also tried to create new lives for themselves and their families, something they shared with congregational members. In sum, they had to find the means to integrate their religious beliefs with their new circumstances which required bridging the demands of the conventional world with their commitments to Prabhupada and Krishna. As one Prabhupada disciple noted,

> Prabhupada taught me a lot. I feel very fortunate to have had the opportunity to learn from him. However, your guru cannot live your life for you, so I believe it is imperative that you become your own being—integrating those teachings that are meaningful to you spiritually, emotionally, and practically. (Centennial Survey 1996)

A devotee woman who defected from the New Vrindaban community stated,

> All of my choices relate to the problem of creating a lifestyle acceptable and sustainable for Westerners while at the same time maintain the Vaisnava principles. Blindly trying to impose Indian culture and lifestyles on Americans does not and will not work. (Disciple of Bhaktipada, Centennial Survey 1996)

Despite having to accommodate to the dominant society, a considerable majority continue to hold firm to their Krishna faith, if not always to their religious practices. Three-quarters (78%) agreed that "my religious faith is of central importance and comes before all other aspects of my life." Although their faith remained strong, their religious practice was more mixed. One-quarter (27%) held daily worship programs in their homes, yet more than half (54%) rarely or never did so. Six in ten (59%) regularly offered their food to Krishna before eating, but a quarter (25%) did so infrequently or never. More than half (57%) chanted "Hare Krishna" each day, but a quarter (23%) did so less than once a week or not at all. With respect to adhering to the regulative principles, a considerable majority abstained from eating meat (90%), drinking alcohol (76%), smoking marijuana (80%), and gambling (90%). A significant portion (61%) occasionally had sex for purposes other than procreation.

Given their commitment to Prabhupada, many former ISKCON members continue to preach his teachings. Nearly six in ten (58%) indicated that they "actively preach to nondevotees at work and/or as part of my daily routine." This represents a commitment to preaching equal to that of full-time ISKCON members and exceeds that of congregational members. As one Prabhupada disciple observed:

> Prabhupada's instructions are the foundation of my existence. I always try to live up to being his disciple by first and foremost being an example for others to follow. I'm also always thinking about what Prabhupada would be preaching if he were here today. Srila Prabhupada was very topical in his preaching, and so I am trying to be innovative in my presentation of his teachings to others. (Centennial Survey 1996)

Another Prabhupada disciple explained that her professional work provided opportunities for presenting Prabhupada's teachings to others.

> I have lost faith in the ISKCON leadership and am not so involved in "ISKCON activities." However, in my own way I tell others about Srila Prabhupada and through my art I try to elevate others spiritually. (1991/1992 Survey)

Although preaching Prabhupada's teachings, former members face a dilemma in how best to guide those expressing an interest in Krishna Consciousness. For many, directing them to ISKCON is not an option. As one former ISKCON member put it, "I will preach love for God, not guru pimping."

Organization Switching

The guru controversies led some devotees to disaffiliate from ISKCON in favor of other Vaisnava organizations associated with Prabhupada's Godbrothers in India (the Gaudiya Math). Most notable have been S. R. Sridara Maharaja and Narayana Maharaja, the latter being a disciple of Prabhupada's Godbrother B. P. Keshava Maharaja. Each was an associate of Prabhupada's both before and after he left India for the United States in 1965.

Following Prabhupada's death, members of the GBC sought the advice of Sridara Maharaja to help clarify the authority of the newly appointed gurus. For more than two years, the ISKCON leaders sought guidance and instruction from Sridara in dealing with a range of philosophical matters (Rochford 1985:245–53). When conflict emerged over the zonal acarya (guru) system, however, some ISKCON leaders and senior Prabhupada disciples blamed Sridara. In 1982, ISKCON's leadership severed relations with Sridara and "declared him the enemy" because his "presentation of Krishna consciousness often differs from that of Srila Prabhupada" (Vishnu, Swami B. B. 2004:182). But as one former ISKCON member and follower of Sridara Maharaja contends, "A more candid explanation for ostracizing Shridara Goswami . . . is perhaps the fact that many members of the [ISKCON] society began to follow him instead of accepting the dictates of the new gurus" (Vishnu, Swami B. B. 2004:183). The change in ISKCON's policy toward Sridara produced ISKCON's first major schism in 1982, when the ISKCON guru Jayatirtha[6] split from ISKCON with one hundred of his disciples to join forces with Sridara Maharaja in India (Rochford 1985:251).[7]

A recent and perhaps more significant threat to ISKCON has been Narayana Maharaja. During the 1990s, nearly two hundred ISKCON members became followers of Narayana. Those joining him were both longtime Prabhupada disciples and disciples of Prabhupada's successors. Moreover, an additional one hundred followers of the ISKCON guru Goura Govinda accepted Narayana as their *siksa* (instructing) guru following their guru's death in 1996 (Collins 2004:224).

In 1994, tensions between Narayana Maharaja and ISKCON came to a head at a celebration in India commemorating Prabhupada's taking sannyasa thirty-five years earlier (Collins 2004:224). During the proceedings, Narayana contended that "there were many higher teachings that Prabhupada could have given had his disciples been more advanced" (quoted in Collins 2004:224). To ISKCON leaders, this statement implied that Narayana was demeaning Prabhupada's teachings as elementary. Moreover, many believed that Narayana Maharaja was simply positioning himself to provide these "higher teachings" to ISKCON's membership.

After a number of high-profile ISKCON gurus and senior Prabhupada disciples began receiving instruction from Narayana, the GBC passed a resolution in 1995 that, while not specifically mentioning Narayana by name, nonetheless effectively banned all ISKCON members from associating with him or his teaching. The resolution also provided for the possible suspension of ISKCON members who failed to comply (Collins 2004:222). Averting what would have been a major schism, the offending leaders agreed to desist from any further involvement with Narayana.

To many devotees, the GBC's punitive response to Narayana and his followers was further evidence of the failings of ISKCON's leadership (Collins 2004:227). As one former ISKCON member who became a follower of Narayana commented,

> ISKCON has become an institution outside of the Gaudiya Vaisnava *sampradaya* [lineage of gurus]. The leaders feel that to allow the members of ISKCON to take guidance from learned Vaisnavas from other institutions within the Gaudiya Math will destroy or weaken ISKCON. Actually the opposite is true. Without taking guidance from senior Vaisnavas, ISKCON will remain an institution that is crippled by material considerations and will remain a very immature and close-minded institution. (Prabhupada disciple, Centennial Survey 1996)

In defiance of the GBC, Narayana and his following of former ISKCON devotees began yearly preaching tours in 1996, targeting ISKCON communities in North America and other Western countries. As one of those who joined Narayana observed,

> Over the next few years, hundreds and hundreds of disaffected ISKCON members assembled at these gatherings to hear from Narayana Maharaja, attracted by his charismatic qualities. Many devotees even renounced their ISKCON "priestlike" gurus . . . and took reinitiation from Narayana Maharaja. . . . Narayana thus poses a serious and ongoing threat to ISKCON. (Collins 2004:225)

To ISKCON leaders, Narayana's recruitment efforts were little more than poaching. But to some disillusioned ISKCON members, Narayana represented an attractive alternative. His charisma contrasted with that of the ISKCON gurus, whose authority had been thoroughly routinized in an effort to reduce the volatility of the guru institution. As one of Prabhupada's original successors acknowledged,

> Thus, there is a real danger for ISKCON, in its zeal to avoid the high profile fall-downs of the recent past, to sanitise and restrain the position of guru to a point where it is no longer recognisable and, indeed, no longer functions as a real spiritual force for good in the [ISKCON] Society. (Goswami, Hrdayananda Dasa 2000:53)

For both former and disillusioned ISKCON members, joining forces with either Sridara or Narayana proved to be an easy transition, given that their teachings are based on the Gaudiya Vaisnava tradition. Leaving ISKCON therefore did not require a fundamental reworking of individual religious identity. Indeed, organizational switching is far more likely when individuals are not obligated to set aside existing "cultural capital" (Stark 1996:135; Stark and Finke 2000:123). In other words, switching organizations is far more appealing when it does not demand extensive resocialization and religious training.

Insurgency, Revival, and Schism

The ISKCON Revival Movement (IRM) emerged in the late 1990s asserting that ISKCON's gurus were neither authorized by Prabhupada nor qualified to serve in their positions. In essence, supporters of the IRM argued that ISKCON had been hijacked as part of a "great guru hoax" (*Back to Prabhupada* 2005a:3). The solution rested on restoring Prabhupada's authority as ISKCON's initiating spiritual master, excluding his "successors." Thus the IRM represents an insurgent group whose mission is to change ISKCON's existing structure of religious authority. Despite the seriousness of their challenge, IRM supporters viewed themselves as reformers determined to "rebuild the original ISKCON, the real Hare Krishna movement, as given to us by Srila Prabhupada" (*Back to Prabhupada* 2005b:15). The founder and primary spokesperson for the IRM spelled out the group's objectives in the following terms:

Organizing all our supporters spread all over the world into centers is a process that will take more time and is not a priority at this stage. We prefer to concentrate on advancing our arguments philosophically, academically, and with the media, rather than just opening a few buildings and starting our own separate movement. Our objective is not to begin a separate group which goes off and does its own thing but to educate every single person who has some contact with ISKCON regarding Srila Prabhupada's position. Therefore our focus is very much ISKCON's current and former members. (Desai, KrishnaKant 2006)

At issue is the IRM's contention that Prabhupada never appointed any of his disciples to serve as diksa (initiating) gurus, but only as ritvik gurus. In their role as ritviks, ISKCON's gurus were authorized to serve only as ceremonial priests initiating new disciples on Prabhupada's behalf. The IRM cites a July 9, 1977, letter approved by Prabhupada in which he indicates how future initiations should be handled in light of his deteriorating health.

His Divine Grace has so far given a list of eleven disciples who will act in that capacity [as ritvik representatives of the acarya]. . . . Now that Srila Prabhupada has named these representatives, Temple Presidents may henceforward send recommendations for first and second initiation to whichever of these eleven representatives are nearest their temple. . . . [T]hese representatives may accept the devotee as an initiated disciple of Srila Prabhupada by giving a spiritual name . . . just as Srila Prabhupada has done. The newly initiated devotees *are disciples of His Divine Grace A. C. Bhaktivedanta Swami Prabhupada,* the above eleven senior devotees acting as His representative.[8] (my emphasis; quoted in Desai et al. 2004:195)

In the absence of documentation to the contrary, IRM supporters accept the July 9 letter as definitive; Prabhupada fully intended to remain in his role as ISKCON's acarya and initiating guru following his death. The IRM refers to this as "the No Change in ISKCON Paradigm," rejecting official ISKCON explanations that Prabhupada intended the appointed ritviks to become diksa gurus after his passing (KrishnaKant 1996; Desai et al. 2004). On this basis, the IRM rejects the very idea that ISKCON's gurus are Prabhupada's rightful successors.

Before the emergence of the IRM, the ritvik position found appeal among a wide range of devotees in North America and worldwide (Rochford 1998a, 1998b). In fact, a loosely organized "ritvik movement" set the stage for the IRM. The ongoing controversies involving ISKCON's gurus convinced many devotees that Prabhupada never appointed any of his successors. As one former ISKCON member and IRM supporter argued, "How could Prabhupada have made such a big mistake? He is a person who according to scripture cannot make a mistake. How could he have made such a mistake by appointing such unqualified people? Obviously, the answer is they weren't appointed."

Half the congregational members (49%) and former ISKCON devotees (56%) participating in the Centennial Survey agreed that "Prabhupada wanted the eleven ritviks he appointed to continue as ritviks after his departure."[9] Moreover, two-thirds (64%) of the former members and half (51%) of ISKCON's congregational members agreed that "disciples of Srila Prabhupada have the right to serve as ritviks, initiating new devotees who would become disciples of Srila Prabhupada."

Estimates by the founder of the IRM suggest that "many hundreds" of devotees worldwide are active IRM supporters (Desai, KrishnaKant 2006). Global interest, if not active support, is suggested by the readership of the IRM's *Back to Prabhupada* magazine. In 2005, it had a reported circulation of ten thousand in more than one hundred countries (Desai, KrishnaKant 2006). But the IRM has only one North American temple in New York City, and it has attracted few devotees, new or old. The IRM's inability to build a more robust movement appears to relate most directly to its position on performing initiations. Although ritvik initiation is the IRM's theological foundation, as of 2005 it had not performed a single ritvik initiation. Indeed, only a small number of ritvik initiations have been performed in North America by the Prabhupada Sankirtan Society, in New York City (Rochford 1998a:112), and by two Prabhupada disciples acting on their own initiative. Neither of the latter are directly aligned with the IRM. The IRM's decision to temporarily forgo ritvik initiations was explained by the IRM's most prominent leader:

> The IRM does not offer a formal initiation ceremony at present, since it is trying to adhere to Srila Prabhupada's wishes in this matter, and form a real bonafide GBC first, which can authorize ritviks in line with the July 9th directive [1977 letter]. A self-appointed ritvik would not be much different to a self-appointed Guru. . . . So the IRM is waiting to

formalize this initiation later on, once a bonafide GBC is put in place. (Desai, KrishnaKant 2006)

Strategically, the IRM set a goal of aligning thirty ISKCON temples worldwide as the basis for gaining the political leverage required to pressure the GBC into endorsing ritvik initiation. Such a strategy is consistent with the IRM's reformist goals and identity. Despite its efforts, however, the IRM has met with minimal success in recruiting ISKCON temples to its cause. In one case in which the IRM gained control over an existing ISKCON temple in India, a violent confrontation resulted when ISKCON members sought to reclaim the temple. In April 2001, IRM's regional headquarters in Calcutta, India, "was stormed by representatives of ISKCON" in an attempt to occupy the temple (Desai et al. 2004:209–12). Fifteen IRM supporters were physically assaulted when approximately one hundred devotees from ISKCON's nearby Mayapura temple tried to evict them, and police arrested seventy-two ISKCON members involved in the takeover attempt (Desai et al. 2004:209).

In 2005, the temple in Bangalore, India, broke ranks with the IRM and began conducting ritvik initiations. As one of those involved in the decision explained,

> You [the IRM] have the audacity to say, "No, Srila Prabhupada. You cannot initiate right now because we have not set up a GBC. We don't have 30 temples. So we can't initiate." But this is complete nonsense. Prabhupada is alive and guiding in every other way but why are we killing him on this issue?[10] Why is he dead on this issue? We must let the world know that Srila Prabhupada is initiating. He is accepting disciples. And we must let people know that this is the real difference between our temples and ISKCON; that *we are the way to Prabhupada.* Prabhupada remains the acarya here. He is the guru. . . . *We are Prabhupada's ISKCON.* They [ISKCON's leadership] are the deviant ISKCON. They are not Prabhupada's ISKCON. (my emphasis; interview 2006)

As these comments suggest, internal divisions within the IRM over conducting ritvik initiations has given rise to a schismatic group. Those associated with the Bangalore temple expect as many as six hundred devotees around the world will become Prabhupada disciples by the end of 2007.[11]

Not surprisingly, the ritvik challenge mobilized ISKCON's leadership in opposition. As support for the ritvik movement grew during the 1980s, the GBC passed a resolution in 1990 against ritvikism, and in 1999, the GBC amended and affirmed its earlier resolution by placing the following into ISKCON law:

> The doctrine that Srila Prabhupada desired to continue to act as diksa guru after his departure from this world and did not want any of his disciples to give diksa in succession after him is a dangerous philosophical deviation. Ritvikism directly goes against the principles of parampara itself (of successive diksa and siksa gurus), which sustains the pure teachings and practices of Krishna consciousness. This principle has been established by Krishna and is upheld by all Vaisnava acaryas. . . . It is utterly erroneous to espouse it, deluding and misguiding to teach it, and blasphemous to attribute it to Srila Prabhupada. No one who espouses, teaches, supports, in any way, or practices ritvikism can be a member in good standing. (ISKCON Law 6.4.7.2, GBC Resolutions 1999)

Because of the deteriorated authority of Prabhupada's guru successors, ritvik initiation poses a potentially serious threat to ISKCON. Aspiring devotees may choose Prabhupada initiation in part to circumvent the precariousness associated with ISKCON's "living" gurus. Given widespread sympathy toward the ritvik philosophy among both current and former ISKCON members, there also is reason to believe that ritvik communities could appeal to a substantial number of devotees in North America and worldwide.

Independent Householder Communities

Another development also contributed to the general demise of ISKCON's communities. Beginning in the mid-1980s, substantial numbers of devotee families relocated to independent and largely self-governing householder communities, many to ISKCON's New Raman-reti (Alachua) community in northern Florida. In 2006, three hundred households and approximately nine hundred devotees were affiliated with the community. Other, smaller independent householder communities include Prabhupada's Village, in rural North Carolina, the Three Rivers community in central California, and the Saranagati community in British Columbia, Canada.[12] Each of these communities attracted longtime ISKCON members, many of whom were Prabhupada disciples seeking distance from the official ISKCON. Because in 2006 the New Raman-reti community was ISKCON's largest North American community, I will briefly focus on its development.

On November 14, 1977, the same day that Prabhupada died in Vrndavana, India, a group of ISKCON devotees purchased a 127-acre parcel of land in northern Florida that became known as New Raman-reti (North Central Florida Krishna Community Resource Directory 2001: 46). The land attracted few residents until the nearby Gainesville temple complex was sold in 1980 and the displaced devotees moved to the Alachua farm. By the mid-1980s only fifteen devotees lived on the property. But this changed dramatically in the late 1980s after ISKCON's most experienced teachers moved to New Raman-reti following the closure of the ashram-gurukula in Lake Huntington, New York. Because householders throughout North America were seeking Krishna-based schools for their children, large numbers moved to the Alachua community. New Raman-reti also attracted many other devotees looking to escape years of dependence on ISKCON management. The cheap land and the prospect of starting their own businesses or finding work in the local economy appealed to many devotees. Each year over the next ten years, twenty to thirty families relocated to New Raman-reti. One woman who moved to the community with her family in 1991 recounted some of the changes that resulted from the influx:

> Various devotees who had left ISKCON and scattered to other places started to migrate here. At first it was very difficult because we had a temple president who was very rigid. Typical ISKCON type: Very political, "My way or the highway sort of person." But in time there were just too many of us who were of a different mind. These were all Prabhupada disciples who had come here. So we started the "Krishna Community Fund" in 1991 and devotees were giving their money to the Fund rather than directly to the temple. So money talks. The Community Fund was giving money to the temple as it saw fit. . . . It was revolutionary. No one had done anything like that before. And we had a town meeting [1991] with about 200 to 250 devotees, and it was a revolutionary experience. Everybody just felt like this big depression moving off of them, that their voice was finally being heard. So a democratic system started. The Krishna Community Fund had a board of directors, and from there we began electing board members for the

community as a whole [in 1992]. And this wasn't happening anywhere else in ISKCON. As I say, it was revolutionary. (interview 2006)

The effort to create a more democratic community with an elected board quickly became a source of conflict with the GBC leadership. The community's GBC representative argued vigorously against an elected board, and in the end he stepped down from his position under pressure from the community.

> There were a lot of very strong feelings about him. He wasn't even welcome to come to the temple and speak for a while. Just because his style of preaching was not encouraging for the way our community was developing. But that changed in time. He started to come and speak [giving morning classes in the temple], but then the devotees would stand up and protest something he said. (interview 2006)

Relationships between community residents and official ISKCON only deteriorated further in the coming years. When another ISKCON leader was appointed as the community's GBC representative, he too faced opposition. In conjunction with the board of directors, community members began considering the idea of selecting their own GBC representative in defiance of GBC policy. As a member of the community's board during this period recounted,

> So the board generated the idea of electing our own GBC. . . . And we wrote something up to that effect. So I was going to Mayapura each year for the GBC meetings. We had a resolution, which I presented [to the GBC] on behalf of the board. And the GBC didn't approve it. They felt they were going to lose too much control and it was too threatening to them. Basically they didn't want to talk about it. That was the general mood. So at that point they made (name) the GBC [who was a resident of New Raman-reti]. (interview 2006)

Conflict with the GBC only escalated in the summer of 2000 when the board of directors unanimously voted to approve a statement of "no confidence" in the GBC. The statement read in part:

> We herein express our lack of confidence in the GBC body and its current state to lead the movement and to adequately represent Srila

Prabhupada. . . . [G]eneral categories of misconduct of the GBC body that are far below acceptable standards include areas such as accountability, managerial competence, responsiveness, and representation. . . . We believe it is essential that any new structure include a GBC body that is accountable to a group or constituency external to itself, since it is clear that the GBC body is unable to evaluate and discipline itself. This board views this statement as a service to the GBC body, and hopes these comments will contribute to a positive reconstruction that will restore moral authority to the GBC body. (ISKCON of Alachua Board of Directors, July 20, 2000)

In April 2001 a more direct challenge was made: "The board of directors is expressing that it does not accept the authority of what currently is called the ISKCON Governing Body Commission (GBC). . . . ISKCON of Alachua (New Raman-reti) will conduct itself peacefully and independently from the GBC" (ISKCON of Alachua Board of Directors, April 19, 2001).

While challenging the authority of the GBC, the fact remained that large portions of the New Raman-reti community viewed the GBC as largely irrelevant and inconsequential. As one community member stated, "I think that if we went down the phone list of the nine hundred or one thousand adult devotees and youth, I think the prevailing attitude would be that the GBC just doesn't matter" (interview 2006). Then he went on to say,

They don't care about the GBC. In this community there is a whole microcosm of everything that is going on in the Vaisnava world. You have got the Gaudiya Math [Narayana followers], you've got ISKCON, you've got fringies, the committed mangal arti crowd [early-morning worship in temple], ritvik supporters, etc., etc. It is all here.

The emergence of independent devotee communities like New Raman-reti allowed many devotees to remain in ISKCON's orbit while retaining control over their lives and those of their families. Such communities were appealing precisely because they provided a safeguard against the influence and intrusions of ISKCON's leadership. The very success of these communities, however, only further depleted the number of residents in ISKCON's other North American communities.

Conclusion

Religious movements require effective and legitimate leadership if they are to grow and prosper (Stark 1996:138). Moreover, rank-and-file members must perceive themselves as active players in that system of authority (Stark 1996:139). As Chaves (1993, 1994) argues, organizational or internal secularization results from the decline of religious authority, and secularization grows from the shrinking influence of social structures whose legitimation rests on the world of the supernatural (Chaves 1994:756). As this and previous chapters have demonstrated, ISKCON's GBC and guru structures of authority lost legitimacy in the eyes of large portions of ISKCON's first- and second-generation members. The resulting crisis of authority had far-reaching consequences for ISKCON's development as a religious organization. Internally, the leadership's weakened authority had a substantial influence on members' commitment and levels of ISKCON involvement. It also gave women the political opportunity to advance their pro-change agenda. In addition, ISKCON's crisis of authority led to individual and group defection, organizational switching, insurgency, schism, and the rise of independent householder communities. By the mid-1980s this outpouring of devotees left ISKCON's North American communities struggling to survive.

In 2000, only about 750 to 900 devotees continued to live in ISKCON's forty-five communities in the United States (Squarcini and Fizzotti 2004:70). The number residing in ISKCON's Canadian communities also remained small. In 1980, ISKCON's Los Angeles community had nearly four hundred adult residents, but in 1994, only sixty (Squarcini and Fizzotti 2004:79). New Vrindaban, which had 377 adults in 1986, saw its numbers drop to 131 in 1991 and to only about 50 in 2004 (Rochford and Bailey 2006). ISKCON's Toronto community had only ten residents in 2004, without a single person having taken up residence during the previous three years (Vande Berg 2005). Similar declines also can be found in Atlanta, Chicago, Detroit, New York, and other major North American communities (Squarini and Fizzotti 2004:79; Vande Berg and Kniss 2005).

The dramatic decline in temple residents, combined with the limited contributions of ISKCON's congregation, left local ISKCON temples with a critical shortage of labor and other resources. Although women were called on to fill a variety of administrative positions, such as temple president, many communities lacked the routine labor required to keep them functioning. By the mid-1980s, virtually all of ISKCON's communities were forced to rely on devotee labor from developing countries to meet their needs (Rochford and Bailey 2006). Many devotees from these countries are eager to relocate to North America in hopes of securing "green cards" and resident status. Yet imported devotee labor has been associated with the further weakening of ISKCON's North American communities (Rochford and Bailey 2006).

By the beginning of the new millennium, what remained of ISKCON's residential communities was populated largely by devotees from overseas.[13] Although imported devotee labor helped offset labor shortages, ISKCON's communities continued to face persistent and grave financial problems. As we will see in the next chapter, ISKCON leaders tried to alleviate this financial crisis by cultivating local congregations of Indian Hindu immigrants. In so doing, however, ISKCON's religious culture and identity underwent yet further change.

8

Hindus and Hinduization

I had a feeling that I never experienced before as a devotee. I felt
like an outsider. Like it wasn't my temple. It was so strange.
— ISKCON devotee reacting to the large number of Indians at a
festival celebrating Krishna's birthday, 2005

It's not about getting money [from Indian supporters]; it's about
serving Krishna. Better to keep the purity and remain poor, than
deviate and get millions of dollars.
— Das, Ragaputra 2005

Asian immigrants are changing the religious mosaic of North
America (Min and Kim 2002), as religion for them serves as both a
means of integration into American society and an institutional support
helping maintain their ethnic identities (Leonard et al., 2005; Warner
and Wittner 1998; Williams 1988). For Indian immigrants, their traditions and cultures as well as their religions have been subject to negotiation in order to construct ethnic identities appropriate to their new sur-
roundings (Knott 1987; Kurien 2002:102). Yet this process of identity
construction often results in strengthening their religious belief and Indian identity (Kurien 2002; Williams 1988:11). Despite the growing literature on immigrant religions in America, the question of how immigrants promote change within established religious organizations has
gained little attention.

Immigrant Indians became vital to ISKCON's survival beginning in the
1980s. In a state of decline, the leadership turned away from the movement's radical goals and lifestyle and focused instead on building congregations of Indian Hindus in its temple communities. In coming to
ISKCON to worship and strengthen their ethnic identities, Indian Hindus
reshaped ISKCON's religious culture and overall mission as a new religious movement.

The Emergence of an Indian-Hindu Congregation

Estimates indicate that in 2005 a considerable majority of ISKCON's approximately fifty-thousand-member North American congregation was of Indian descent. Only a small portion, however, can be considered committed ISKCON devotees. Instead, most are patrons whose involvement is limited to intermittent temple worship and financial contributions supporting local ISKCON temples.[1] Large numbers of other Indians attend ISKCON-sponsored festivals celebrating major Hindu holidays such as Janmastami (Krishna's birthday) as their only form of ISKCON involvement. A visit to most ISKCON temples on any given Sunday would reveal that 80 percent or more of those in attendance are Asian Indian immigrants and their families, whereas on major festivals that percentage often approaches 90 percent.[2] Yet this remarkable growth in ISKCON's Hindu congregation represents a relatively recent development in the movement's North American history.

During ISKCON's formative stages of development in the late 1960s and early 1970s, relatively few Indians could be found in ISKCON's temples. Prabhupada remained ambivalent about involving Indian Hindus in his incipient movement, short of their becoming fully committed ISKCON members. Early on he generally ignored Indian immigrants in America, fearing that ISKCON would be overly identified with Hinduism. As Prabhupada wrote to one of his disciples in April 1970, "Factually this Krishna Consciousness movement is neither Hindu religion nor any other religion. It is the function of the soul" (Prabhupada 1992:1577). In a 1969 conversation with several of his followers at New Vrindaban, Prabhupada stressed that ISKCON was not a Hindu movement.

> I don't want a Hindu temple. Our constitution is different. We want everyone. Krsna consciousness is for everyone. It is not a Hindu propaganda. People may not understand. And actually, till now in our [ISKCON] society there is not a single other Hindu than me (laughter). Is that not? (June 9, 1969, quoted in Dasi, Hare Krsna 2004)

Prabhupada also openly questioned the spiritual commitment of Indians who immigrated to the West, believing that their primary motive for coming to North America was "to earn money" and that the "best thing will be to avoid them as far as possible" (Prabhupada 1992:

1570).[3] Only after ISKCON became well established in North America did Prabhupada encourage Indians and other Hindus to become involved in the movement.

Despite the general disinterest shown by Prabhupada and his followers, increasing numbers of Indian immigrants were drawn to ISKCON's temples to worship. This was largely because when Indian immigration to the United States increased after President Lyndon Johnson rescinded the Oriental Exclusion Act in 1965, there were virtually no established Hindu temples in the country beyond those offered by ISKCON (Eck 2000:118; Williams 1988:132).[4] The same can be said for Canada, where substantial numbers of South Asian professionals immigrated during the 1960s and 1970s and were joined by Hindus from East Africa, South Africa, Fiji, Mauritius, Guyana, and Trinidad (Coward 2000:152-53).[5]

Indian immigrants found ISKCON attractive because the young American converts affirmed the value of the Hindu tradition in their new environment. As one Indian man suggested, "There is just respect that these Westerners are doing things better. They can recite the *slokas* [verses] from the Gita better than Indians do." Many saw the asceticism of ISKCON members as familiar reminders of the holy men in India and were impressed by the devotees' knowledge of Sanskrit, traditional Hindu rituals, Indian music, and the Vedic literatures (Williams 1988: 131). They also were attracted by the elaborate deity worship found in ISKCON's temples. Being vegetarians, immigrant Hindus also frequented ISKCON's restaurants, which served authentic Indian meals ritually sanctified as prasadam. Of greatest significance was the shared belief that participation in ISKCON's temple programs would help preserve their religious and ethnic identities. The temple thus served to maintain cultural traditions and ethnic identity because of the direct relationship between Hinduism and Indian cultural and subcultural traditions (Min 2005: 107). It also helped keep Indian Hindus away from the allure of American materialism (Williams 1988:131). As one Indian man who took initiation from Prabhupada commented,

I came to this country (USA) for material advancement in 1969. In 1970, I met Srila Prabhupada. Since then I realized how fortunate I was. Many times since 1970 to today, I had many desires and opportunities to fall down [into material life] like the rest of my friends, but

Srila Prabhupada's protection and mercy have saved me. (Centennial Survey 1996)

An Indian from Detroit also pointed to the corrupting influence of American culture and how his ISKCON involvement served as an antidote:

You don't want to look like you are an oddball. So you want to blend in. No matter what price you have to pay you want to blend in. You know you will be accepted if you do. So you go to the cafeteria with your buddies, or the boss has a Christmas party. But these things are so corrupting. Once you are corrupted it goes downhill from there very quickly. You start immediately rationalizing everything. Not only rationalizing but after a while you start believing in these things. And then you stop thinking about your culture. So I am here at [the ISKCON] temple and I am thinking of my culture. The Indian community needs ISKCON for its spiritual revival. (interview 1990)

Despite their presence in ISKCON's temples, ISKCON members made little effort to communicate with their Hindu visitors or to otherwise involve them in the life of the community. Indians visiting ISKCON's temples largely shared this disinterest because congregational participation, so much a part of the American religious experience, represented a significant departure from traditional Hindu religious practice (Kurien 1998:42; Min 2005:100). In India, Hinduism is practiced primarily as a "domestic religion" emphasizing family rituals, with temple worship accorded less importance (Min 2005:100; Rangaswamy 2000:246). Until the mid-1970s, Indian Hindus generally came and went from ISKCON's temples after taking darshan of the deities.[6]

Official ISKCON recognition of Hinduism and its Hindu supporters came only in the mid-1970s when ISKCON faced a variety of threats from the anticult movement and governmental officials. To defend itself against accusations of being a dangerous cult, the leadership asked ISKCON's Indian supporters to speak to the movement's authenticity as a traditional Hindu religious group. On other occasions, ISKCON called on its Indian supporters to respond to the discriminatory actions of government officials. In 1980, for example, city officials seeking to deny ISKCON a permit to stage its annual Rathayatra festival in west Los Angeles were confronted by Indian Hindus charging religious discrimination.

City officials quickly backed down and allowed the festival to proceed as planned. Having seen Indian Hindus come forward in support of ISK-CON, the movement's leaders thereafter sought to publicly align ISKCON with Hinduism and its Hindu patrons (Rochford 1985:270).

ISKCON introduced the Life Member Program to North America in the mid-1970s to formally ally with its Indian-Hindu supporters. Becoming a life member required a donation of $1,111, and in 1984 there were 1,684 life members in the United States, most of whom were Indian immigrants (Williams 1988:134). As "life members," Indian Hindus gained authorized access to ISKCON temples to worship and to socialize with other immigrant families. Few Indians, however, became full-time members or took positions of organizational responsibility, and only a small number became disciples of Prabhupada or one of his successors.[7] The Sunday feast, once an occasion for preaching and recruitment, was essentially handed over to emerging Hindu congregations in locations with substantial Indian immigrant populations. For example, it was not uncommon during the late 1970s in Los Angeles to find several hundred Hindus at the temple for Sunday worship and the feast to follow.

Given the increasing presence and importance of the movement's Indian-Hindu supporters, in 1980 ISKCON's North American GBC declared its intention to alter the public image of ISKCON from that of a "cult" to "a denomination of the Hindu church" (Rochford 1985:271). This effort was meant to bring greater legitimacy to the movement while encouraging financial support from its growing Hindu congregation. Hindu contributions quickly became critical as book distribution revenues dropped precipitously in 1980 and continued to slide thereafter. As one temple president stated, "The growing importance of Indian people in ISKCON is because of a lack of a proper economic infrastructure. That is what it boils down to. The leaders had no plans for maintaining the temples. Zero plans" (interview 2005).

In 1982, Indian Hindus in Detroit contributed $100,000 to the Bhaktivedanta Book Trust (Rochford 1985:268). During that same year, the Hindu congregation in Philadelphia contributed about $1,000 per month toward temple expenses (Rochford 1985:268). Hindu members of ISKCON's Houston temple provided much of the funding that allowed the community to buy the house being used as a temple in 1982 (Williams 1988:266). Hindu funds were equally critical to the building of the multimillion-dollar Radha-Krishna Temple of Understanding at

New Vrindaban in the mid-1980s, with wealthy Indian Hindus substantially funding the project (Rochford and Bailey 2006).

As ISKCON's financial troubles deepened still further in the mid-1980s, the Indian Hindus' financial contributions grew in importance. ISKCON launched an active campaign to expand its Hindu congregation in hopes of bringing economic stability to its impoverished North American communities (Rochford and Bailey 2006; Zaidman 2000: 205–19). When confronted with a lawsuit, the Robin George brainwashing case in Los Angeles, which included charges of false imprisonment, infliction of emotional distress, wrongful death of George's father, and libel, ISKCON was able to raise funds to defray its legal expenses and a substantial financial settlement (for details of the case, see Bromley 1989; Shinn 1987:123). Two Indian ISKCON members, one a GBC member and U.S. immigrant, and the other, a well-known guru from India, visited ISKCON temples throughout the United States seeking donations. The GBC member involved described what happened:

> I had some success with Lokantha Maharaja, who at the time was helping in the fund raising, going from temple to temple standing up and making an appeal. And we were getting contributions of $50,000, $30,000 . . . from various temples. This helped with the legal expenses but it wasn't enough to pay the final judgment. (interview 2005)

On the heels of this successful fund-raising effort, movement leaders established the ISKCON Foundation in 1991. As the foundation's former director explained, "So we saw this opportunity for the George case to be used as a vehicle to turn every temple around. We saw the George case as a blessing in disguise. Krishna is giving us a chance to come up to a much higher level." The foundation's primary mission was to raise money to support ISKCON's communities by actively encouraging the involvement of Indian Hindus in ISKCON temples. But despite their obvious financial need, some temples resisted the foundation's efforts, as the past director explained:

> We were starting to present these ideas and some temples liked them and some didn't. It had a lot to do with the local GBC [representative] and local guru, how much control they were willing to give up. Because this effort was meant to empower other people and some leaders didn't

want that to happen. They felt threatened by giving them power. (interview 2005)

Making use of personal contact with potential donors, as well as phone calls and a direct mail campaign involving thousands of Hindus across North America, the ISKCON Foundation successfully mobilized the support of a significant number of Hindus.[8] A major part of the foundation's strategic plan was to establish advisory boards in each of ISKCON's North American communities. Influential and affluent Hindus comprised the majority membership of these temple boards, and most were successful in enlisting the support of local Indian immigrants. As a result, temple revenues increased substantially in many locations. Most ISKCON temples in North America thereafter operated on what one ISKCON leader characterized as a "Hindu economy." In 1988, for example, congregational members and visitors to the Philadelphia ISKCON temple contributed 48 percent of the temple's total income. In 1991, that percentage had grown to 62 percent, and in 1992, 67 percent. Contributions in dollars increased from $54,000 in 1988 to $111,000 in 1992 (Zaidman 1997:341). Dependence on Indian financial support has grown even more in recent years. In 2005, the temple president of a major ISKCON community in the United States stated, "In the case of this temple, 95 percent of the funds supporting the temple are coming from the Indian congregation. Only 5 percent are from the American devotees." Not surprisingly, the financial support provided by Indian-Hindu congregations expanded their power and influence within local ISKCON temples. As the temple president just quoted admitted, "The whole temple becomes dominated by Indians. Because they have put their money there [in the temple] you are going to have to go their way. Obviously you have to give them a say."

Hindus and Westerners in Comparative Perspective

Because Hindus immigrating to the West come from different regions, language groups, and sects practicing diverse rituals, Hinduism outside India is often practiced as an ethnic religion (Burghart 1987; Williams 1988). Hinduism thereby becomes general in form rather than regional and sectarian. Knott (1987:178) refers to this process as one of "standardization" producing something akin to a "text-book Hinduism."[9] Such a pattern can be found in Hindu temples in both Great Britain and North America (Burghart 1987; Williams 1988). Yet ISK-CON temples are dedicated to neither an ethnic or an ecumenical form of Hinduism; rather, they are dedicated exclusively to the worship of Krishna and his incarnations. Although Indian immigrants are clearly familiar with the forms of worship, teachings, and religious practices associated with Krishna, many do not consider Krishna to be the supreme god (Zaidman 1997:340). Instead, they favor worshipping a variety of Hindu gods and acknowledge different Hindu traditions as equally valid. As one Indian commented on the Centennial Survey, "With all Hindus, Hindu unity should be the foremost concern, irrespective of their affiliations with other demigods [gods other than Krishna]."[10]

Members of ISKCON's Indian congregation generally admire Prabhupada because of his success in bringing the Hindu tradition to the world. As an Indian temple president commented in a 2005 interview,

> The Indians really respect Prabhupada because he has converted thousands of Christians and Jews into Hindus. In India that is really what they respect Srila Prabhupada for. This one man had such an impact globally. He has shown the greatness of the Hindu tradition to the whole world. One man has converted so many people to my culture.

Although they respect Prabhupada, many of ISKCON's Indian-Hindu supporters do not embrace his teaching. As one longtime ISKCON member and Prabhupada disciple of Indian ancestry explained,

> Many Indians do not fully understand Srila Prabhupada's unique qualities, that he was the leading proponent or teacher of our Vedic philosophy. They don't for the most part understand that or his teachings. Rather, they fall back on the more ritualistic aspects that they grew up with, going to temples but carrying on with what they grew up with in India. In my view, these are often compromised understandings of the Vedic teachings, not in keeping with Prabhupada's teachings. (interview 2005)

The 1996 North American Centennial Survey allows for a systematic comparison of the religious orientations and patterns of the ISKCON involvement of 106 Indian Hindus and 318 other ISKCON members (see

appendix 2, table A.3).[11] Indian Hindus expressed less commitment to
ISKCON's religious beliefs, the movement's preaching mission, and the
authority of Prabhupada's scriptural commentaries. With respect to religious practice, Indian Hindus participated far less often in ISKCON's collective religious practices and were less likely to wear traditional dhotis
or saris (religious clothing), adhere to the four regulative principles, and
chant daily rounds. They did, however, hold morning worship programs
at home more frequently than did other ISKCON members.[12] Although
about equally committed as other members were to the authority of the
GBC and ISKCON's gurus,[13] Indian Hindus were less committed to ISK-
CON's purposes and goals. They also placed greater emphasis on democratic forms of governance than did other ISKCON members. Last, Indian Hindus spent far fewer hours performing volunteer work in their
local temple community and placed less value on devotee relationships
than did other ISKCON members.

In essence, the Indian Hindus affiliated with ISKCON in most cases do
not share the movement's sectarian religious orientation and are less
committed to ISKCON and the broader devotee community. Representative of this is that one-quarter of the Indians taking part in the Centennial Survey indicated that they were not ISKCON members, despite worshipping at an ISKCON temple. An Indian temple president noted about
the Indian congregation in his temple:

> Most accept that Krishna is the supreme personality of Godhead. . . .
> But they are not ISKCON on the basis of philosophy. All Hindus are
> brought up with a certain faith and that sticks to them. When they
> come to a Hare Krishna temple and you try to impose your faith into
> them, and your style of *puja* [deity worship] and arti, and so on, they
> are not totally in sync with it.

An Indian Hindu from Southern California explained how his Hindu
beliefs remained at odds with those represented by ISKCON:

> It is a tragedy that ISKCON has chosen to become "non-Hindu" for rea-
> sons other than religious considerations. ISKCON believes in [the] Var-
> nashram system, yet considers itself solely for Vaisnavas, not other
> Hindus. What happened to other varnas, which constitute the bulk of
> Hindus? How can ISKCON survive as a separate cult without the basic
> four castes? (Centennial Survey 1996)

An Indian life member from Toronto expressed his disagreement with the preaching strategies emphasized by Prabhupada.

> I believe in Krishna and the Gita. I don't 100 percent agree with Srila Prabhupada's philosophy, e.g., distribution of free food to attract others even if they don't subscribe to the Gita, or distribut[e] books freely, which end up in a garage sale or in the garbage. (Centennial Survey 1996)

As these findings reveal, ISKCON's North American temples consist of two distinct and parallel communities. The first is made up of mostly Western converts dedicated to Prabhupada's religious teachings and overall vision for ISKCON. The second is composed of Indian Hindus who view ISKCON's communities as places of worship and ethnic identification.[14]

Divided Communities and Collective Estrangement

The different orientations of Indian Hindus and ISKCON's Western devotees have produced strains between the two groups which only have intensified as Indian Hindus have gained power and influence in ISKCON's temple communities. As one temple president stated:

> The temples are becoming Hindu temples because they put their money there and they are more involved than the American congregation. They come and wash the pots [for the Sunday feast] and are more involved in everything than the Western congregation. So the whole temple becomes dominated by Indians. The American devotees must get more involved in the temple and make their presence felt. Come do service. Sing, dance, chant and contribute part of their income. If not, this is the way things are going to continue going. (interview 2005)

Any observer of an ISKCON community on Sunday will note the limited interaction between Western devotees and Indian Hindus:

> There is not very much interaction unfortunately between the Indians and the devotees on Sunday. And there is a need for a lot more. I have been telling every single temple president here, "We need to build up

our Indian congregation because the finances of the temple are not in good shape. So one thing I want you to do for heaven's sake is to go to them and say, 'How do you do?'" Introduce yourself to all of them. If you did this for a few months, you would reduce so much resistance. (interview 1990)

A researcher of ISKCON's Philadelphia temple during the early 1990s found that 40 percent of the temple residents reported that they had no relationship with Indian visitors on Sunday other than to acknowledge them by saying, "Hare Krishna." Sixty percent, including some devotees in the temple hierarchy, admitted to holding bitter and highly critical views of the Indians. One reason stemmed from the refusal of many Hindus to accept temple residents as legitimate devotees, for many denied the very possibility that Westerners could be priests or brahmins.[15] In addition, the funds contributed by Indian congregational members were directed to projects related to the temple, not to improving the living spaces and situations of temple residents. The funds also were not used to advance ISKCON's traditional preaching mission (Zaidman 2000: 215). Apart from these reasons is that the Indian Hindus who come to ISKCON's temples to worship and feast on Sundays do so mainly so they can socialize with other Indian people. In the United States, Indians are the most spatially dispersed immigrant group (Portes and Rumbaut 1996:40), which creates a barrier to ethnic formation (Kurien 2002: 104). ISKCON's Sunday programs provide structured opportunities for Indian Hindus to communicate and make contacts with members of the Indian community. In recognition of this, the Indian temple president of one ISKCON community explained his strategy for involving Indians in the temple congregation:

> The temple is a spiritual place for worship but it is also provides for a social get-together for the Indians on Sunday. They want to go and meet some influential people. A lot of people when I invite them to the temple I say some influential person is coming and they say, "Oh, OK, I will definitely be there." So when I invite them I tell them who is coming, especially if there are people they might want to rub shoulders with. So that is how it works. So I try to target top-notch and recognized Indians in [city]. Bank Presidents. Big hotel owners. Because I know others will follow. (interview 2005)

Apart from the limited interaction between Western devotees and Indian Hindus, there also are fewer Westerners choosing to attend the Sunday temple program because of the large Indian presence. At a 2005 community meeting of a dozen longtime Western devotees, each said that they only infrequently attended the Sunday feast. Moreover, when one of them acknowledged that he "would never bring a new [Western] person to the temple because they would be put off" by the overwhelming number of Indians, others quickly nodded their heads in agreement. As the GBC representative for the community stated,

> It is common to meet intelligent, good devotees who say, "I just go to the temple when I want to see the deities. But otherwise I just can't relate." . . . Calling up the Indians [in the temple] to get their little gifts because they donated [funds] for the puja. Any Western person would be put off. This has become a very common response.

Indians also find reason to feel estranged at the Sunday program. Many find the loud kirtans and active dancing that forms part of the Western devotees' worship to be disagreeable and even offensive. According to an Indian temple president,

> They want to change the way that you [Westerner devotees] dance in the temple; jumping up and down, screaming and shouting at the top of your voice. They think this is very monkey like. It is very off-putting to them. If you go to any Hindu temple that is not the way it is. One doesn't pray to God like that. The way to pray to God is very sober, with awe and reverence. So because of the way the Westerners worship in the temple, you are turning away part of your congregation who are afraid to bring their friends to the temple. This same group of people who are the ones putting large sums of money toward supporting the temple. . . . In fact, they have voiced this to me, "Prabhu, is there another way we can do the artis?" So you have to take these things seriously. (interview 2005)

Differences between Indian Hindus' vision of the temple and that of temple residents have occasionally produced conflict. Hindus who view ISKCON communities largely as sites of worship see little need for more than a limited number of religious specialists to serve as pujaris and teachers, in addition to temple administrators. Because of this, temple residents are often viewed as unnecessary expenses rather than evidence of ISKCON's vitality as a missionary movement. One issue entails the financial support provided to temple pujaris and other devotees working in the temple communities. As the former director of the ISKCON Foundation reported,

> It is obvious to the Indians that funds were necessary to support the deities, the grounds, and that the temple building needed to be kept up. It was also obvious that the mortgage had to be paid, utilities, insurance, but when it came to supporting the devotees who were full-time pujaris, they always had a lot of questions. Why do we need so many people? What do they do all day? Why don't they have some other source of income? I remember fighting against that viewpoint. It still goes on from what I can tell. (interview 2005)

As one Indian commented, "In other [non-ISKCON] temples in the U.S., the Indians see that there are only one or two pujaris who come from India and are given simple accommodations. That is all it takes from their perspective."[16]

Questions about support for temple residents are part of a broader concern about how the funds collected from the Hindu congregation are used by temple authorities. As one Indian man commented on the Centennial Survey,

> If you raise some money then you want to tell those who contributed what you have done with it before you ask for more. Tell people, "Thank you very much for the money. We want to tell you what we did with it." If people see that the money was spent wisely, they will want to give some more.

Two-thirds (64%) of the Indians responding to the Centennial Survey agreed that "I would be more involved in ISKCON, and more likely to contribute, if there were a better accounting of how money is spent." Growing out of this and other concerns, a considerable majority (84%) believed that "local temple management should be the responsibility of an elected board of directors." Elected temple boards would place greater control over ISKCON's communities in the hands of Indian-Hindu congregations.

Indian advisory board members have exerted pressure meant to influence management decisions within ISKCON's temple communities. Board members in Philadelphia, for example, found reason to complain about the performance of temple vice presidents, and on one occasion they successfully pressured for a resignation. This level of involvement in temple management exceeded the power initially given to temple advisory boards (Zaidman 1997:343). Staffing decisions in temple communities have resided with ISKCON leaders, with Indian congregational members traditionally remaining outsiders to ISKCON's authority system and thus without a voice (Zaidman 1997:343). To the extent that local Hindu congregations can exert their newfound power on temple decision making, however, this may be changing and seems all the more likely given that an increasing number of Indians are now serving as temple presidents in major ISKCON communities such as in Atlanta, Chicago, Dallas, Houston, and San Diego.

The Hinduization of ISKCON's Religious Culture

ISKCON's temple communities have faced growing pressure to conform to the religious orientations of their increasingly influential Indian-Hindu congregations. As a result, ISKCON's traditional religious culture has been subject to negotiation and change.

Nurit Zaidman detailed a number of negotiations between Indian advisory board members and local ISKCON officials in Philadelphia during the early 1990s. One negotiation related to organizing an evening for Durga, a Hindu goddess. When board members asked the temple president to conduct a puja for Durga in the temple room, the request produced some apprehension, as Durga, like other demigods, is not worshipped in ISKCON temples. After some negotiation, the temple president allowed the program to take place, but in a rented hall. Another condition was that Krishna be symbolically represented as the supreme god and given a higher status than Durga. Yet not all aspects of the event were controlled to fit ISKCON standards, as the actual arti ritual performed was not in accordance with ISKCON ritual standards (Zaidman 1997:346).[17]

Other examples of Indian-Hindu influence on ISKCON's religious culture have emerged in recent years. On several occasions, festivals held at ISKCON's Spanish Fork temple in Utah were criticized by ISKCON members concerned that these events unduly catered to the Hindu community, at the expense of ISKCON's religious beliefs. In both 2004 and 2005, the Spanish Fork temple celebrated Shiva Ratri, complete with storytelling and a sacred bathing ceremony for Lord Shiva. Included, too, was the chanting of Shiva's 108 names (Das, Caru 2004b:1). The advertisement for the 2004 festival read in part, "Shiva Ratri is one of the most auspicious of days in the Hindu calendar. . . . In the Hindu pantheon, Lord Shiva is the 'Destroyer of Evil'" (Das, Caru 2004b:1). One devotee critic of the festival complained that "the only mention of Krsna's name is that the celebration is to take place in a Krsna temple. In some places the article [advertisement] comes very close to pronouncing Lord S[h]iva to be the Supreme Lord" (Dasi, Hare Krsna 2004:1). Dasi also expressed surprise that the announcement for the Shiva Ratri festival was posted on February 1, the day before Lord Nityananda's "appearance day" (birthday): "And yet there was no announcement for a festival for Lord Nityananda at the ISKCON Spanish Fork temple. Apparently energies have been diverted to something else" (Dasi, Hare Krsna 2004:2–3). Nityananda is considered an incarnation of Krishna by ISKCON members.[18] In response to this criticism, the president of the Spanish Fork temple noted, "If the Hindus, who are our biggest natural supporters all over the world, are going to worship Lord Shiva anyway, isn't it better we bring them to do it gorgeously in the Krishna temple, rather than someplace else where they will not get the Krishna overview" (Das, Caru 2004a:2)?

Yet there are unintended consequences associated with allowing Hindu ritual to gain a foothold in ISKCON's temples.

> The problem is that every new element of ritual and Hindu tradition that is brought in means that another element of what Srila Prabhupada gave us is gradually pushed aside. We may have an opulent temple, with a Shiva Ratri festival and meticulous observance of various aspects of Hindu practice and tradition—but at the same time we are losing energy to pursue Srila Prabhupada's social programs of building self-sufficient Krsna conscious communities. (Dasi, Hare Krsna 2004:2)

A second event, the Holi/Gaura Purnima festival, held at the Spanish Fork temple, likewise provoked an outcry when advertisements appeared to minimize the birthday of Caitanya Mahaprabhu, considered an incarnation of Krishna by ISKCON members. Holi is a religious occasion celebrated by Hindus both inside and outside India. But only followers of the Gaudiya Vaisnava tradition, of which ISKCON is a part, celebrate Gaura Purnima. One devotee responded to the advertisement for the 2005 "Holi/Gaura Purnima" festival by commenting, "Notice, if you will, the Lord's appearance is third on the list and 'coincides with Holi' (not the other way around)." He added, "Gaura Purnima is on Friday [March] the 25th, not Saturday the 26th, at least in North America. . . . So what gives?" (Das, Ragaputra 2005:1). What gives is that the Holi/Gaura Purnima festival attracts as many as eight hundred visitors to the Spanish Fork temple. As the temple president noted, "Without the element of the colors, I doubt there would even be a fraction of that number" (Das, Caru 2004a:2).[19]

A recent and perhaps more dramatic example of the influence of Indian-Hindu congregations on ISKCON's religious culture is the building of a new ISKCON temple near San Diego, California. The Indian congregation raised millions of dollars to help build the temple, but it will not strictly conform to ISKCON tradition, as it will include traditional Hindu images of Shiva and Ganesh with accompanying samskaras and pujas "performed regularly for the Indian community" (Das, Ragaputra 2005). One member of the San Diego temple community claimed that such a concession represented "kowtowing to the material conceptions of the Indian community" (Das, Ragaputra 2005:2). He added, "The Indian community has a lot of money and is willing to fork it over for the projects that fit in with their notions of 'Hindu dharma.' But we are not Hindus. We are devotees of Krishna, the Supreme Personality of Godhead" (Das, Ragaputra 2005:2).

Hinduization and the Demise of Preaching

Preaching has been a defining element of ISKCON's religious culture. Much of the public controversy that surrounded the movement during the 1970s and 1980s resulted from the devotees' literature distribution efforts and what was perceived as ISKCON's aggressive recruitment tactics. Although ISKCON's recruitment in North America started to fall dramatically beginning in the mid-1970s, preaching has remained emblematic of ISKCON's identity as a new religious movement. Yet as Western devotees moved out of ISKCON's temple communities during the 1980s and Indian Hindus gained dominance, preaching was no longer an organizational priority. An Indian temple president stated:

Throughout ISKCON the temples are becoming Hindu temples. The Indians don't take to Krishna Consciousness for the most part. But Prabhupada came to this country to attract Americans, not Hindus. My biggest frustration and failure is that I have not been able to attract Americans to the community. (interview 2005)

Without sufficient labor in the temples and facing a financial crisis, ISKCON's communities shifted their priorities to serving the religious and ethnic needs of Indian congregations. What this meant was that ISKCON's temples emphasized deity worship at the expense of preaching. As one GBC representative and guru remarked,

The most insidious influence of the Indian presence is the growing laziness that has resulted where we have abandoned Prabhupada's mission to preach. We thought it would be the opposite. With funds provided by the Indians we would be free to preach more, not less. Now we are free *not* to preach. (his emphasis).

As this leader explained in a meeting of temple residents in 2005,

The decision was made that deity worship must be maintained but that the preaching would be reduced. The problem is that this is exactly opposite of what Prabhupada wanted. Prabhupada said, "Reduce the deity worship and increase the preaching. The deities keep the devotees spiritually strong so they can preach." We find ourselves relying on a congregation [of Indian Hindus] who desire nice deities so they can worship. They give money so we have to satisfy their desires. We are not exactly employees but in many ways that is true. We have given up our autonomy and independence and become uninterested in preaching. The risk is that the temples will be transformed into third-class mundane institutions because of the exclusive focus on deity worship rather than preaching. . . . This is an important historical moment for ISKCON. Will we be transformed into something else, or preserve what Prabhupada wanted?

The demise of preaching goes beyond the question of deity worship, however. The number of Indians present on Sundays has made the temple an unattractive place to bring Westerners interested in Krishna Consciousness. As the leader just quoted commented, "It is an ISKCON cliché for someone to say, 'I met this intelligent young person but I don't want to invite them to the temple.'"

Because of the dilemma posed by the transformation of the Sunday feast into a Hindu event, some ISKCON communities have sought innovative ways to preach to non-Indians. In the Dallas ISKCON community, for example, the temple holds separate feasts and worship services at different times on Sunday for Indians and Westerners. The Atlanta temple is also considering separate Sunday programs. Moreover, the temple in Atlanta is creating a separate space in the community devoted exclusively to Western preaching. As the spiritual leader of the community reported,

> We are going to turn this house into the "Bhakti-yoga Center." . . . The idea is to just imagine that we have just come to Atlanta, forget the Indian congregation, forget the old Western devotees, forget the deity worship, forget all of that. Just imagine a couple of us just arriving in Atlanta and we have this house. So that is what we are going to do early next year. We are going to launch this as a Bhakti-Yoga Center to preach to Westerners. (interview 2005)

Hinduization and Uneven Transformation

Despite the ongoing Hinduization of ISKCON's North American communities, the movement's leadership has generally been slow to respond. In part this is because as one leader commented, "It's just coming on the radar because it [Hinduization] is just beginning to change the culture of the temple." Also, ISKCON's religious culture is not being transformed consistently across ISKCON's North America communities. Some communities have been able to rely on Indian-Hindu support while avoiding significant compromise. These latter communities tend to be those whose leadership has consistently preached Prabhupada's teachings to the Indian community rather than being satisfied with only receiving their financial contributions. An ISKCON leader commented:

> In places where in the cultivation of the Indian community there was more preaching, there was more of a concern to give something to the Indians. In those cases there was a natural filtering where those Indians actually came forward to commit to ISKCON. These are the Indians who

know what we are about. In Houston and Dallas many Indians have become committed because Tamal [Krishna Goswami] preached. North Carolina and LA [Los Angeles] the same thing. These are examples where there was good preaching. You have a lot of Indian preaching, a lot of Indian support but no compromise. (interview 2005)

A temple president made much the same point but also admitted that few Indians have accepted the movement's teachings because they have not formed personal relationships with the Western devotees, those best able to preach Prabhupada's message.

Because of their deep-rooted childhood upbringing, it is really hard for them to digest the whole philosophy of Srila Prabhupada without having close association with devotees. And 99 percent of the Indian congregation doesn't have that association. Those that do get that association can have a systematic study of [Prabhupada's] Bhagavad Gita and they can then appreciate Srila Prabhupada from a whole different perspective. (interview 2005)

Although preaching ISKCON's sectarian beliefs to the Indians has converted some to Prabhupada's teachings, it seems unlikely that large numbers will become active ISKCON devotees. For the majority is not seeking a new religion, even one that is a part of their Hindu tradition. Rather, ISKCON's temples provide a place to worship in the company of other Indian people. And as the preceding examples illustrate, it is ISKCON that is changing to accommodate its Indian supporters. Unwilling to alienate its Hindu supporters from concern for losing financial support, ISKCON's leaders are likely to continue acquiescing to the "Hindu dharma." To do otherwise risks the possibility that ISKCON's Hindu supporters will transfer their allegiances to established Hindu temples or construct temples of their own.[20] Yet in continuing to compromise elements of its religious culture and overall mission, ISKCON's temples seem destined to become ethnic churches. As one devotee critic concluded,

But when they [Hindus] are attracted, it is we who should be giving them Srila Prabhupada's teachings about how to be a Vaisnava—*not that we should leave Srila Prabhupada's teachings, and take up their lifestyles of Hinduism.* . . . If we do that, we do a disservice to both them and ourselves, and to Srila Prabhupada's Krsna consciousness mission.[21] (my emphasis, Dasi, Hare Krsna 2004:3)

Conclusion

Once a radical and controversial new religion, ISKCON in North America has evolved into a new denomination in order to survive. ISKCON's Indian-Hindu congregation has clearly helped rescue a failing religious organization. In pursuit of needed financial resources in the face of decline, Prabhupada's movement is steadily advancing toward becoming a Western sect of Hinduism. Today ISKCON provides temples, leadership, and religious specialists for a sizable number of Indian Hindus throughout North America. In so doing, however, ISKCON has progressively aligned itself with the religious orientations of its Indian supporters and negotiated away elements of its traditional religious culture. By compromising elements of its core teachings to implement innovations meant to ensure the organization's survival, ISKCON has lost the basis for generating member commitment and loyalty (see Finke 2004). For most of its Indian supporters, ISKCON represents a place of worship and ethnic identification rather than a source of organizational commitment. For its traditional Western members, temple communities have become sources of estrangement reducing rather than promoting commitment. In this form, ISKCON appears unlikely to attract significant interest among a new generation of Americans seeking alternative religious paths. Organizational maintenance in the form of a Hindu revival is transforming a new religion that once symbolized the radicalism of the 1960s.

In the next chapter, I move from looking at ISKCON's transformation to consider the Western members who remained aligned with the organization. As ISKCON was evolving into an ethnic church, its long-standing members were establishing a place for themselves and their families in American society. But worldly accommodation brought with it a new round of cultural development as devotees sought community for themselves, their children, and the future of Prabhupada's movement.

9

World Accommodation

Looking at our movement, the lines with the outside society have definitely softened and are bleeding into the colors of the outside society. I don't think there is any question about that.
—Prabhupada disciple, interview 2006

My focus at first was just preaching to nondevotees. And at this point my focus is almost entirely on dealing with community. Prabhupada said that we should take care of the devotees we have. And this is where things are going.
—Prabhupada disciple, interview 2006

An important if underdeveloped topic in the study of new religions is the factors that influence their development over time (Bromley and Hammond 1987; Rochford and Bailey 2006; Stark 1996; Wilson 1987). Such an oversight is especially conspicuous given that new religions are susceptible to rapid and dramatic changes that promote organizational transformation (Barker 2004). Scholars have considered two overlapping approaches with respect to the development of new religions. The first identifies and analyzes the factors that influence their success and failure (Bromley and Hammond 1987; Stark 1987, 1996; Wilson 1987).[1] The second approach focuses less on organizational outcomes in favor of describing the social processes that advance accommodation with mainstream societies (Rochford 2007). This approach considers how internal weaknesses and/or external opposition lead to change and transformation (Chancellor 2000; Introvigne 2000:46-47; Mauss 1994; Melton 2000:44-51).

In the midst of ISKCON's being overtaken by Indian-Hindu immigrants during the 1980s and 1990s, its long-standing members were establishing lives in American society. Worldly accommodation brought about a new round of cultural development centered on reshaping ISKcon's traditional religious culture to fit the changing needs of families and the larger devotee community.

Mapping Change in New Religions

Scholars have debated the characteristics defining new religious movements (Barker 2004; Bromley 2004; Melton 2004; Robbins 2005). Barker (2004:99) argues that new religions collectively share significant internal characteristics growing out of their "newness." These include charismatic authority, first-generation membership, and a degree of volatility that make them subject to ongoing change (Barker 2004). Melton (2004:81) contends that new religions are unique not because of shared intrinsic attributes related to their newness but because of tension in their relationships with the dominant churches. From the vantage point of the traditional faiths, new religions are "unacceptably different" and thus religious outsiders (Melton 2004:79).

Bromley (2004:92–93) also defines new religious movements in relational terms, arguing that a low level of alignment with dominant societal institutions and cultural orientations distinguishes them from other forms of religion. Given this misalignment, new religions generally exist in an elevated state of tension with the larger culture (Bromley 2004; Stark 1996; Wilson 1990). In rejecting conventional institutions and cultural patterns, new religions are branded as deviant, radical, and perhaps even dangerous. By contrast, dominant religious groups are firmly aligned with the culture of the prevailing society and take an active role in its construction and legitimation (Berger 1969; Bromley 2004:92).[2]

These definitions provide a basis for mapping change in the careers of new religions. Being new movements with collective goals that are world transforming in nature, new religions are inherently fragile and unstable enterprises. Externally, given their radical goals and lifestyles, they face ongoing opposition. Internally, the need to build alternative religious worlds is burdened with difficulties. Yet as Stark (1996:137) contends, "In order to grow, a religious movement must offer a religious culture that sets it apart from the general, secular culture." In building a culture that supports their religious beliefs, new religions try to build structures of integration and separation (Kanter 1972; Kraybill 2001). Culture thus promotes individual identity and group solidarity while simultaneously establishing group boundaries meant to separate the faithful from the "evils" of the outside world. From an insider's perspective, what is "true," "moral," and "good" exists within the religious community; outside there is "darkness," "pollution," and "danger." A "wall of virtue," whether symbolic or physical, is constructed in which the religious community places "the oppressive and morally defiled outside society in sharp contrast to the community of virtuous insiders" (Sivan 1995:18). At the same time, however, the outside society is targeted for conversion and social change in accordance with religious beliefs.

Although culture is a core concept in the social sciences, its definition continues to be debated (Swidler 1986, 1995; Wuthnow and Witten 1988). What is clear is that every group develops at least a rudimentary culture based on shared experiences. In the broadest sense, culture consists of "a system of knowledge, beliefs, behaviors, and customs shared by members of an interacting group to which members can refer and which they can employ as a basis of further action" (Fine 1995:128– 29). But beliefs and the behaviors that grow from them rest on a foundation of social institutions. Institutions are unyielding structures that both constrain and offer opportunities to individuals, and individuals act in culturally uniform ways largely because they must negotiate the same institutional hurdles (Swidler 1995:36). By shaping the social contexts in which individuals operate, institutions influence behavior from the "outside in" (Swidler 1995:25). Political and economic institutions, marriage, family, and education all represent normative structures that form the basis of social order. As is well known, however, social movements are characteristically changeable, with the metaphor of "movement" epitomizing their continuous flux (Johnson and Klandermans 1995:4). As a result, institution building remains a tenuous and uncertain enterprise, one with an ongoing potential for social conflict.

Radical beliefs require oppositional forms of social organization if they are to endure over time. The challenge for religious movements is to produce cultures that sustain "oppositional consciousness" (Mansbridge and Morris 2001) by providing alternative ways of life that challenge society. ISKCON was not alone in its battle to build alternative institutions supportive of its religious culture. Each of the major new religions that gained prominence in the 1960s also struggled to develop institutional structures capable of sustaining members in a communal context. For the most part, this resulted from an inability to develop domestic cultures that supported family life. Such a critical deficit posed serious problems as many new religions faced what Barker (2004:98) refers to as "inverted disproportionality," or the presence of a larger number of children born within than the number of first-generation converts. Indeed, the fortunes of The Family (Children of God), the Unification Church ("Moonies"), as well as ISKCON, eroded significantly as families began leaving the communal fold to secure an independent life.

In 2001, The Family's membership included 8,900 "Charter members" residing communally as full-time members, 3,100 "Fellow members" living and working outside the movement, and more than 64,000 "Outside members" ranging from "live-out disciples" to those whose involvement is limited to financial contributions (Shepherd and Shepherd 2002:5–6). After The Family completed restructuring in 2003, its Charter member population declined by 2,360. Less committed Charter members became Fellow members or newly created Missionary members. Among the trends related to declines in member commitment was a decrease in communal households, outside employment, children attending secular schools, and expectations that second-generation members would not maintain the Charter members' standards of discipleship (Amsterdam 2004).

Evidence suggests a similar trend for the Unification Church. Introvigne (2000:47) found that the church in Asia and the United States has relatively few full-time members but a much larger congregation of "Home Church" members. The latter are largely householders living and working outside the church's communities to support their families. As "associate" members, their commitment and involvement in the Unification Church varies widely, with some being little more than movement sympathizers (Barker 1995:228). Given this diversity, it no longer remains clear who is and is not a "real" Unificationist, even to those affiliated with the group (Barker 1995:227).

The failure to build and sustain communally based cultures to support families grows out of at least two factors. The first is the overall mission. Some leaders and rank-and-file members alike resisted the idea of shifting organizational priorities away from recruitment and missionary work. Although this posture was reversed in The Family, it was only after recruitment slowed measurably and significant numbers of second-generation youths began leaving the movement (Chancellor 2000:205–6). ISKCON's leaders resisted far longer, even as recruitment dwindled and the movement rapidly declined. The second factor turns on economic resources. ISKCON and some of the other established new religions became financially unstable during the 1980s (on The Family, see Chancellor 2000), in the midst of large and growing numbers of children. Without a stable economic base, the challenge to adequately meet the needs of children and parents in a communal context was enormous. Lacking internal structures of support, most parents and children had little choice but to seek employment, schooling, and recreation in the conventional culture (Amsterdam 2004; Chancellor 2000; Introvigne 2000:46–47). Moreover, new members with families often permanently remained living and working in the conventional society (Rochford 2000). Mainstream social institutions therefore became an ever present force in members' daily lives.

Because culture is situated (Fine 1995:130), it is activated in the social contexts in which individuals and groups exist in time and space. As the institutional challenges faced by Krishna devotees began to change, their cultural resources were repackaged to fit their new circumstances. When they moved out of the communal context to establish new lives, they faced the inevitable challenge of integrating their Krishna beliefs with the cultural blueprint of American society. The result was both greater cultural continuity with the dominant society and the emergence of new cultural repertoires reflecting their changed realities.

Culture Failure and Worldly Accommodation

World accommodation is the outcome of a developmental path in which new religious movements move away from their world-transforming objectives and make peace with the world (Wallis 1984:35–36). In Bromley's (2004) terms, accommodation is a growing alignment with mainstream institutions and cultural conventions, whereby societal rejection and the goal of promoting social change through conversion are displaced, if not rejected.[3] The scope and influence of religious beliefs narrow, being limited largely to individual religiosity and the community of like-minded believers. As one ISKCON devotee remarked, "We have many members who view Krishna Consciousness as their religion, rather than a complete way of life." Such a statement is emblematic of the dramatic changes that ISKCON's membership has undergone over the past three decades.

We have already seen how ISKCON and the majority of its member-ship rejected traditionalist models of sex roles in favor of the American norm of gender equality. But other changes of significance also resulted as devotees established lives in the conventional culture. As one ISKCON member of thirty years explained,

> It is just a matter of practicality, having to survive in the world. Devo-tees have to be concerned about occupations because our ISKCON soci-ety doesn't have the financial structure or the positions that you find in the larger society. So people dealt with the world as devotees in their hearts, performing activities in the bigger society, receiving a paycheck, developing new relationships, supporting political candidates, and do-ing all the things people do out of practical need. (interview 2006)

A second-generation devotee reflected on her struggles to integrate Krishna Consciousness with her everyday life in the mainstream culture. Her words point to some of the same challenges Dasa faced when he left New Vrindaban in the mid-1980s:

> I initially rejected my Hare Krsna way of thinking in order to mix with the outside world. Eventually, experience and philosophical reasoning showed me that it wasn't an "either/or" situation in which I had to re-ject one viewpoint to accept another. It was just a matter of broadening my own vision to encompass both worlds. (Kafle 2001:43)

The North American Centennial Survey sheds more light on how dominant institutional involvements have aligned devotees with main-stream American culture. Sixty-one percent of the devotees employed in secular jobs and 45 percent of those who were self-employed agreed that "I identify with many of the values and lifestyles of the outside so-ciety, along with my Krishna conscious values and lifestyle." Moreover, 70 percent of those working in nondevotee settings and 59 percent of the self-employed agreed that "I have increasingly had to accommodate to the daily routines and lifestyle of the outside society."[4] These findings suggest that involvement in conventional institutions—in this case, the world of work—have drawn devotees toward the values, lifestyles, and routines of the dominant culture. The same can be said for the devotee young people who made the transition from the gurukula into public education in the absence of ISKCON secondary schools. As we saw, devotee youths engaged in a complex set of negotiations with their non-devotee peers, leading many to exchange their ISKCON collective identity for social acceptance. Given that today the majority of ISKCON's children attend public schools, mainstream institutions and culture constitute major influences in their lives.

The retreat into the outside society produced not only accommodation but also collective efforts to create new cultural forms consistent with devotees' changed circumstances. Much of this cultural work was oppositional in nature, challenging those elements of ISKCON's traditional culture that diminished the significance of family in devotional life.[5]

Social Movement Havens and Emerging Cultural Repertoires

Fantasia and Hirsch (1995:158) argue that the transformation of a movement's traditional culture depends on two developments. First, internal social conflict must reach a level of intensity in which participants are pushed outside their normal everyday routines. This view is consistent with Swidler's (1986) argument that "unsettled" times growing out of crisis lead to the rejection of old cultural models in favor of emergent cultural forms. Second, "free spaces" or "havens" must be present to facilitate the collective renegotiation of a movement's existing culture. By definition, free spaces are removed from hegemonic cultural forms and those who champion them. It is in this sense that social movement havens are sites of oppositional cultural formation (Fantasia and Hirsch 1995:159).

ISKCON's history in North America has clearly been one of ongoing conflict over marriage and family life. The legacy of neglect and abuse is a tragic reminder of the power wielded by the leadership in its efforts to preserve ISKCON's traditional goals of preaching, book distribution, and conversion. The exit of large numbers of householders following ISKCON's financial collapse in the 1980s opened "social and spatial preserves" (Fantasia and Hirsch 1995:158) that allowed for new forms of cultural production to emerge. Devotee enclaves formed in areas surrounding ISKCON's temple communities. These enclave communities, composed of householders and their children, defined ISKCON's shift to a congregationally based movement. As social movement havens, they allowed for a culture of dissent to emerge. No longer subject to the authority and control of the leadership, householders rejected ISKCON's antifamily ideology in favor of ideals that elevated the status of families in devotional life. As might be expected, ISKCON's leadership became a focal point of discontent.[6] The emergent ideology promoted family and community over ISKCON's traditional objectives and sources of religious authority. Emerging cultural work was of two broad types. The first was a reworking of ISKCON's traditional religious culture in an attempt to make it more compatible with the needs and routines of family life. The second was grassroots initiatives directed toward providing new cultural resources to support families and the broader devotee community. Each of these forms of cultural production turned away ISKCON's foundational goals in favor of building community in support of devotee families.

Reworking Religious Culture

The most immediate challenge to ISKCON's traditional religious culture pertained to the leadership. The abuse of children and women and the misuses of power, scandal, and corruption all undermined the legitimacy of ISKCON's guru and GBC leadership. As we have seen, large portions of devotees of all types questioned and often rejected the authority of ISKCON's leaders. As one devotee who remains committed to ISKCON was forced to admit,

> At this point even if the GBC collapsed tomorrow, it wouldn't matter. The movement would go on. . . . ISKCON is becoming less relevant to the members. There is the management structure, the bureaucratic structure, and then the general members. But most devotees don't see the relevance of the GBC as a managing authority. As one devotee said in a morning [temple] class, "I don't see what relevance the GBC has in my life. What does it mean that I accept the GBC?" (interview 2006)

As the leadership's legitimacy came under fire, ISKCON's traditional goals of preaching, book distribution, and conversion lost their significance. Many rejected these goals in part because they associated them with the leadership's control of the organization. But more pragmatic reasons were involved as well. As one congregational member associated with the New Raman-reti (Alachua) community commented,

> Twenty years ago I was one of those devotees who was trying to change the world in the sense that I was dedicated to book distribution and doing what was asked of me without really thinking twice about it. I was dedicated to the movement as a whole. When the calamity started to surface with the gurus, abuse, so many levels of calamity, you shift your priorities. You start to realize that you can't do this work of giving others Krishna Consciousness unless there is a foundation and level of support at a very basic level around you. . . . But when you are hurt and beleaguered and you don't have enough money to pay the bills and you don't have enough money for a plate of pasta, then your ability to think about changing the world is going to be greatly diminished. (interview 2006)

A substantial portion of the congregational members responding to the Centennial Survey indicated that they no longer considered traditional forms of preaching to be a priority. Two-thirds (68%) agreed that "I have little desire to go out in public and distribute books and preach."

Given the changes in the daily routines of its membership, ISKCON's traditional religious culture has been challenged in other ways. Because most adults hold full-time jobs in addition to family obligations and their children most often attend non-ISKCON schools, morning temple programs have suffered from a lack of attendance for years. As we have already seen, religious practice became largely privatized within devotee households. As a result, many devotees remained marginal to the life of their temple community. In an effort to reinvolve its congregational members, some ISKCON communities have altered their morning program schedule. A devotee from one such community explained:

> In most temples the morning program goes until 8:30 or 9 o'clock in the morning. That in and of itself is prohibitive for almost everybody. Here in [name of community] the temple program is over every morning at 7:30. . . . You could certainly go to the whole morning program and be at work at eight. Kids can get to school, adults to work. But if you suggest this to other temples, they are aghast. How can you

interfere with Prabhupada's program? But this is something we can do. Make the morning program more in harmony with people's lifestyle. (interview 2006)

Because the temple no longer serves as the foundation of religious life, religious education, which was once so much a part of temple life, has found new outlets. Following the pattern of many established religious groups, seminars, workshops, and courses in the philosophy and lifestyle of Krishna Consciousness have proliferated. As one devotee commented, the temple-based renunciate culture of the past no longer appeals to most devotees.

> There is still an infatuation with the sannyasi culture but it is basically just that—infatuation. I don't see devotees flock to hear these renounced preachers. There just isn't a strong connection between that culture and their daily lives. I hate to say it, but it is more entertainment. There is a move in ISKCON definitely toward seminars, toward helping people practically and spiritually to live Krishna Consciousness in their lives. . . . Often times these days, devotees are substituting these courses for the training once provided in the temples. I see these educational programs as a measure of our success really, that we are adopting a culturally accepted way of teaching adults. (interview 2006)

Seminars and workshops often are organized around major festivals that attract large numbers of devotees. Every spring, for example, the New Vrindaban community sponsors a two-day Festival of Inspiration that brings in several hundred devotees from around North America, most all of whom are Westerners. Two dozen or more seminars and workshops encompassing a great variety of topics are held. For instance, the 2006 program included sessions like "Distant Learning in ISKCON: How to Get Our Congregation to Read and Study Srila Prabhupada's Books," "The Transcendental Mechanics of Chanting," "Srila Jiva Goswami and Vedanta Philosophy," "Why Can't We Just Get Along? How to View and Respond to Conflicts in Devotional Life," "Spiritual Care in ISKCON," and "Taking Krishna Consciousness out of the Temple." In the summer of 2006, ISKCON's second generation held the first Kulimela festival at New Vrindaban. The festival had workshops on a broad range of topics, including "Yoga and Mantra Meditation," "Classical Indian Dance with a Progressive Edge," "Understanding Therapeutic Process," "Business and Women in the Working World," "Building Healthy Relationships," and "Spiritual and Community Development."

More dramatic changes to ISKCON's religious culture have also been suggested. Based on interviews with thirty-one leaders and senior devotees, an internal report on the future of ISKCON in the United States proposed that the movement step back from its Indian cultural roots in order to appeal more widely to Westerners. The proposed changes also have relevance to devotees whose lives intersect with the conventional society.

> A few interviewees suggested that ISKCON get away from being so blatantly Indian. Cultural chauvinism, where Indian culture is considered inherently spiritual and Western culture is considered inherently polluted, is hostile to the West and in turn evokes hostility from the West toward ISKCON. Interviewees felt that ISKCON should present itself as a universal spiritual science, rather than as something that is ethnically Indian, fanatical, and out of touch with the 21st century. Suggestions . . . include eliminating "gender bias," doing away with "the floor culture," where everything is done on the floor, modifying loud and passionate kirtanas, preparing healthy food as opposed to heavy, oily, and spicy [Sunday] "feasts," and not insisting that members wear Indian clothes. (Senior Devotees Speak about the Present and Future of ISKCON USA, August 2002)

Festivals have always been an integral part of ISKCON's religious culture. Like collective rituals, festivals celebrate community and promote group solidarity. As ISKCON's communities became increasingly fragmented, festivals gained greater importance. Gathering together at festivals, often scheduled to overlap with educational seminars and workshops, devotees renew friendships, worship together, take part in kirtans, and feast on prasadam. Festivals such as New Vrindaban's annual Festival of Inspiration, the newly established Kulimela,[7] and the Prabhupada Memorial Festival held yearly in Los Angeles each attract hundreds of devotees for two to three days of celebration. One of the organizers of the 2006 Prabhupada Memorial Festival explained that the event "gather[s] Srila Prabhupada's family under one roof, to re-inspire through association with fellow devotees and through hearing of his [Prabhupada's] pastimes, and to re-kindle our love and gratitude for him" (Kumar, Rasa 2006). The Kulimela festival also sought to re-awaken a sense of common identity between second-generation devotees and their parents' generation. Dasa, who served as one of the festival organizers, stated its purpose:

> It is a means to legitimize and affirm the second generation's presence in the greater devotee society. It is one way our generation is attempting to serve and improve our community. Kulimela is meant to be an inclusive event, drawing on devotees from all walks of life. Through positive examples, we hope to demonstrate what is possible when people from different generations work together for a common goal.

The most significant event in the annual festival calendar is the Festival of India and the Rathayatra parade that accompanies it. The event is staged in a dozen cities in North America throughout the summer months. Devotees pull temple deities placed on large carts through the streets while they sing, dance, and play instruments. Many hundreds of devotees attend these festivals in cities like Chicago, Los Angeles, Montreal, New York, San Francisco, Toronto, and Washington, D.C.

Beyond efforts to rework and reinvigorate portions of ISKCON's traditional religious culture were new forms of cultural production directed toward strengthening families as well as the broader devotee community. Many of these cultural innovations were modeled on mainstream institutions.

New Forms of Cultural Production

The goal of community development spawned the growth of a number of grassroots initiatives by devotees throughout North America. Collectively, they produced a number of community resources to serve the psychological, social, and family needs of devotees.[8] As a board member of the New Raman-reti community in Florida observed,

> As our priorities have changed, we have had to look to where our problems exist. If people have been hurt in their lives or their children have been hurt, the tendency is to revert into the family or to revert into the community or to revert into oneself because there is a need for healing.

Doing the things that are already there in our philosophy: revealing your mind in confidence, inquiring confidentially, having intimate relationships, developing certain qualities. Flipping the whole thing around and realizing the importance of community and home and that these things take a lot of time and effort. (interview 2006)

Given the "need for healing," counseling and therapy services have proliferated throughout the movement, aided by the substantial number of devotees who have gone back to school to gain professional training and credentials. As one woman commented, "In most communities you will find devotees to go to for family counseling or personal counseling. So this has become much stronger within our movement, where twenty years ago it was a dirty word."[9]

In 2002, ISKCON's North American Office of Communications sponsored a conference, Therapy and Social Care: A Krsna Conscious Perspective. Conference participants played a lead role in organizing the growing number of ISKCON professionals in the field of counseling and mental heath care. The Vaisnava Alliance of Care Providers and a national system of peer-counseling were established to help devotees with problems in their lives (Dasa, Aghari and Dasi, Candramukhi 2002).

In 2004, the North American Grhastha Vision Team formed to serve the needs of devotee families. Members of the group are trained in marriage and family dynamics, and many are licensed counselors and therapists. The group's initial goal has been to improve the quality of devotee marriages. Members of the Vision Team provide formal instruction to couples planning to marry and also to those newly married. In addition, the group successfully lobbied ISKCON's leadership on behalf of devotee families. In 2005, the GBC passed resolution 417, which endorsed the grhastha ashram and committed leaders to the welfare of devotee families. The resolution stated in part:

We also affirm the importance in ISKCON of nurturing strong marriages, encouraging harmony in families, improving the welfare of children, ensuring the protection and care of women, discouraging divorce, and enlivening grihastha[10] men and women in Krishna's service. We hereby pledge ourselves, and will encourage our regional and other senior leaders to . . . [p]romote an environment conducive to successful Krishna conscious family life in ISKCON temples and communities. . . . Confront and correct any preaching or teaching that undermines the health and strength of the grihastha ashram, or discriminates against spiritually based grihastha life. (Vaisnava Family Resources 2006)

The Grhastha Vision Team has also persuaded temple presidents in Canada to perform temple marriage ceremonies only if the devotee couples have first received premarital education. The group is working to secure a similar agreement from temple presidents in the United States.

Other groups that have emerged include Children of Krishna, whose motto is "Helping Hare Krishna Youth to Help Themselves." The group formed in 1996 to provide therapy, educational, and other forms of support for young people abused in the gurukula. The organization's services are now available to all ISKCON youths in need, and Children of Krishna has awarded grants of more than $285,000 (Children of Krishna 2006). Vaisnavas CARE (Counseling, Assistance, Resource, and Education) is a nonprofit organization of Vaisnava health care professionals dedicated to supporting and assisting terminally ill devotees and their families. The group includes devotee doctors, nurses, and psychologists, as well as volunteers dedicated to incorporating ISKCON's religious beliefs into the care of the dying (Vaisnavas CARE, Inc. 2006). In 2006, a hospice facility opened in Vrndavana, India, to care for the growing number of terminally ill devotees choosing to die in sacred surroundings in the care of other devotees. In 2003, CARE (Community Action Resources Effort, Inc.) was formed to help members of the New Ramanreti community suffering from economic, family, and personal hardships. The program maintains a hot line for community members and in other ways seeks to reach out to those in need in the congregation.[11]

As this discussion demonstrates, world accommodation has gone hand in hand with the production of new cultural repertoires supportive of families and community development. When they were pushed out of the movement's oppositional world to establish lives in the conventional society, householders reworked ISKCON's traditional culture to make it responsive to new institutional demands. The resulting cultural agenda elevated families as the foundation of devotee life. From radical beginnings that placed preaching and conversion above the needs of families, the Hare Krishna has evolved into an American religious community centered on family life. Remarkably, this community has remained largely marginal to its organizational roots. For as ISKCON's long-standing members were working to create a religious culture more responsive to the needs of families, ISKCON was moving toward becoming an ethnic church. As a result, the devotee community that formed along ISKCON's institutional borders represents the future of Prabhupada's movement in North America.

ISKCON and the Fate of New Religions

Eileen Barker (2004:99) raised the provocative question "When do new religions stop being new? . . . [I]n the twenty-first century the Unification Church, ISKCON, and Scientology are beginning to look old." Bromley's (2004) approach to defining new religions provides one response. If new religious movements are unique by virtue of their low level of alignment with dominant institutions and cultural-symbolic patterns, they become "old" as they emerge out of the "contested spaces within society" (Melton 2004:75) and begin a process of accommodation. Collectively, ISKCON and the other major new religions have been drawn toward conformity with American society as their members have become involved in mainstream institutions in the absence of communally based domestic cultures. As a result, boundaries with the outside society have necessarily been redrawn. Images of a "corrupt" and "demonic" society requiring reform and transformation become difficult to sustain when adults and children are bound by ongoing societal involvement. Yet as ISKCON's case demonstrates, societal accommodation holds the potential for stimulating new forms of cultural production in keeping with members' changed lives.

Although Bromley's (2004) concept of alignment allows for tracking the development of new religions, it fails to stress an essential point. Like all social movements, new religions are dedicated to promoting or resisting change in society (Turner and Killian 1987: 223). At their core, new religions are oppositional movements that seek to change, if not transform, society (Bromley 1997; Kent 2001; Rochford 2007). This oppositional stance is the source of their tension and misalignment with the normative foundations of mainstream society. Yet some religious groups and communities maintain relatively low levels of alignment with the dominant society without a commitment to social change. One only need mention the Amish to make the point. Although in various ways the Amish way of life is misaligned with society's institutions and cultural conventions, the Amish have no interest in changing American society (see Kraybill 2001). Bromley mistakenly fails to place the concept of alignment within a broader framework of social protest, but he is not alone in this oversight. In his influential model detailing why religious movements succeed or fail, Rodney Stark (1996:134) defines religious movements as "social enterprises whose primary purpose is to create, maintain and supply religion to some set of individuals." Clearly, this definition encompasses the goals of virtually every religious group and denomination that has existed historically. As Stark and other scholars (Mauss 1994; Wilson 1990) have acknowledged, what distinguishes new religions is their oppositional stance toward society. In challenging society, new religions provoke tension and become targets of countermovements, local and national governments, and publics concerned with the threat they represent.

New religious movements grow old and die or are transformed when they give up the fight to promote social change. Growing societal alignment is simply a symptom of turning away from protest and goals of changing society in line with religious beliefs. Given that new religions are quintessentially social movements, the significant question is how, and under what circumstances, they are transformed into religious *organizations and/or communities*.[12]

This study of ISKCON's development in North America has underscored how the radical project of promoting world transformation dies when the social environment that fosters and sustains it falters. Radical religious beliefs centered on promoting social change require cultures of opposition if they are to endure. Communities of opposition promote radical identities and model the religious world that the movement seeks to advance. Because the new religions of the 1960s generally failed to integrate families into their oppositional worlds, they were beset by internal turmoil, as well as significant change, when their members left the communal fold and began a process of worldly accommodation. ISKCON provides a dramatic example, as the mass exodus of householders from its communities during the 1980s set the organization on a course of decline and potential failure. ISKCON survived only by developing a new constituency of Indian-Hindu immigrants to support its impoverished communities. As this was occurring, longtime devotees existing on the periphery of ISKCON started reworking elements of the movement's religious culture to sustain a community facing new realities. Today, Prabhupada's vision and teachings live on, but increasingly outside the organization that he founded to promote Krishna

Consciousness in America. The fate of Prabhupada's legacy lies primarily with independent communities like New Raman-reti and with the many devotee families throughout North America socializing the next generation of Krishna devotees while remaining a part of American culture. It may also lie with the ritvik movement should it form temples and communities dedicated to Prabhupada. The struggle ahead will no doubt require still more cultural work to keep this widely disparate community united in the service of Prabhupada and Krishna. All best wishes.

Appendix 1

Commitment, Involvement, and Leader Authority Measures

Figure 1 details the commitment, involvement, and leader authority dimensions, variables, and measures used in the analyses presented in chapters 2, 5, 7, and 8. The data are from the Prabhupada Centennial Survey conducted in North America in 1995/1996. I used principal component factor analysis with varimax rotation to construct each of the indices and selected those items with significant factor loadings that comprised distinct dimensions. Classification of the commitment and involvement dimensions was derived in part from Kanter's (1968, 1972) commitment categories and Glock and Stark's (1965:18–38) dimensions of religiosity.

The following provides a brief conceptual rationale for each of the various dimensions and subdimensions:

I. Commitment Dimensions

1. *Commitment to Krishna Conscious Religious Beliefs.* If a member is to remain committed to a religious organization, he or she must ultimately become cognitively committed. While this often is viewed in rational-calculus terms in which members are portrayed as weighing the relative costs and benefits of participation (Burke and Reitzes 1991; Kanter 1972), more is involved for "identity transforming organizations" (Greil and Rudy 1984) such as ISKCON. To become cognitively committed normally requires that members undergo a process of conversion (see Lofland and Stark 1965; Snow and Machalek 1984). ISKCON members are expected to incorporate the beliefs of Krishna Consciousness into all aspects of their everyday lives and to pursue the movement's spiritual objectives as a first priority. Krishna Consciousness thus becomes a global interpretive frame (Snow et al. 1986:475). Included items

address the importance of specific aspects of the Krishna conscious philosophy as well as its overall significance as a master interpretive frame.

2. *Commitment to Preaching.* Preaching and the recruitment of new members have traditionally defined ISKCON's mission as a new religious movement. For most of ISKCON's North American history, ISKCON members distributed Prabhupada's writings and recruited new members in public places such as airports. As devotees became more independent beginning in the 1980s, this preaching broadened to include the varied contexts that comprise their everyday lives (in the workplace, educational institutions).

3. *Commitment to ISKCON.* Organizational commitment refers to a member's degree of loyalty to ISKCON. Committed members identify with ISKCON and are willing to sacrifice on its behalf because they see the organization and its purposes and goals as aligned with the self.

4. *Commitment to the Truth of Prabhupada's Books.* Prabhupada's writings and commentaries on the Vedic scriptures represent the theological basis of ISKCON. Most ISKCON members consider Prabhupada's writings as "truth" and attempt to live their lives accordingly.

5. *Importance of Devotee Relationships.* Individual religious belief, as well as group commitment, depends on maintaining relationships with other believers (Lofland and Stark 1965; Snow and Phillips 1980). Items measure the importance placed on involvement with other ISKCON members and the devotee community more generally.

II. Collective Involvement and Participation

1. *Collective Religious Practices.* Group ritual enhances communion within religious communities (Kanter 1968:510). As Durkheim (1965: 47) noted long ago, collective religious rites function to unite believers into a "moral community." They thus function to build esprit de corps, anchoring member identity to the group (Blumer 1951; Turner and Killian 1987:337–43). ISKCON's collective religious life is an especially rich one, with distinctive religious clothing, daily worship services, and classes on the philosophy of Krishna Consciousness.

2. *ISKCON Volunteer Work.* If a religious group is to survive, it must find ways to ensure that adherents devote time, energy, and resources to the organization. Through the process of investment, members become integrated into the collectivity and come to understand that they have a stake in its success (Kanter 1968:504–5). One such measure is the

amount of time ISKCON members spend on unpaid labor in their local temple community.

III. Individual Involvement and Participation

1. *Private/Household Religious Practices.* Like group ritual, individual forms of worship represent expressions of religious meaning that serve to deepen members' conviction and commitment. For ISKCON devotees, daily chanting of the Hare Krishna mantra is the primary means of individual worship, although other practices and activities are followed as well, as indicated in figure 1.

2. *Follow the Regulative Principles.* When accepting a spiritual master and becoming initiated into Krishna Consciousness, an ISKCON devotee vows to avoid eating meat, taking intoxicants, gambling, and involvement in illicit sex (i.e., sex outside marriage and for purposes other than procreation). The regulative principles are deemed essential by the Vedic scriptures for spiritual advancement and provide the normative standards for behavior within ISKCON.

IV. Leader Authority and Governance

1. *Authority of the Gurus/Guru Institution.* As Chaves (1993, 1994) argued, the decline of religious authority defines secularization. At the individual level this means that there is a "decrease in the extent to which actions of persons are subject to religious control" (Chaves 1993: 7). Given the political turmoil following Prabhupada's death, and the politics surrounding the ascendancy of the nuclear family during the 1980s, the overall authority of ISKCON's leaders has been challenged (Rochford 1998a, 1998b), with the guru successors to Prabhupada a particular focus of concern. The measures identified in figure 1 determine how ISKCON members view the authority of the gurus and the guru system more broadly.

2. *Bureaucratic Control of the Gurus.* Because of the ongoing controversies surrounding ISKCON's gurus, pressures have grown from within the membership to control the guru institution in an effort to limit its volatility. Enforced limits on the gurus' material lifestyle and mandated GBC reviews of individual gurus have been called for.

3. *Authority of the GBC.* Issues of religious authority also apply to ISKCON's structure of governance (the GBC). Like ISKCON's gurus the

GBC has increasingly come under fire by the rank and file. Some claim that the GBC does not represent their interests and concerns and question the very legitimacy of the GBC body and its ability to effectively govern the movement.

4. *Democratic Governance.* Because of a lack of trust in the GBC, ISK-CON members have increasingly called for more democratic forms of governance. These include demands that GBC members be elected to office rather than appointed, the body be restructured to ensure greater representation for an increasingly diverse membership, and an impartial system of justice be provided.

FIGURE I
Summary Dimensions and Measures

I. *Commitment Dimensions*

1. Commitment to Krishna conscious religious beliefs

   My religious faith is (check one):
   (1) Only of minor importance to my life.
   (2) Important but no more important than certain other aspects of my life.
   (3) Of central importance and comes before all other aspects of my life.

   At this point in my life I am *most committed* to:
   (a) Advancing in Krishna Consciousness.
   (b) Improving my *sadhana* (i.e., religious practice).
   (c) Following the four regulative principles.
   Ranges from (0), not at all committed, to (5), strongly committed.

   How would you characterize the *strength of your commitment* to:
   (a) The practice of Krishna Consciousness.
   Ranges from (0), not at all committed, to (5), strongly committed.

2. Commitment to preaching

   I have little desire to go out in public and distribute books and preach.
   Ranges from (1), agree strongly, to (4), disagree strongly.

   I actively preach to nondevotees at work and/or as part of my daily routine.
   Ranges from (4), agree strongly, to (1), disagree strongly.

   At this point in my life I am *most committed* to:
   (a) Preaching Krishna Consciousness.
   Ranges from (0), not at all committed, to (5), strongly committed.

3. Commitment to ISKCON

   How would you characterize the *strength of your commitment* to:
   (a) ISKCON leadership and present structure.
   (b) ISKCON's purposes and goals.
   Ranges from (0), not at all committed, to (5), strongly committed.

I have a sense of pride about being a member of ISKCON.

Ranges from (4), agree strongly, to (1), disagree strongly.

Whatever ISKCON's past or present faults, it still represents Prabhupada, and on that basis I will forever be connected to ISKCON.

Ranges from (4), agree strongly, to (1), disagree strongly.

My identity as a person is defined largely by my ISKCON involvement.

Ranges from (4), agree strongly, to (1), disagree strongly.

4. Commitment to the truth of Prabhupada's books

I accept as truth Prabhupada's translations of and commentaries on the Srimad Bhagavatam and other Vedic scriptures.

Ranges from (4), agree strongly, to (1), disagree strongly.

There are philosophical statements in Prabhupada's books that I don't accept fully.

Ranges from (1), agree strongly, to (4), disagree strongly.

5. Importance of devotee relationships

To what degree have the following *positively influenced* your willingness to be connected to and/or involved in ISKCON?
  (a) Association with other ISKCON members.
  (b) Warmth and support I receive from devotees in my local ISKCON community.
  (c) Cooperatively working together with other ISKCON devotees.

Ranges from (0), no influence, to (5), major influence.

At this point in my life I am *most committed* to:
  (a) Maintaining my relationships with other devotees.
  (b) The well-being of my local ISKCON community.

Ranges from (0), not at all committed, to (5), strongly committed.

II. *Collective Involvement and Participation*

1. Collective religious practices

How often do you:
  (a) Attend Mangala arti?
  (b) Attend Guru Puja?
  (c) Attend Bhagavatam class?
  (d) Take part in kirtan?
  (e) Wear dhoti or sari?

Ranges from (6), daily, to (1), rarely or never.

2. Volunteer work in local ISKCON community

Do you spend time doing regular unpaid duties in your local ISKCON temple community?
  (1) No.
  (2) Yes.

If yes, on *average* how many hours a week do you spend performing unpaid duties?
  ____ hours per week.

III. Individual Involvement and Participation

1. Private/household religious practices

    How often do you:
    (a) Chant japa?
    (b) Offer your food?
    (c) Read Prabhupada's books?
    (d) Listen to tapes of Prabhupada?
    (e) Hold morning program at home?

    Ranges from (6), daily, to (1), rarely or never.

2. Follow regulative principles

    Do you:
    (a) eat meat?
    (b) eat eggs?
    (c) eat meat products?
    (d) consume alcohol?
    (e) smoke marijuana?
    (f) take LSD, cocaine, or other drugs?
    (g) use tobacco?
    (h) drink caffeinated coffee or tea?
    (i) gamble?
    (j) have illicit sex, inside or outside marriage?

    Ranges from (4), no, to (1), often.

IV. Leader Authority and Governance

1. Authority of the gurus/ guru institution

    To what degree have the following *positively influenced* your willingness to be connected to and/or involved in ISKCON?
    (a) Spiritual potency of ISKCON's present gurus.

    Ranges from (0), no influence, to (5), major influence.

    To what degree have the following *limited* your ability or desire to remain actively involved in ISKCON?
    (a) Lack of respect for ISKCON's current gurus.

    Ranges from (5), no influence, to (0), major influence.

    The "reform movement" of the mid-1980s basically resolved the guru controversies within ISKCON.

    Ranges from (4), agree strongly, to (1), disagree strongly.

    The atmosphere of controversy surrounding the new gurus following Prabhupada's disappearance had a profound negative influence on my commitment to ISKCON.

    Ranges from (1), agree strongly, to (4), disagree strongly.

    In my understanding, Prabhupada appointed the first eleven gurus as ritviks with the idea that they would become regular initiating gurus after his departure.

    Ranges from (4), agree strongly, to (1) disagree strongly.

I respect the spiritual potency and authority of ISKCON's current gurus.
Ranges from (4), agree strongly, to (1), disagree strongly.

The grand disciples of Srila Prabhupada are fully connected to the parampara.
Ranges from (4), agree strongly, to (1), disagree strongly.

2. Bureaucratic control of gurus

Standards limiting an ISKCON guru's material lifestyle should be enforced.
Ranges from (4), agree strongly, to (1), disagree strongly.

Aspiring ISKCON gurus should be required to pass the Bhaktivedanta degree.
Ranges from (4), agree strongly, to (1), disagree strongly.

ISKCON's initiating gurus should be subject to regular reviews by the GBC.
Ranges from (4), agree strongly, to (1), disagree strongly.

3. Authority of the GBC

To what degree have the following *limited* your ability or desire to remain actively involved in ISKCON?
(a) Lack of trust in the GBC.
Ranges from (5), no influence, to (1), major influence.

When you have important decisions to make in your life, how often do you seek guidance from:
(a) The local GBC representative?
Ranges from (1), never, to (5), always.

The GBC represents my interests and concerns as a devotee.
Ranges from (4), agree strongly, to (1), disagree strongly.

I accept the GBC as the legitimate governing authority within ISKCON.
Ranges from (4), agree strongly, to (1), disagree strongly.

The GBC is a closed and elitist group.
Ranges from (1), agree strongly, to (4), disagree strongly.

GBC decisions have little or no relevance to my life as a devotee.
Ranges from (1), agree strongly, to (4), disagree strongly.

4. Democratic governance

Members of the GBC should be elected to office rather than appointed to the GBC.
Ranges from (4), agree strongly, to (1), disagree strongly.

The GBC should be structured to ensure representation for a greater variety of devotee viewpoints.
Ranges from (4), agree strongly, to (1), disagree strongly.

ISKCON needs to have a well-functioning and impartial system of justice to deal with problems and abuses.
Ranges from (4), agree strongly, to (1), disagree strongly.

Devotees should have the right to congregate freely and discuss any and all issues of mutual concern, no matter how controversial.

Ranges from (4), agree strongly, to (1), disagree strongly.

Local temple management should be the responsibility of an elected board of directors.

Ranges from (4), agree strongly, to (1) disagree strongly.

Appendix 2
Data Tables

*Mean Differences for Full-Time and Congregational
Members with and without Children (mean scores)*

	Full-Time Members				Congregational Members		
	Children				Children		
	No		Yes		No		Yes
I. Commitment Dimensions							
1. Commitment to Krishna Consciousness	20.31 (131)		19.97	(117)	16.29 (49)		17.45 (89)
2. Commitment to preaching	9.32 (131)		9.16	(117)	7.31 (49)		7.62 (89)
3. Commitment to ISKCON	17.07 (131)		17.21		15.08 (49)		15.15 (89)
II. Collective Involvement/ Participation							
1. Collective religious practices	24.04 (131)		20.72***	(117)	12.04 (49)		13.07 (89)
2. Service/volunteer work in ISKCON community							
a. Percentage who volunteer	88%	(105)	82%	(91)	43% (20)		53% (45)
b. Mean number of hours per week	33.27	(92)	16.88***	(85)	6.28 (16)		4.07 (36)
c. Median number of hours per week	30.00	(92)	10.00***	(85)	4.00 (16)		3.50 (36)
III. Individual Involvement/ Participation							
1. Private/household religious practices	22.16 (131)		22.87	(117)	17.51 (49)		19.85* (89)
2. Follow regulative principles	39.36 (131)		38.97	(117)	36.14 (49)		36.70 (89)
IV. Leader Authority							
1. Authority of the gurus/guru institution	23.28	(96)	21.29**	(106)	20.49 (12)		19.90 (34)
a. Need more bureaucratic control of gurus	9.18	(96)	9.58	(106)	8.85 (12)		9.71 (34)
2. Authority of the GBC	18.97 (131)		17.03***	(117)	16.35 (49)		15.89 (89)
a. Need for more democratic governance	14.57 (131)		15.40**	(117)	15.19 (49)		15.72 (89)

* $p < .05$, ** $p < .01$, *** $p < .001$.

TABLE A.2

Select Comparison of Congregational and Former ISKCON Members (mean scores)

	Congregational Members	Former Members
I. Leader Authority		
Authority of the GBC	15.6 (82)***	11.9 (87)
Authority of the gurus	19.8 (37)**	16.6 (78)
II. Commitment		
Commitment to ISKCON	14.6 (82)***	11.4 (87)
Commitment to Krishna Consciousness	16.7 (82)	16.6 (87)
Commitment to preaching	7.2 (82)	7.9 (87)
Truth of Prabhupada's books	6.7 (82)	6.9 (87)
III. Religious Practice		
Private religious practices	18.4 (82)	18.4 (87)
Follow regulative principles	36.2 (82)	36.1 (87)

** $p < .01$, *** $p < .001$.

TABLE A.3

Select Comparison of Indian Hindus and Other ISKCON Members (mean scores)

	Indian Hindus	Other Members
I. Religious Commitment and Involvement		
a. Commitment to Krishna Consciousness	17.1 (106)	19.0 (318)***
b. Commitment to preaching	8.1 (106)	8.6 (318)*
c. Collective religious practices	14.4 (106)	19.2 (318)***
d. Following regulative principles	36.7 (106)	38.1 (318)***
e. Commitment to the truth of Prabhupada's books	6.7 (106)	7.2 (318)***
f. Read Prabhupada's books[a]	3.5 (101)	4.4 (310)***
g. Wear traditional dhoti or sari[a]	2.8 (100)	4.1 (309)***
h. Hold morning worship at home[a]	3.9 (96)***	2.5 (255)
i. Chant japa[a]	5.0 (98)	5.4 (310)**
II. ISKCON Commitment and Involvement		
a. Commitment to ISKCON's purposes and goals[b]	3.7 (100)	4.0 (307)*
b. Authority of the GBC	16.8 (106)	17.4 (318)
c. Authority of the gurus	21.5 (27)	21.8 (215)
d. Democratic governance	15.7 (106)**	15.1 (318)
e. Hours of ISKCON volunteer work/week	3.9 (106)	11.7 (318)***
f. Importance of devotee relationships	16.5 (106)	17.7 (318)**

* $p < .05$, ** $p < .01$, *** $p < .001$.
[a] Ranges from (6) daily; (5) 5–6 days; (4) 3–4 days; (3) 1–2 days; (2) less than weekly; (1) rarely or never.
[b] What is the strength of your commitment to: ISKCON's purposes and goals?
Ranges from (0), not at all committed, to (5), strongly committed.

Notes

1. *Bhakta* means devotee. The term is typically applied to devotees who have not taken initiation from a guru and precedes their Christian name.

2. For an account of the research methods used in my initial study of ISK-CON, see Rochford 1985:21–42 and Rochford 1992.

3. The Prabhupada Centennial Survey was an international survey of two thousand current and former ISKCON members from fifty-three countries. This book includes only the respondents from Canada and the United States, however, given its focus on ISKCON's North American development.

4. Geertz (1973:93) argues that cultural patterns are "models" that "have an intrinsic double aspect: they give meaning, that is, objective conceptual form, to social and psychological reality both by *shaping themselves to it and by shaping it to themselves*" (my emphasis).

5. Caitanya and his followers were known as the Gaudiya school of Vaisnavism because of their Bengali origin and to distinguish them from other Vaisnava traditions (Squarcini and Fizzotti 2004:45). Gauda is the ancient name for the area corresponding to much of present-day Bengal (Squarini and Fizzotti 2004:87).

6. Although distribution of Prabhupada's books provided the primary source of revenue for ISKCON's communities, other funds came from the sale of Spiritual Sky incense. In 1969 in New York City, ISKCON members began producing and distributing incense as a way of raising money to support the community. Incense sales remained an important source of revenue until the late 1970s when Spiritual Sky Scented Products was sold.

1. Dasa's life history is based on three separate interviews conducted between 1998 and 2005. In December 1998, I interviewed Dasa for ten hours over two days. In May 2000 we spoke once again, for a four-hour period. And in November 2005 I conducted a three-hour phone interview with Dasa. All the interviews were tape-recorded and transcribed. Note that Dasa is the name I chose to protect this man's anonymity.

2. The Fisher mansion was transformed into an ISKCON temple and cultural center and was financed by two ISKCON members, one a grandson of Henry Ford and the other, the daughter of Walter Reuther, the former president of the United Auto Workers.

3. The Bhagavad Gita, a sacred Hindu text, describes Krishna giving spiritual knowledge to his friend and disciple Arjuna on the battlefield of Kuruksetra. The two sides in the conflict were the Kurus and the Pandavas.

4. To encourage devotees involved in either "picking" or book distribution, scores were computed according to how much money an individual collected in a given day. Success at collecting funds was an important basis for establishing status in the devotee community.

5. Unfortunately, the saga of Dasa's mother's death does not end here. In 1986, workmen digging a trench for a pipeline accidentally dug up her remains, as she had been buried in an unmarked grave. Because of an ongoing murder investigation at New Vrindaban, her body was exhumed and impounded by the state as evidence. Tragically, her body was misplaced, and it took Dasa until 1993 before he was able to locate and claim it. Her body was then cremated, and Dasa and his brothers and sisters placed the remains in the rose garden at Prabhupada's Palace. In the summer of 2005, Dasa and his siblings held a memorial service for their mother at New Vrindaban. They installed a bench in her name with an iron trellis surrounding it along a path circling the pond near the temple.

6. In 1991, Bhaktipada was convicted of racketeering and mail fraud. In July 1993, his conviction was overturned when an appellate court ruled that the district court had wrongly allowed evidence of child molestation and other irrelevant matters to be presented during the trial, evidence that unduly prejudiced the jury. In April 1996, Bhaktipada went back to court after refusing a plea bargain offered by the government. Although he accepted no responsibility for the murders of two former New Vrindaban residents, in the middle of the trial he pleaded guilty to one count of federal racketeering and was sentenced to twenty years in a federal prison. In 1997 the sentence was reduced to twelve years because of Bhaktipada's failing health. Eight years later, on June 16, 2004, Bhaktipada was released from federal prison in North Carolina. He now lives with a handful of his followers at the Sri Sri Radha Murlidara temple in New York City. For a more detailed account of Bhaktipada's legal troubles and how they affected New Vrindaban, see Doktorski 2003 and Rochford and Bailey 2006.

7. At the previous reunion, one leader confronted a number of second-generation devotees. According to Dasa, he "said something to the effect that 'you are all a bunch of dancing monkeys. Dancing in the lap of maya.'" In response, several of the youths at the reunion drafted a letter of protest to the leader in question. As Dasa reported, "He never responded to any of us. But he never stepped out and said anything during a reunion again, either."

8. I participated in these meetings as well.

9. The temple president was concerned that the newsletter being produced by Dasa and his peers would have the same hard-hitting content as its predecessor, ISKCON *Youth Veterans,* which was highly critical of ISKCON and its leadership. It also publicized child abuse in the gurukula and was instrumental in mobilizing ISKCON's second generation. Many first-generation devotees found the publication offensive because of its content and the outspoken nature of its editor.

10. The demise of communalism and the shift toward a congregation of independent householders occurred much later at New Vrindaban than in other ISKCON communities in North America.

11. *Arti* is a religious ceremony performed several times a day in either the temple or devotees' homes, in which the devotees sing and play instruments while worshipping and making offerings to the deities on the altar.

NOTES TO CHAPTER 2

1. Perhaps ironically, these avoidance strategies may have only heightened awareness of the opposite sex. As this woman devotee observed, "What happened to me was that all I thought about was men and saris. 'There's a man. Is my sari on right? Is it the right color? Do I have any hair showing in the front [coming out from where the sari is wrapped around the head]?' And that was all I thought about. I stopped thinking about Krishna and Prabhupada."

2. ISKCON members often spell "Krishna" as "Krsna." I use "Krishna" throughout the book, except where "Krsna" appears in quoted materials.

3. During ISKCON's initial years in America, devotees wanting to marry sought Prabhupada's permission and blessing. In 1972, however, Prabhupada refused to personally sanction any more marriages, citing the growing number of marital problems among his disciples, including separation and divorce. In a 1972 letter he wrote, "I am so much disgusted with this troublesome business of marriage, because nearly every day I receive some complaint from husband or wife . . . so henceforth I am not sanctioning any more marriages" (Prabhupada 1992:866).

4. The combination of marriage being a loss of status for men, marriages being arranged for reasons other than compatibility, and pressures to commit oneself fully to ISKCON at the expense of family responsibilities has played a significant role in ISKCON's rate of divorce. Estimates by ISKCON members suggest that from one-third to two-thirds of all ISKCON marriages end in divorce. My 1991/1992 Family Survey found that one-third of all marriages ended in divorce or separation, a figure actually lower than the rate of divorce in the United States, where one out of two marriages ends in divorce (Riley 1991:156). In fact, my findings may actually underestimate the rate of divorce, since it seems

likely that a greater proportion of those who defect from ISKCON are divorced from a devotee spouse. Marital and family problems are one reason that devotees leave ISKCON, temporarily or permanently (Rochford 1991:91).

5. These findings on marriage and family life should be taken as reasonable estimates rather than precise figures, because neither the 1980 nor the 1991/1992 surveys were based on probability samples.

6. Based on the yearly numbers of devotees initiated by Prabhupada in North America, recruitment fell beginning in 1974 (Prabhupada Disciple Database 2006). Although no statistical data on ISKCON's recruitment fortunes during the 1980s are available, I can report the following: First, ISKCON members widely acknowledge that the movement has attracted relatively few new members over the past three decades. My own observations agree with this observation. Second, a comparison of data from the 1980 and 1991/1992 surveys provides indirect evidence of ISKCON's recruitment fortunes during that twelve-year period. A comparison of the median age and the median year when my devotee respondents joined ISKCON suggests that few members were recruited. The median age of ISKCON's membership in 1980 was between twenty-six and twenty-seven, and in 1991/1992, the median age rose to between thirty-seven and thirty-eight. During the twelve years between the two surveys, the median age of the movement's membership increased by almost exactly the same number of years. Equally revealing is the small change in the year that devotees reported joining ISKCON. In 1980, the median year joined was 1975, and in 1991/1992 the median was between 1976 and 1977. These two findings suggest that ISKCON had little success attracting new members during the 1980s.

7. During the 1970s and early 1980s, ISKCON leaders rejected attempts by devotee businessmen to develop income-producing business enterprises (Rochford 1985:224–25, 1989:166–67). Business was viewed as "materialistic" and, perhaps more important, as potentially competing with book distribution. Therefore, because of the leadership's generally unfavorable attitude toward business, ISKCON was left without an alternative means of support when book distribution revenues dropped dramatically within the span of only a few years.

8. Although far from common knowledge, Prabhupada did tell some of his senior disciples as early as 1972 that married devotees should be required to "produce some *outside* income and live *outside* the temple" (my emphasis) (Prabhupada 1992:866). But neither instruction was followed, as the movement's leaders found reason to disregard Prabhupada's directives. First, the prevailing sentiment of the time was that any devotee who lived outside the temple community was destined to slip into maya and thereby leave Krishna Consciousness. Second, the temple presidents were reluctant to encourage devotees to become financially independent. In addition to the loss of control this implied, it also would have reduced the number of devotees collecting money on sankirtan to support the community.

9. Two ashram-based gurukulas for high school–aged men and women were located in ISKCON's northern Florida community. The other, in Baltimore, served the educational needs of half a dozen elementary school–aged boys. Worldwide, only India's Vrndavana and Mayapura schools remain as ashram gurukulas for adolescent boys.

10. In 1975, when I began my research on the Los Angeles ISKCON community, it was considered scandalous for a householder and his family to move even a few blocks away from the temple community. Such a devotee was referred to as a "fringie," an appropriate description to the extent that those so characterized were looking to become more involved in the outside culture. One rarely hears this term used in ISKCON communities any longer, which in itself is a telling statement about the nature of ISKCON's development during the 1980s and 1990s.

11. Table A.1 reports the mean scores for a number of commitment and involvement measures for full-time and congregational members based on family status. For a list of the table's commitment and involvement dimensions, variables, and specific measures, see appendix 1.

12. There is evidence that the trends reported here can also be found in ISKCON's communities around the world; see Rochford 1995, 2000.

13. *Varna* represents four general divisions in society based on occupation and social standing. *Brahmanas* are society's spiritual leaders and educators; *ksatriyas* are its administrators and protectors; *vaisyas* produce foodstuffs and are responsible for protecting cows; and *sudras* are responsible for a variety of skilled and unskilled tasks, including working in the fields and helping people of other varnas. *Ashram* refers to living arrangements that facilitate spiritual activities and growth. The *brahmacari* and *brahmacarini ashrams* are for unmarried male and female renunciates committed exclusively to spiritual advancement; the *grhastha ashram* is a living arrangement for a husband, wife, and children that allows them to structure their lives so that Krishna Consciousness remains at the center of their everyday life; the *sannyasi ashram* is composed of renunciate men devoted to the lifelong pursuit of spiritual learning and practice and full-time preaching; and the *vanaprastha ashram* houses those retired from family and work responsibilities who devote their remaining days to spiritual activities. For a more detailed discussion of varnashram, see Prabhupada 1974, 1992: 2525–71.

NOTES TO CHAPTER 3

1. Because it was assumed that adolescent girls would marry at an early age, none were sent to India for further schooling. At ISKCON's New Vrindaban community in West Virginia in the late 1970s, for example, it was not uncommon for girls as young as thirteen to get engaged or married. When many of these

marriages failed, and girls and their parents began to resist the idea of early marriage, adolescent girls began attending local public schools. Because ISK-CON had no secondary schools for girls and few acceptable alternatives (home schooling), outside schooling became a solution, even if not always a preferred one. Chapter 4 discusses the effects of public education on ISKCON's second generation.

2. Results of the ISKCON youth ministry survey should be considered with caution. The questionnaire was mailed to eight hundred youths and adults who grew up in the movement, but an unspecified number of those who took part in the survey had not attended the gurukula when it was based on the ashram. There also is reason to suspect that those who were abused were more likely to take part in the survey, if only to have their experience acknowledged. Moreover, with 115 returned questionnaires, the response rate was only 14 percent.

3. Note that I do not use devotee's real names, in order to protect their anonymity. In a few instances in which I quote from published sources, I do use real names, including the author's. However, in every case, I avoid using the names of alleged abusers in published and unpublished sources, including the VOICE website. The latter source was an Internet site established by ex-gurukula students to expose the child abuse that they and their peers suffered. This website was very controversial within ISKCON before it ceased operation. Because ISK-CON's leaders were concerned about the adverse public relations impact of VOICE, it pressured the leadership to respond constructively to the problem of child abuse and to the young people abused as children.

4. The sexual abuse of children apparently was not limited to teachers and others working in the gurukula, as there are reports that bramacaries were involved in molesting children in India (Brzezinski 1997). Allegations also persist that some male leaders associated with the Mayapura, India, gurukula were sexually abusing children (Brzezinski 1997; Prabhupada Anti-defamation Association 1993).

5. This situation contrasts sharply with that of other groups that communalized children and child rearing. In the Oneida community founded by John Humphrey Noyes in northern New York during the mid-1800s, children also were raised separately from their parents in a community school. Yet as Kephart explains, this system of communal child rearing was based on "ample affection and kindness . . . [and] that childhood in the Old Community was a happy and exhilarating experience" (1963:268). This suggests that the communalization of children and child rearing is not in itself neglectful or abusive. For a discussion of children in the *kibbutzim*, see Spiro 1958; Talmon 1973.

6. One second-generation devotee commenting on an earlier draft of this chapter stated, "I agree 100 percent. Every day in the morning, sankirtan scores [were] read out to inspire the devotees and praise the individuals who [did]

good collecting money, or distributing the most books. Never, never ever [were] the teachers' praised, or the kids who [did] good at school."

7. It also resulted in long-term emotional consequences for some second-generation youths. As one reported,

> We don't want to trust anyone else with our feelings, our emotions, our love . . . because we "know" that that person will just turn around and hurt us. . . . They'll leave, they'll reject us. . . . "They don't really care about us . . ." we think. I'm twenty-six years old. I'm still struggling to trust someone on an emotional, "feelings" level, and to share my feelings with them. It's hard for me. Damn hard. Being raised by twenty-six parents/caretakers from age seven to fifteen makes it damn hard to place my love and trust in someone again. (personal communication 1998)

8. Some ISKCON members drop the final "a" in Prabhupada's name, as in this quotation. For both stylistic reasons as well as to avoid confusion, hereafter I have corrected the spelling in quoted materials.

9. The questioning of Prabhupada's role in the child abuse in the gurukula has surfaced as an issue among second-generation youths, to which the VOICE website paid considerable attention. Those implicating Prabhupada charge that he knew that children were being physically punished yet failed to intervene directly or have leaders under him stop such behavior. It does seem clear from Prabhupada's letters that he was aware, as early as 1972, that children in the gurukula were being physically punished (see, for example, Prabhupada 1992: 797, 799). There also is evidence suggesting that he did intervene (Prabhupada 1992:797). In a 1972 letter to a disciple who had complained that her child was being mistreated in the Dallas gurukula, Prabhupada wrote:

> But you may be assured that I am always anxious about the welfare of my disciples, so that I am taking steps to rectify the unfortunate situation. . . . [C]hildren should not be beaten at all, that I have told. They should simply be shown the stick strongly. So if one cannot manage in that way then he is not fit as a teacher. . . . [H]e must have two things, love and education. So if there is beating of child, that will be difficult for him to accept in loving spirit, and when he is old enough he may want to go away— that is the danger. (1992:793)

Yet physical punishment and various forms of abuse only escalated in the following years. Some former gurukula students believe that Prabhupada "did not implement appropriate measures to guarantee the safety of children in his movement from his disciples. [And] that the programs he established and interpretations of his words greatly fostered an environment under which child abuse flourished" (Hickey et al. 1997).

10. The lack of a decisive response by the authorities to allegations of abuse also is typical of some other religious organizations. The noted author, sociologist, and Catholic priest Andrew Greeley wrote the following in the forward to

Jason Berry's book *Lead Us Not into Temptation: Catholic Priests and the Sexual Abuse of Children*: "Bishops have with what seems like programmed consistency tried to hide, cover up, bribe, stonewall; often they have sent back into parishes men whom they knew to be a danger to the faithful. . . . Catholicism will survive, but that will be, despite the present leadership and not because of them" (1992:xii–xiv). Also see Staff of the Boston Globe, 2002.

11. This raises another issue about parental involvement. Many children who attended the gurukula did not have close relationships with their parents, which may have dissuaded some from telling their parents about the neglect and abuse in the gurukula, including their own abuse.

12. In one instance, parents sending their child to the Vrndavana gurukula developed a strategy to circumvent the monitoring system. Responding to rumors about child abuse and the censuring of student mail by the administration, the parents and child developed a code that would sound the alarm if harmful things were occurring. In a letter to his parents, the student would request that pizza be sent to him through the mail. This served as a request for the child to be removed from the school.

13. A fourth factor warrants a brief comment, which is a selective understanding of Prabhupada's views on disciplining children held by some teachers and others working in the gurukula. Simply put, some teachers felt that corporal punishment was fully sanctioned by Prabhupada as a means to deal with unruly children. Some evidence appears to support such a conclusion, but a close inspection of Prabhupada's ideas about child discipline suggests that overall he was not in favor of physical punishment. It is worth noting, however, that Prabhupada's letters and conversations, now widely available from ISKCON's Bhaktivedanta Book Trust, were not widely available during this period. Most members of ISKCON, including gurukula teachers, had limited and certainly incomplete information concerning Prabhupada's views on child discipline and other issues.

14. I am aware of one influential ISKCON member whose son was sexually molested.

15. In 1990, ISKCON's GBC passed resolution 119, which established a system for investigating, reporting, and preventing incidents of child abuse throughout the movement. At an influential meeting of former gurukula students, leaders, and community members in ISKCON's northern Florida community in 1996, former students spoke about their often traumatic experiences growing up in ISKCON's schools. This emotional meeting led to the formation of Children of Krishna, an organization that helps former gurukula students with educational and vocational needs, as well as therapy for mental health issues. In 1998, the GBC ratified the report of the ISKCON Child Protection Task Force, which established a central office to coordinate child protection within ISKCON. The nonprofit organization incorporated in Florida is known as either the Association

for the Protection of Children (APC) or the Association for the Protection of Vaishnava Children (APVC) (Das, Dhira Govinda 2004:1).

16. Not surprisingly, the lawsuit resulted in considerable anguish and debate within the movement. Many devotees both inside and outside ISKCON expressed anger at ISKCON's leaders, who were viewed as ultimately responsible for the abuse. Others directed their anger at the plaintiffs and other former gurukula students supporting the Turley lawsuit. Yet the most vocal and angry responses were provoked because the original complaint filed in 2000 in the U.S. district court directly implicated ISKCON's founder, Srila Prabhupada, in the abuse. The complaint stated:

> The founder of the institution, Prabhupada, was informed in 1972, at a time when he totally controlled the institution, that extensive physical and sexual abuse of minor ISKCON children was occurring, but he concealed the wrongdoing from the public, parents and all but a handful of chosen advisers. (2000:15)

Although most existing and former ISKCON devotees were willing to acknowledge the abuse that occurred, few could accept the idea that Prabhupada had any knowledge of the abuse or had helped cover it up. Although Prabhupada was aware of some physical punishment being administered to children in the gurukula, I have found no evidence that he knew of the sexual abuse. The fact that the case never made its way into open court dissipated what otherwise promised to be an explosive situation.

NOTES TO CHAPTER 4

1. The historical record amply demonstrates how religious communities have met with varying degrees of success in their efforts to retain the young into adulthood. On the Shaker's adopted children, see Bainbridge 1982 and Foster 1991; on Amana, see Barthel 1984; on the Amish, see Kraybill 2001; and on Oneida, see Carden 1969 and Mandelker 1984.

2. I should emphasize that the public high school negotiations reported here apply to only a very specific time period in ISKCON's history. Today, most devotee young people attend public elementary and secondary schools and generally have more extensive involvement in the dominant culture than did those ISKCON youths who transferred from the ashram-gurukula into public education during the 1980s.

3. The literature on religious conversion has focused on the interrelationship among interaction, identity, and changing consciousness, and empirical studies have identified social interaction and affective social bonds as keys to the conversion process (Lofland and Stark 1965; Snow and Phillips 1980). Snow and Phillips concluded "that conversion in general is highly improbable in the absence of affective and intensive interaction" (1980:444). Conversion thus takes

place when a person comes to believe what one's friends believe (Lofland and Stark 1965). Social ties play a role in the conversion process in yet another way. Conversion is more likely if the ties to persons supporting one's previous identity and worldview are neutralized. Such attachments represent countervailing sources of commitment, capable of undermining the conversion process (Lofland and Stark 1965; Rochford 1985:79–83, 87–122). The need to counteract these out-group ties appears especially relevant to conversion to communally organized religious groups, especially those defined as "peculiar" or "threatening" (Snow and Phillips 1980:441–42).

4. Three-quarters (74%) of those surveyed were born in the movement, and the remainder accompanied one or both parents into the movement, most at an early age. All the respondents had previously attended one or more ISKCON schools or were doing so at the time of the survey. All but two at some point had attended an ashram-based gurukula. The average number of years attended was 6.7, with a range of 1 to 13 years. Unless otherwise indicated, quoted materials in the chapter are from the Second Generation Survey.

5. Researchers have found that the identity of women making the transition into college is strongly influenced by the "culture of romance" (see Holland and Eisenhart 1990; Silver 1996:12).

6. Each of the six young people in my Second Generation Survey who attended either a private or religious high school also took measures to avoid revealing their ISKCON identity. Attending school outside one's neighborhood appears to provide certain advantages for concealing an ISKCON identity. Peer relationships can be more easily avoided, given the distance students typically live from one another. Moreover, these relationships are also more readily subject to self-presentation strategies directed toward concealment. For example, one ISKCON mother whose daughter attended a Catholic high school told me that she held birthday parties and other social gatherings for her daughter at a park near the ISKCON community where she lived. By contrast, a local public school is a community institution, and hence interactions between classmates naturally spill over into the neighborhood. This fact makes concealment difficult to sustain over the long run for those who attended local public schools.

7. It appears that a limited number of ISKCON youths actively sought to become integrated into the outside culture upon entering the public high school. I found three cases in which ISKCON youths saw the public high school as a stepping-stone toward leaving ISKCON. One of two reasons were cited: the young person had experienced abuse—physical, psychological, or sexual—during his or her days in the gurukula, and/or one or both parents had defected from the movement or had otherwise been mistreated by ISKCON authorities.

8. One exception to this can be found in ISKCON communities located in rural locations where effectively managing an ISKCON identity becomes difficult, if not impossible. In one ISKCON farm community located in rural Pennsylvania,

for example, devotee youths entered the local public high school with the locals' full knowledge that they were Hare Krishnas. ISKCON students were routinely ostracized and found themselves at the bottom of the school social hierarchy. To the extent that they established friendships, they were with working-class youths, who themselves were situated at the lower rungs of the status system. ISKCON parents have painfully revealed how these young devotees often began drinking alcohol, taking drugs, and expressing a general resistance to learning. In short, they began to acquire the habits and attitudes of their newly acquired working-class friends.

9. By the early 1980s it was common for first-generation ISKCON members to wear conventional clothes when leaving the devotee community to work or run errands.

10. At the first gurukula alumni reunion I attended in Los Angeles in 1992, I was surprised to find so many of those present using Christian names. However, owing to a recent change in some young people's relationship to ISKCON, this trend has begun to reverse itself. At the gurukula reunion held at New Vrindaban in 1994, several young people told me that there was a trend away from using Christian names. Immediately before this discussion, a young man in his mid-twenties scolded a teenager who made the mistake of calling him by his Christian name. The symbolism here of reverting to devotional names is significant and speaks to one way that the gurukula reunions serve to revive the collective identity of some second-generation devotees.

11. Of the eighty-seven second-generation ISKCON youths surveyed, only seven indicated that they had ever consumed meat, and of these, only three regularly ate it.

12. Some male devotee youths did report hanging out together, but apparently only after their nondevotee classmates became aware of their ISKCON identity. Having been discredited, associating with other devotee students became a means of defending against the possibility of harassment and/or rejection by other students.

13. One other factor that facilitated the efforts of ISKCON youths to pass resulted from the process of commonsense classification itself. The task of categorization in everyday life normally does not involve an empirical test to determine whether a particular person actually fits the criteria for inclusion. Rather, the use of membership categories relies on an "if-can" test (see Sacks 1972). As West and Zimmerman explained, "This test stipulates that if people can be seen as members of relevant categories, then categorize them that way" (1987:133).

14. I excluded those still in high school to highlight how role transitions initiated during the high school years influenced subsequent identification with ISKCON and Krishna Consciousness. It should be obvious that influences beyond the public high school experience may have also been significant in shaping identification with ISKCON and Krishna Consciousness. Unfortunately, the

Second Generation Survey does not permit us to determine precisely the separate influence of high school and post–high school factors on collective identity.

NOTES TO CHAPTER 5

1. Knott (1995) argues that the acceptance of conventional attitudes favoring gender equality by scholars and movement insiders has unduly influenced assessments of women's lives in ISKCON. The use of such conventional criteria virtually ensures a critical conclusion and one that distorts ISKCON's purpose and mission. In resisting conventional gender roles, ISKCON is trying to draw a boundary between itself and the modern world. This and related challenges to dominant beliefs and lifestyles is what distinguishes ISKCON as a new religion (see Bromley 2004; Rochford 2007). My interest here is if and how activist women have drawn on conventional notions of "gender equality" in their efforts to promote social change.

2. Both men and women used a variety of interactional strategies to maximize their success at distributing Prabhupada's books and other products in public locations. Some of these practices were deceitful and highly controversial both inside and outside the movement (Rochford 1985:171–89), and the public controversy further rigidified ISKCON's public image as a deviant and threatening cult (Rochford 1985:186).

3. The author also noted that because of the degrading ways in which devotee women were seen and treated, intelligent women stopped joining ISKCON. Moreover, this mistreatment generated considerable "bad press" for the movement (Devi Dasi, Jyotirmayi 2002:4).

4. Survey data presented throughout the chapter do not include Asian Indians. I chose to exclude them because they were neither involved in nor directly affected by the issues discussed here. The influence of Indian Hindus on ISKCON's evolving religious culture is discussed in chapter 8.

5. This statement produced a number of challenging responses on the Internet from women supporting a pro-change agenda. Note how in the following response "austerity" and the need "to submit to authority" are radically reinterpreted:

> I thought that not much could shock me anymore. . . . But this left me completely speechless and stunned. It is mind-blowing that someone even considered neglect and abuse as a means for spiritual advancement. . . . Please, I beg women in ISKCON to educate themselves in the differences between assisting someone in their spiritual life, and being a victim of emotional, spiritual, [and] physical abuse. (Dasi, Subhadra-Mayi 2004:1)

As discussed later in the chapter, pro-change women actively tried to educate other women in an attempt to facilitate the interpretive shift apparent in the preceding woman's comments.

6. Opponents have disputed the significance of these accounts depicting Prabhupada's interactions with his earliest female disciples. None of these early interactions was tape-recorded, and thus they rely on the memories of the women involved. This stands in stark contrast to later years when virtually all of Prabhupada's lectures and personal conversations were tape-recorded and thus preserved. Some critics also have noted that during ISKCON's early days, Prabhupada only gradually introduced the rules and regulations of Krishna Consciousness to his followers. As one critic commented, "Srila Prabhupada was never more lenient than he was in the 60s and early 70s" (Devi Dasi, Sita 2002:1). Although there is truth in this statement (see Goswami, Satsvarupa Dasa 1980; Rochford 1985:155–56), it also is true that these anecdotal accounts were convincing to many women who sided with pro-change activists.

7. But the last sentence of this letter reads, "Of course women, generally speaking are less intelligent, better she has heard nicely then she will speak nicely" (Prabhupada 1992:2585). This line was omitted when Jyotirmayi Devi Dasi (2002:9) quoted the letter in her influential paper outlining the history of women during Prabhupada's times. Such an omission means little to my argument here, as I am concerned with the discourse of dissent rather than with the accuracy of that discourse. Obviously, for ISKCON members opposed to the pro-change agenda, such an omission has very different connotations.

8. I should emphasize that devotee women have always been a vital source of labor in ISKCON's communities. In addition to distributing Prabhupada's books and preaching in public, they have contributed in significant ways to the day-to-day functioning of temple communities. The difference now is that women are being called on to perform those tasks traditionally allocated to men. Such a pattern parallels those of conventional denominations that have granted women ordination because of shortages of male clergy (Chaves 1997; Nesbitt 1997).

9. Immediately following the GBC meetings, many felt it would be a gesture of goodwill to allow a woman for the first time to give Srimad-Bhagavatam class in the temple in Mayapura, India, where the GBC meetings were being held. But the temple authorities strongly opposed the idea, arguing that this was against local custom and would negatively influence the local people's views of ISKCON. After a heated debate, the temple authorities relented and a senior woman was allowed to give the class. Such a response points to the ways that gender equality has remained a contentious issue despite reform, the topic of the next chapter.

NOTES TO CHAPTER 6

1. Ardhabuddhi Dasa is the fictitious name used by the person who leaked the correspondence between members of the GHQ to the larger devotee commu-

nity. In Sanskrit, "Ardhabuddhi" means "half-wit" or "half-brain." This name was chosen specifically because GHQ members portrayed women as less intelligent than men. Much of the information presented in this chapter is from the leaked e-mail correspondence published on the website "Vaisnava News Network" (VNN) on November 18, 1998, under the title "Conspiracy to Terminate the ISKCON Women's Ministry." Unless otherwise indicated, quotations appearing in the chapter are from the leaked GHQ correspondence published on VNN. Other sources of information were derived from subsequent letters and essays written by supporters and opponents of the GHQ published by VNN and other ISKCON-affiliated websites. The latter includes anonymous discussion groups and forums, from which material is quoted here without specific citation, as the groups no longer exist on the Internet.

2. Those who accept "mayavada" philosophy are considered "impersonalists" because they believe that God is formless rather than being a person. Prabhupada and his followers portray mayavadins as foolish and ignorant. For a discussion of Prabhupada's treatment of mayavadins in his writings, see Lorenz 2004:117–21.

3. As discussed in chapter 5, pro-change activists uniformly rejected the "feminist" label. In response to this rejection, one GHQ member stated, "Now for those who object to the term feminist, I ask one question: What exactly is the difference between the occupational freedom and independence demanded by some members in ISKCON and the non-devotee feminist platform of occupational equal rights? I have come to the conclusion that there is none" (Dasa, Jivan Mukta 1998:3).

4. *Apasiddhanta* means a false philosophical conclusion, and *apa* means deviant.

5. Knott (2004:297–301) identifies three distinct meanings of dharma: Vedic, Hindu, and Krishna conscious. GHQ's understanding and use of dharma conforms most closely to the traditional "Vedic" way of life. In Vedic varnashram-dharma, men serve God through their spiritual master, and women, through the men who protect them—serve their fathers, husbands, and sons. Under such a system the husband serves as the wife's spiritual master. The "Hindu" system of varnashram-dharma also is historically situated but in the present age of *kali yuga*. In this age of material gratification, oppression becomes commonplace as represented by the caste system. Women still are required to serve, but instead of receiving spiritual guidance and protection in return, men tend to exploit them. This view of dharma recognizes that in the current age, men and women cannot readily conform to Vedic ideals. The "Krishna conscious" view of dharma also recognizes the sheer difficulty, if not impossibility, of realizing Vedic ideals in the contemporary era. Both sexes thus use the Vedic system as a model for establishing varnashram-dharma. Men and

women take initiation from a guru, marry, and although women are responsible for bearing and raising children and men for supporting them, both are expected to serve Krishna through their respective spiritual masters. Women are not required to fully submit to their husband's authority, but instead both husband and wife seek to serve their guru and Krishna as their first priority. In the Vedic period, a woman rendered service to her husband; in the present age service is rendered to God through the spiritual master.

6. Chaves (1997:50–53) argues that denominations granting women ordination do so in part to appease external audiences for whom gender equality represents a highly valued social norm.

7. Several days after this message was posted, one member suggested that the group stop using words like feminazi, and other "slighting words," "lest they slip out and further outrage the hot-tempered *purvakshins*"(term used to characterize opponents favoring feminism, and male-female equality) (September 29, 1998, GHQ Conference).

8. The Manusamhita is said to be the work of Manu, the progenitor of humankind and a lawgiver. The work is controversial because of its misogynistic statements, and many scholars reject the text as an accurate portrayal of Vedic culture (Goswami, Hrdayananda Dasa, personal communication, 2005).

9. Lorenz (2004:122) found that 9 percent of Prabhupada's statements about women in the Bhagavad Gita and in five selected volumes of his Srimad Bhagavatam (i.e., Bhagavata Purana) emphasized the need to place restrictions on women to avoid giving them freedom. Moreover, 56 percent of Prabhupada's statements focused on women as sex objects. Lorenz notes further that Prabhupada's "negative" statements about women are largely inconsistent with the scriptural commentaries of other interpreters of these texts.

10. Such dismissive rhetoric regarding pro-change women is hardly limited to ISKCON. A representative of the Roman Catholic Church had the following to say about women activists pushing for ordination in the church: "'Some of these women are well intentioned, but the bulk of them are power-hungry witches,' says a Vatican functionary. They have no concern for the church and for souls" (Labi 1998:8).

11. Several GHQ members noted that ISKCON leaders had failed to follow their own rules when they appointed a woman to be the GBC representative and the women's minister. They claimed that GBC rules mandate that any person appointed to positions of ISKCON leadership "should have no record of moral turpitude" (Swami, Bhakti Vikasa 1998).

12. Ravindra Svarupa Das also pointed to the child abuse legal case in Dallas as another example of Prabhupada's being on trial on charges that he both knew about the abuse and failed to intervene.

13. Other issues discussed by the group included statements by Prabhupada

that women are nine times lustier than men and that increased sexual activity by men lessens their potency, leaving them unable to conceive boys. The later is the basis for Prabhupada's statement that "the whole world is increasing woman population" (quoted in Dasa, Jivan Mukta 1999a).

14. Two women were admonished by their gurus for their role in the challenge to Prabhupada's writings and authority (COM 2000a; Dasi, Dhyana-Kunda 1999). In one case, apologies were made, and the woman in question sought forgiveness from her guru (COM 2000a). Yet there is no evidence that public apologies were made for the challenge to Prabhupada's teachings and authority, a fact that added fuel to the GHQ's virulent tone. In fairness, Dhyana-Kunda Dasi did address publicly those offended by her remarks by stating, "For many devotees Prabhupada is the dearmost person and even more than that. And yet I 'analyzed' him in the same way I would analyze any other human being. I tried my best to make it clear that my statements are subjective, that it is me who has a problem. I didn't try hard enough. I am sorry for *that*" (my emphasis; Dasi, Dhyana-Kunda 1999:2).

15. Ameyatma Das's (2000) editorial "The Fire of Sati" also demanded that "GBC men" who failed to respond should step down from their positions or otherwise be removed. One GBC representative from India did resign, but for somewhat different reasons: "I don't know Ameyatma Prabhu personally. Nevertheless, I hear his voice as the echo of the helpless cry of many sincere followers of Srila Prabhupada. I feel extremely regretful about my inability to do anything to defend Srila Prabhupada's honor and protect his ISKCON. Therefore, I hear by [sic] submit my resignation from the GBC as one of its members" (COM 2000b).

16. The GHQ's website (http://www.qhqd.org) disappeared from the Internet in the aftermath of the 2005 GBC meetings.

NOTES TO CHAPTER 7

1. In the years following Prabhupada's death, gurus dominated the GBC's membership. In 2000, 83 percent of ISKCON's GBC members were initiating gurus. Moreover, two-thirds (66%) were sannyasis, and three-quarters either had never been married or had no children (Das, Kalakantha 2000). Given the GBC's membership profile, emerging guru controversies had direct implications for the GBC's authority as well as for the guru institution.

2. Satsvarupa Dasa Goswami still is an ISKCON guru, but as of 2005, he was not initiating new disciples.

3. The sample of former ISKCON members is weighted toward those who remained in the devotee networks, either inside or outside ISKCON. This is because the Centennial Survey questionnaires were distributed through devotee networks. Although considerable effort was made to include a wide range of

former members, it is clear that those who were no longer involved in devotee relationships were unlikely to participate in the Centennial Survey.

4. Questions relating to the gurus were asked only of respondents initiated by Prabhupada or one of his successors, which accounts for the smaller number of congregational members for the "authority of the gurus" dimension in table A.2.

5. Regression analyses, including a range of factors posited as influencing ISKCON commitment (gender, having children, year joined ISKCON, commitment to Krishna Consciousness, involvement in devotee relationships, views of the leadership), found that by far the strongest influence on former members' commitment was the authority attributed to the GBC. Those holding critical views of the GBC were far less committed to ISKCON. Former members who placed less emphasis on devotee relationships also were less committed to ISKCON. Among full-time and congregational members, ISKCON commitment was most strongly influenced by involvement in devotee relationships, the authority placed in the GBC, and commitment to Krishna Consciousness (Rochford 1998a).

6. In my book *Hare Krishna in America,* I refer to Sridara as "Maharaja Swami" and to Jayatirtha as "Foreign guru."

7. Following a series of meetings between representatives of ISKCON and Sridara Maharaja in 2001 and 2002, the GBC approved a resolution that stated in part, "Resolved, That the impression that may exist in some circles that the GBC Body regards Shripad B. R. Shridara Maharaja as responsible for ISKCON's accepting the zonal-acharya system is erroneous" (quoted in Vishnu, Swami B. B. 2004:186–87).

8. The letter was signed and presumably written by Prabhupada's personal secretary, Tamala Krsna Goswami. At the bottom of the letter is the note: "Approved: A. C. Bhaktivedanta Swami" (Desai et al. 2004:195).

9. Twenty-five percent of ISKCON's full-time members also agreed that Prabhupada wanted the eleven ritviks to remain in that capacity following his death.

10. Most devotees seek Prabhupada's guidance and inspiration by reading his books, listening to his lectures, and praying and worshiping. On this basis, Prabhupada remains "alive" to his disciples and followers.

11. As leaders of the Bangalore temple began offering Prabhupada initiation, they reconsidered the prevailing "ritvik" terminology. As one stated, "It is a term that has been badly used and mislabeled. We should say rather than we are using Prabhupada's system of initiation. It is Prabhupada's ISKCON, and we are going to use Prabhupada's system of initiation. Drop the terminology of ritvik because it is a political trap" (interview 2006).

12. Unlike New Raman-reti, Prabhupada's Village, Three Rivers, and Saranagati are not official ISKCON communities.

13. In December 2005, except for the community's spiritual leader, none of the residents of ISKCON's Atlanta temple was American born. Of the ten full-

time residents, most were from South America; two were from India; and one was from England.

NOTES TO CHAPTER 8

1. Patrons support religious organizations, but their participation is less visible and regular. Their involvement is limited to occasional meetings and services and the provision of moral and material assistance. Patrons do not take positions of organizational responsibility, nor are they subject to the authority of leaders. They are more likely to show up on mailing lists than to be involved in personal relationships with other categories of members (Beckford 1985:83–84). Given their limited roles, patrons generally are not considered "members" by more committed and involved participants. Acknowledging their patron status, devotees typically refer to the Hindus who visit ISKCON temples as "guests." Such a characterization raises questions about the extent to which the majority of ISKCON's Indian-Hindu supporters can reasonably be considered congregational members.

2. There are exceptions, however. The movement's largest community in the United States, located in northern Florida, has relatively few Indian Hindus who attend temple activities on Sunday or on other occasions.

3. Prabhupada's views of Hinduism and the role of Indian-Hindu immigrants in his movement are far from consistent. For a discussion of Prabhupada's views of Hinduism and whether ISKCON should be considered a Hindu religious movement, see Brzezinski 1998.

4. By quietly rescinding the Oriental Exclusion Act to allow Hong Kong refugees to enter the United States, President Johnson permitted Asian immigration quotas to rise to those for western Europe (Melton 1987:52). Between 1951 and 1960, only 1,973 Indians immigrated to the United States, but that number grew considerably to 27,189 between 1961 and 1970, to 164,134 between 1971 and 1980, and to 250,786 between 1981 and 1990 (Yearbook of Immigration Statistics 2004). In 2000 the Indian population in the United States was more than 1.6 million, double the 1990 population (U.S. Bureau of the Census 2000). Although there are no figures detailing the percentage of Indian immigrants belonging to various religions, indirect evidence suggests that Hindus are underrepresented in comparison to Sikh and Christian immigrants (Kurien 2002:101). One estimate suggests that about 65 percent of the Indian immigrants in the United States are from Hindu backgrounds (Fenton 1988:28), even though Hindus represent more than 80 percent of the population in India (Kurien 2002:101).

5. The "continuous journey" legislation of 1908 allowed Canada's federal government to effectively ban South Asian immigration. South Asians seeking

immigration to Canada were required to have a "continuous" ticket from their country of origin. But no shipping companies covered the entire route from South Asia to Canada, and thus the purchase of a continuous ticket was impossible (Coward 2000:152).

6. Vande Berg and Kniss (2005) provide an example of how this continues in a different form in the Chicago ISKCON temple. ISKCON devotees favoring the more up-scale professional Indians from the suburbs typically overlooked working-class Indians from the surrounding neighborhood who came to the temple. Being slighted in this manner, the "Devon Avenue Indians" generally ignored both Western devotees and the suburban Indians.

7. Although we don't know exactly how many Indian Hindus in North America have been initiated by an ISKCON guru, a 1993 estimate placed the number at approximately five hundred (Zaidman 1997:337).

8. Initial efforts by the foundation to gain the support of Indian Hindus met with some resistance, however. In completing a feasibility study that used interviews with one hundred prominent Indian-Hindu supporters, it became clear that many were estranged from ISKCON because of the movement's leadership problems, ISKCON's poor public image, and ongoing concerns about how their financial contributions were being used.

9. Knott (1987) discusses negotiations among Gujaratis, Punjabis, and Hindus from other Indian states who joined together to establish a temple in Leeds, England. The small size of the Indian population in Leeds brought together Hindus from varying linguistic and cultural backgrounds. The diversity in ethnic and caste divisions, as well as religious orientations, led to a process of "standardization" by which certain beliefs and practices gained prominence while others were neglected for the sake of unity. As Knott concluded, "This process, commensurate as it is with the gradual erosion of ethnically related religious and cultural interests, is the price of its [Hinduism's] survival as a socially meaningful tradition in a new location" (1987:179). Also see Kurien 1998.

10. Kurien (1998) contends that the sectarianism emerging among Hindus in the United States is of two kinds. In major metropolitan areas where there are substantial numbers of Indian Hindus from a particular region in India, it is not uncommon for sectarian groups and temples to form. This may even include different groups forming around separate castes (1998:45). In locations where the Indian-Hindu population is diverse, "sectarianism" is based largely on language and subcultural differences (1998:55).

11. Appendix 1 lists the questionnaire items for each of the summary measures in table A.3. Among the Indian Hindus surveyed, a quarter (23%) indicated that they were full-time ISKCON members, half (49%) life members or congregational members, and a quarter (25%) non-ISKCON members. Four percent were former ISKCON members. One-fourth (28%) were initiated disciples

of Prabhupada or one of ISKCON's successor gurus, a percentage substantially higher than for the overall population of Indian Hindus affiliated with ISKCON. Because the Centennial questionnaires were distributed within ISKCON's communities, the Indian Hindus most active in ISKCON were more likely to be targeted.

12. Many Hindus maintain small altars in their homes where they worship deities that may or may not be found in ISKCON temples.

13. Only those who were initiated disciples responded to the questions relating to the authority of the gurus, which accounts for the smaller number of cases reported in table A.3.

14. The phenomenon of parallel congregations having separate religious and social agendas also has been noted for American converts and Asian immigrants practicing Theravada Buddhism in Chicago and Los Angeles. Numrich (1996:72–75) found marked differences between adult Asian immigrants and American converts with respect to religious behavior and attitude. Although the two congregations intersected at times, interaction between them was minimal (Numrich 1996:76).

15. Members of the Indian congregation did, however, consider the temple president to be a brahmin, as he is a highly respected ISKCON guru and GBC representative with a Ph.D. in religion. Given these qualifications, the Indians in the congregation accepted his authority and right to interpret and rule on religious issues (Zaidman 1997:344).

16. As suggested in chapter 7, most ISKCON temples rely on devotees from India and other developing countries to serve as pujaris and to meet other temple needs.

17. Vande Berg and Kniss (2005) demonstrated that a major part of the religious training that leads some Indian immigrants to become ISKCON *devotees* is coming to accept Krishna as supreme and superior to other Hindu gods. Given the religious backgrounds of most Hindus immigrating to America, this represents a significant transformation in belief and one that most are unwilling to make.

18. Because the Gaudiya Vaisnava tradition is monotheistic, all the expansions of the lord such as Balarama, Krishna's brother, are considered forms or incarnations of Krishna. Nityananda is considered Balarama and thus ontologically identical with Lord Caitanya (Goswami, Hrdayananda Dasa, personal communication 2005).

19. Among other things, Holi involves the throwing of dry colors on people celebrating the occasion. It should be noted that this festival, like others at the Spanish Fork temple, attracts interested college students and Mormons from the surrounding community, in addition to Indian Hindus.

20. In 2000, there were more than four hundred Hindu temples in the United States (Eck 2000:222), many located in urban areas where ISKCON has temples. Canada also has a substantial number of Hindu temples. In Ontario

alone, there were fifty Hindu temples and organizations in the early 1990s, the majority of which were in the Toronto area (Coward 2000:156).

21. Hinduization appears to be occurring in the United Kingdom in a fashion that mirrors changes in North America, as can be seen in the following comments:

> It is undoubtedly a worrying trend in the UK and elsewhere to jump on the Hindu bandwagon. . . . [D]ue to the vast financial input of the Hindu community ISKCON's core values are watered down and are in danger of getting lost altogether. In not more than one generation much will have disappeared. Money obliges, especially if it is coming repeatedly from the same source. Srila Prabhupada wanted the help of the Indian community no doubt but he didn't want the preaching to the Westerners [to] stagnate or [be] directed entirely towards the Hindus. . . . There is no immediate need any more to distribute books as the temples are secure because of donations from the Hindu community. . . . Hardly any [Western] devotees are being made either. (Patel 2006)

NOTES TO CHAPTER 9

1. Stark (1987, 1996) defines success in terms of power and influence, so new religions are deemed successful to the extent that they "dominate one or more societies" (Stark 1987:12). But this definition rules out nearly all new religions that have arisen historically, a fact that weakens the empirical usefulness of Stark's model of success and failure. Kanter (1968:502) offers a more realistic definition suggesting that utopian communities—secular or religious—are successful if survive a generation, or twenty-five years. Having celebrated its fortieth anniversary in 2006, ISKCON has been successful on the basis of longevity. Yet as we have seen throughout this book, it has undergone profound changes in its goals and identity as a religious movement.

2. Sectarian religions occupy a middle ground between dominant and new religions in that they reject the legitimacy and authority of the traditional churches yet have widely varying degrees of alignment with society's institutions and cultural patterns (Bromley 2004:92–93). For a comparative discussion of cults, sects, and new religions, see Rochford 2007.

3. As one devotee commented, "I think the spark is still there that brought 80 percent of the devotees into the movement. It is just a matter of what they can realistically do with that spark in their life at this time. If they are not in a position to act on those past motivations, why ask them to do so?"

4. The corresponding percentages for those working in ISKCON or devotee work settings are smaller but still substantial. Forty percent agreed that they identify with many of the values and lifestyles of the outside society, as well as those of Krishna Consciousness. Forty-two percent agreed that they have

increasingly accommodated to the routines and lifestyles of the conventional society. These findings point to the ways that American society has generally pen-
etrated the lives of ISKCON's membership.

5. It is worth noting that organizationally, ISKCON has tried to alter its public definition in order to gain greater legitimacy in American society. The head
of ISKCON's North American Office of Communications actively sought to increase public acceptance through interfaith work, talking with members of
other religious traditions, and working with scholars of religion, journalists,
and anticult groups. The pursuit of organizational legitimacy has brought about
greater accommodation between ISKCON and the mainstream culture.

6. I have spent countless hours over the years listening to devotees complain
bitterly about the failings of the leadership. Such discourse helped forge a culture of dissent that in time led to collective efforts to rework the movement's
traditional culture.

7. The Kulimela festival held at New Vrindaban in June 2006 attracted as
many as seven hundred first- and second-generation devotees. A reported 450
former gurukula students attended, and another one hundred young people
aged eighteen or younger also participated.

8. One program that the leadership did sponsor was a movementwide dispute resolution program introduced in 2002. The GBC approved and provided
funding for the program (Zack 2002:5–6). Under the leadership of an outside
authority on mediation, training courses were held in the United States, Europe,
and India, resulting in the certification of seventy devotee mediators. In the program's first year, nearly one hundred cases were mediated (Zack 2002:6). By all
accounts the program has been a success. The GBC has itself used devotee mediators to resolve differences among its members (Zack 2002:11).

9. During ISKCON's early years, devotees believed that personal problems
had spiritual origins and related solutions. By rededicating themselves to the
cause of book distribution and/or performing individual *sadhana* (a religious
practice such as chanting), they could resolve their personal troubles. Professional counseling was discouraged. So when devotees began to seek counseling
during the 1980s and 1990s, a controversy emerged when some devotees
claimed that nondevotee counselors were sources of harm because they did not
understand Krishna Consciousness. Such debate has subsided in recent years because of the widespread availability of professionally trained devotee therapists.

10. "Grihastha" is an alternative spelling for "grhastha."

11. The ongoing effort to create resources to serve the varied needs of the
devotee community has by no means replaced outside sources of aid. In cases of
domestic violence, child abuse, and other specialized needs, outside professionals are routinely turned to for assistance. One example is that some members of
ISKCON's New Raman-reti community have taken parenting classes offered at a
nearby Baptist church.

12. I am inclined to accept Robbins's (2005:108) view that "new" should be applied to groups that are chronologically new, regardless of their pattern of development. He argues against Bromley's implicit argument that new religious movements that move toward alignment with conventional institutions and cultural patterns cease to exist as new religions. I would hasten to add, however, that these groups no longer represent movements but, instead, new religious organizations or communities.

Glossary

acarya: guru and head of a religious institution

apa: deviant

apasiddhanta: a false philosophical conclusion

arti (arati): ritual performed as part of deity worship

ashram (asrama): place of residence or one of four stages of life in traditional Hinduism (student, householder, retired, and renounced)

ashram-based gurukula: Krishna boarding school

Back to Godhead: magazine started by ISKCON's founder in India and continues to be published and distributed worldwide

Bhagavad Gita: philosophical treatise forming an episode of the Hindu epic, the Mahabharata, in which Krishna introduces *bhakti-yoga,* or salvation through surrender to Krishna

Bhagavata Purana: see Srimad Bhagavatam

bhakta: a devotee who practices bhakti-yoga

bhakti-yoga: a devotional form of Hinduism practiced by ISKCON members

brahmacari: unmarried celibate male student

brahmacarini: unmarried celibate female student

brahmin (brahmana): intellectual or priestly class in the Vedic system of varnas

brahmin initiation: second initiation

chapatis: round thin wheat tortilla

darshan (darsana): visual contemplation of the deity

dasa (das): male servant

dasi: female servant

dharma: duty of rendering service to God (Krishna)

dhoti: strip of cloth worn by men on the lower portion of the body

diksa initiation: first initiation

disciple: one who has taken initiation from a guru

Durga: a Hindu goddess

fringie: less committed ISKCON member who is considered materialistic

Gaudiya Math: institution of Bengali Vaisnavism founded in 1915 by Bhaktisiddanta Saraswati, the guru of ISKCON's founder Bhaktivedanta Swami Prabhupada

GBC: Governing Body Commission

GHQ: General Headquarters

Godbrother: male devotee who shares the same guru

Godsister: female devotee who shares the same guru

grhastha (grhasta): a married devotee with or without children

grhastha ashram: one of the four stages of life; married people or householders

guru: a spiritual teacher or guide who initiates disciples in the tradition's teachings and practices

gurukula: school established by a guru

gurukuli: student who attended an ISKCON gurukula

Hare Krishna (Hare Krsna): the first two words of the mahamantra for which ISKCON has come to be known

Hare Krishna movement: also known as the International Society for Krishna Consciousness (ISKCON)

Hare Nam: public chanting

harinama-diksa: first initiation

householder: married devotee with or without children

IRM: ISKCON Revival Movement

Janmastami: Krishna's birthday

japa: chanting of the Hare Krishna mantra on prayer beads for personal spiritual benefit

karatals: small hand cymbals

karma: the effect of one's actions, good or bad, that determine the place and condition in which one is reborn

karmies: materially minded nondevotees

Kartika: a major Hindu festival

kirtans (kirtanas): congregational singing and chanting, usually with musical accompaniment

ksatriya: a warrior or administrator in the Vedic social system of varnas

life member: patron member of ISKCON who contributes funds

Mahabharata: Hindu epic and a basis for much of India's popular religion

mahamantra: the Hare Krishna mantra and core religious practice of

ISKCON members: Hare Krishna Hare Krishna, Krishna Krishna, Hare Hare, Hare Rama Hare Rama, Rama Rama, Hare Hare

mangal arati(arti): early-morning ritual honoring the deities performed in the temple or at home

mantra: a word or group of words, such as Hare Krishna, considered to have transcendental power

Manusamhita: said to be the work of Manu, the progenitor of humankind and a lawgiver, controversial because of its misogynistic statements

mata: mother

maya: illusion or material energy that results from forgetting one's relationship with Krishna

mayavada (mayavadins): impersonalist philosophy that maintains there is no difference between God and other living beings

mrdanga: a traditional two-headed Indian drum used in kirtans

New Raman-reti: ISKCON (Alachua) community in northern Florida

New Vrindaban: ISKCON community in West Virginia

prasadam: vegetarian food sanctified by being offered to Krishna

puja: ritual worship of the deity

pujaris: temple priests who serve the deities

Ramayana: one of two great Hindu epics, concerns the deeds of Rama

Rathayatra: a festival in which temple deities are paraded in the streets on a cart

ritvik-guru: ceremonial priest

Ritvik movement: followers believe that Prabhupada remains ISKCON's initiating guru after his death and that his guru successors initiate on his behalf in their role as rivik-gurus

sadhana-bhakti (sadhana): disciplined spiritual practice

sadhu: a holy or saintly person

salagrama: a smooth round black stone regarded as an image of worship

sampradaya: religious tradition

samsara: the repeated cycle of birth and death

sankirtan: preaching, chanting in public, and book distribution

sannyasi: one who has totally renounced society and its material attachments

Sanskrit: an Indo-European classical language of India and a liturgical language of Hinduism, Buddhism, and Jainism

Saranagati: Non-ISKCON devotee community in British Columbia, Canada

sari: women's garment consisting of cloth draped to form a skirt and a head or shoulder covering

sastra (shastra): sacred teaching or scripture

sastric: scriptural source

shika: a tuft of hair on the back of an otherwise shaved head

Shiva (Siva): creator and destroyer deity

siksa guru: instructing guru

slokas: verses from the scripture

Srimad Bhagavatam: composed by Vyasadeva and considered by most Vaisnavas as their primary scriptural source

sudra: skilled/unskilled laborers in the Vedic social system of varnas

Swamiji: a name for Prabhupada used by his earliest followers

Tulasi: a plant considered sacred

Vaisnava: a worshipper of Visnu (Krishna)

vaisyas: a merchant or farmer class in the Vedic social system of varnas

varna: social/occupational classes in traditional Indian society (Brahman, ksatriya, vaisya, and sudra)

varnashram: the Vedic social system, composed of occupations (varnas) and four stages of life (ashrams)

VAST: Vaisnava Advanced Studies

VNN: Vaisnava News Network, an Internet website

zonal acarya system: a system that emerged after Prabhupada's death that gave new ISKCON gurus spiritual and political authority over individual zones or territory

References

Aidala, Angela. 1985. "Social Change, Gender Roles, and New Religious Movements." *Sociological Analysis* 46:287–314.

Amsterdam, Peter. 2004. "The Family—Restructuring and Renewal: An Overview of Organizational Changes—1994–2006." Paper presented at the CESNUR International Conference, Waco, Tex.

Anonymous. 1998. "The GHQ Conspiracy."

Anonymous a. 1996. Letter. VOICE website, December 28 (no longer operating).

Anonymous b. 1996. Letter. VOICE website, December 28 (no longer operating).

Avantika. 2004. "Comments: Fallout from Satsvarupa Maharaja Falldown." *Hare Krishna Cultural Journal,* May 27. Available at http://siddhanta.com/cgi-bin/comment_gate.cgi?entry_id=24.

Back to Prabhupada. 2005a. "The Great Guru Hoax: Parts 1 and 2." *Back to Prabhupada: The Magazine of the Real Hare Krishna Movement,* special summary issue.

Back to Prabhupada. 2005b. "IRM: The Respected Voice of Reform in ISKCON." *Back to Prabhupada: The Magazine of the Real Hare Krishna Movement,* special summary issue.

Back to Prabhupada. 2005c. "Proof 4—One Guru Falls = No Gurus Authorized." *Back to Prabhupada: The Magazine of the Real Hare Krishna Movement,* special summary issue.

Back to Prabhupada. 2005d. "Who Is Really Destroying ISKCON." *Back to Prabhupada: The Magazine of the Real Hare Krishna Movement,* no. 9 (autumn).

Bainbridge, William. 1982. "Shaker Demographics 1840–1900: An Example of the Use of U.S. Census Enumeration Schedules." *Journal for the Scientific Study of Religion* 21:352–65.

Balch, Robert, and Joanne Cohig. 1985. "The Magic Kingdom: A Story of Armageddon in Utopia." Paper presented at the annual meeting of the Society for the Scientific Study of Religion, Savannah, Ga.

Barker, Eileen. 1995. "The Unification Church." In *America's Alternative Religions,* edited by Timothy Miller, 223–29. Albany: State University of New York Press.

Barker, Eileen. 2004. "Perspective: What Are We Studying? A Sociological Case for Keeping the 'Nova.'" *Nova Religio* 8(1):88–102.

Barthel, Diane. 1984. *Amana: From Pietist Sect to American Community.* Lincoln: University of Nebraska Press.

Beck, Guy. 2004. "Hare Krishna Mahamantra: Gaudiya Vaishnava Practice and the Hindu Tradition of Sacred Sound." In *The Hare Krishna Movement: The Postcharismatic Fate of a Religious Transplant,* edited by Edwin Bryant and Maria Ekstrand, 35–44. New York: Columbia University Press.

Beckford, James. 1985. *Cult Controversies: The Societal Response to the New Religious Movements.* London: Tavistock.

Becker, Howard. 1963. *Outsiders.* New York: Free Press.

Berger, Bennett. 1981. *The Survival of the Counterculture.* Berkeley: University of California Press.

Berger, Peter. 1969. *The Sacred Canopy: Elements of a Sociological Theory of Religion.* New York: Anchor Books.

Berger, Peter, and Thomas Luckmann. 1967. *The Social Construction of Reality.* New York: Anchor Books.

Blumer, Herbert. 1951. "Collective Behavior." In *Principles of Sociology,* edited by A. M. Lee, 166–222. New York: Barnes & Noble.

Bromley, David. 1988. *Falling from the Faith: Causes and Consequences of Religious Apostasy.* Newbury Park, Calif.: Sage.

———. 1989. "Hare Krishna and the Anti-Cult Movement." In *Krishna Consciousness in the West,* edited by David Bromley and Larry Shinn, 255–92. Lewisberg, Pa.: Bucknell University Press.

———. 1997. "Constructing Apocalypticism: Social and Cultural Elements of Radical Organization." In *Millennium, Messiah, and Mayhem,* edited by Thomas Robbins and Susan Palmer, 31–46. New York: Routledge.

———. 2004. "Whither New Religious Studies: Defining and Shaping a New Area of Study." *Nova Religio* 8(2):83–97.

Bromley, David, and Phillip Hammond. 1987. *The Future of New Religious Movements.* Macon, Ga.: Mercer University Press.

Brown, Phil, and Faith Ferguson. 1995. "'Making a Big Stink': Women's Work, Women's Relationships, and Toxic Waste Activism." *Gender and Society* 9(2):145–72.

Brzezinski, Jan. 1997. Letter. VOICE website, January 5 (no longer operating).

———. 1998. "What Was Srila Prabhupada's Position: The Hare Krsna Movement and Hinduism." *ISKCON Communications Journal* 6(2):27–49.

Burghart, Richard. 1987. *Hinduism in Great Britain: The Perpetuation of Religion in an Alien Cultural Milieu.* London: Tavistock.

Burke, Peter, and Donald Reitzes. 1991. "An Identity Theory Approach to Commitment." *Social Psychology Quarterly* 54:239–51.

Cable, Sherry. 1992. "Women's Social Movement Involvement: The Role of

Structural Availability in Recruitment and Participation Processes." *Sociological Quarterly* 33:35–47.

Capps, Donald. 1992. "Religion and Child Abuse: Perfect Together." *Journal for the Scientific Study of Religion* 31(1):1–14.

Carden, Maren L. 1969. *Oneida: Utopian Community to Modern Corporation.* Baltimore: Johns Hopkins University Press.

Chancellor, James. 2000. *Life in the Family: An Oral History of the Children of God.* Syracuse, N.Y.: Syracuse University Press.

Chaves, Mark. 1993. "Intraorganizational Power and Internal Secularization in Protestant Denominations." *American Journal of Sociology* 99:1–48.

———. 1994. "Secularization as Declining Religious Authority." *Social Forces* 72(3):749–74.

———. 1997. *Ordaining Women: Culture and Conflict in Religious Organizations.* Cambridge, Mass.: Harvard University Press.

Children of ISKCON et al. vs. the International Society for Krishna Consciousness (ISKCON) et al. 2000. Filed in U.S. District Court, Dallas, June 12. Available at http://www.rickross.com/reference/krishna/complaint0606.pdf.

Children of ISKCON et al., vs. the International Society for Krishna Consciousness et al. 2001. Filed in Texas State Count, October. Available at http://www.wturley.com/homeframes/iskcon/petition.pdf.

Children of Krishna. 2006. Available at http://www.childrenofkrishna.com.

Cockburn, Cynthia. 1991. *In the Way of Women: Men's Resistance to Sex Equality in Organizations.* London: Industrial and Labor Relations Press.

Collins, Irvin. 2004. "The 'Routinization of Charisma' and the Charismatic." In *The Hare Krishna Movement: The Postcharismatic Fate of a Religious Transplant,* edited by Edwin Bryant and Maria Ekstrand, 214–37. New York: Columbia University Press.

COM. 2000a. "HH Bhakti Caru Swami Resigns from the GBC." Vaisnava News Network (VNN) website, February 4. Available at http://www.vnn.org/world/WD0002/WD04-5407.html.

COM. 2000b. "Ravindra Svarupa Steps on a Land Mine." Vaisnava News Network (VNN) website, February 17. Available at http://www.vnn.org/editorials/ET0002/ET17-5493.html.

Coser, Lewis. 1974. *Greedy Institutions: Patterns of Undivided Commitment.* New York: Free Press.

Costin, Lela, Howard Karger, and David Stoesz. 1996. *The Politics of Child Abuse.* New York: Oxford University Press.

Coward, Harold. 2000. "Hinduism in Canada," In *The South Asian Religious Diaspora in Britain, Canada, and the United States,* edited by Harold Coward, John Hinnells, and Raymond Williams, 151–72. Albany: State University of New York Press.

Daly, Mary. 1985. *The Church and the Second Sex.* Boston: Beacon Press.

Das, Abhirama. 2000. "Official Report on the Kartik Vrindavan Incident." Chakra website, February 14. Available at http://www.chakra.org/discussions/IntFeb23_04.html.

Das, Ameyatma. 1998. "The So-Called Conspiracy against the Women's Ministry." Vaisnava News Network (VNN) website, November 20. Available at http://www.vnn.org/world/WD9811/WD20-2531.html.

———. 2000. "The Fire of Sati." Vaisnava News Network (VNN) website, February 29. Available at http://www.vnn.org/editorials/ET0002/ET29-5575.html.

Das, Caru. 2004a. "Exchange of Views." Chakra website, February 23. Available at http://www.chakra.org/discussions/IntFeb23_04.html.

Das, Caru. 2004b. "Shiva Ratri, the Night of Lord Shiva." Chakra website, February 1. Available at http://www.chakra.org/announcements/eventsFeb01_04.html.

Das, Dhira Govinda. 2004. "ISKCON Child Protection Office Report." Vaishnava News Network (VNN) website, July 28. Available at http://www.vnn.org/world/WD0407/WD28-8672.html.

Das, Kalakantha. 2000. "Unofficial Statistical Abstract of ISKCON's Governing Body Commission." Unpublished paper, director, GBC Secretariat, May.

Das, Krishna-kirti. 2005. "Language, Ideology, and the Women's Movement in ISKCON." *Hare Krishna Cultural Journal,* February 23. Available at http://siddhanta.com/archives/culture/2005_02.html.

Das, Ragaputra. 2005. "The Hindufication of ISKCON." Chakra website, March 31. Available at http://chakra.org/discussions/IntMar31 05.html.

Das, Ravindra Svarupa. 1994. "Cleaning House and Cleaning Hearts: Reform and Renewal in ISKCON" (two-part essay). *ISKCON Communications Journal* 3:43–52, 4:25–33.

———. 2000a. Letter presented in "Ravindra Svarupa Steps on a Land Mine," Vaisnava News Network (VNN) website, February 17. Available at http://www.vnn.org/editorials/ET0002/ET17-5493.html.

———. 2000b. "Restoring the Authority of the GBC." *ISKCON Communications Journal* 8(1):37–43.

Dasa, Aghari, and Candramukhi Dasi. 2002. "Krsna Conscious Co-Counselling : A Peer- Counselling Model for Vaisnava Society." *ISKCON Communications Journal* 10 :13–24.

Dasa, Anuttama. 2001. "Press Release: $400 Million Suit against Hare Krishna Dismissed," October 2. Available at http://www.iskcon.com/press/2oct01.html.

———. 2005. "Press Release: Courts Confirms Hare Krishna Chapter 11 Reorganization." Available at http://www.iskcon.com/press/index.html.

Dasa, Ardhabuddhi. 1998. "Conspiracy to Terminate the ISKCON Women's Ministry." Vaisnava News Network (VNN) website, November 18. Available at http://www.vnn.org/world/WD9811/WD18-2521.html.

Dasa, Basu Ghosh. 2005. "Why the 'Women in ISKCON Resolution 2000' Needs Amending." *Hare Krishna Cultural Journal,* February. Available at http://siddhanta.com/archives/culture/2005_02.html.

Dasa, Jivan Mukta. 1998. "Gurus, Wives and Equal Rights." Vaisnava News Network (VNN) website, November 25. Available at http://www.vnn.org/editorials/ET9811/ET25-2555.html.

———. 1999a. "Change Prabhupada's Sexist Books." Vaisnava News Network (VNN) website, May 3. Available at http://www.vnn.org/world/WD9905/WD03-3779.html.

———. 1999b. "I Just Have a Big Problem Trusting Persons." Vaisnava News Network (VNN) website, December 6. Available at http://www.vnn.org/editorials/ET9912/ET06-5033.html.

———. 1999c. "ISKCON Law: What about Husbands?" Dharma-kshetra, February 29, http://www.qhqd.org (no longer operating).

———. 1999d. "The Myth of Equal Rights—Section 1 Parts 1–4." Dharma-kshetra, November 24, http://www.qhqd.org (no longer operating).

Dasa, Manu. 1998. Gurukula alumni database.

Dasa, Murali Vadaka. 1992. "Morning Class." Dallas ISKCON temple, November 7.

———. 1994. "All Dressed up with No Place to Go." Paper presented at ISKCON's North American Board of Education Conference, Alachua, Fla.

Dasi, Dhyana-Kunda. 1999. "Follow up to Jivanmukta's Article." Vaisnava News Network (VNN) website, December 23. Available at http://www.vnn.org/editorials/ET9912/ET23-5137.html.

Dasi, Hare Krsna. 2004. "The Hinduization of ISKCON?" Chakra website, February 12. Available at http://www.chakra.org/discussions/IntFeb12 04.html.

Dasi, Pranada. 1999. "Do the Women Deserve This?" Chakra website, November 12. Available at http://www.chakra.org/discussions/IntNov12 04.html.

Dasi, Rukmini. 2000. "Presentation by Rukmini Dasi." *ISKCON Communications Journal* 8(1):16–20.

Dasi, Saudamani. 2000. "Presentation by Saudamani Dasi." *ISKCON Communications Journal* 8(1):12–13.

Dasi, Subhadra-Mayi. 2004. "In Response to 'Our Unquestioning Service Is Our Glory.'" Chakra website, December 17. Available at http://www.chakra.org/discussions/IntDec17 04.html.

Dasi, Sudharma. 2000. "Presentation by Sudharma Dasi." *ISKCON Communications Journal* 8(1):13–16.

Dasi, Syamasundari. 1999. "Be Arjuna and We'll Be Draupadi." Vaisnava News Network (VNN) website, November 25. Available at http://www.vnn.org/editorials/ET9811/ET25-2556.html.

Dasi, Visakha, and Sudharma Dasi. 2000. "Women in ISKCON: Presentations to the GBC, March 2000." *ISKCON Communications Journal* 8(1):1–4.

Dasi, Yasomati-stanya Payi. 2004. "Our Unquestioning Service Is Our Glory." Chakra website, December 9. Available at http://www.chakra.org/discussions/ODiscDec09 04.html.

Dawson, Lorne. 1998. *Comprehending Cults: The Sociology of New Religious Movements.* New York: Oxford University Press.

Deadwyler, William (Ravindra Svarupa Das). 2004. "Cleaning House and Cleaning Hearts : Reform and Renewal in ISKCON." In *The Hare Krishna Movement: The Postcharismatic Fate of a Religious Transplant,* edited by Edwin Bryant and Maria Ekstrand, 149–69. New York: Columbia University Press.

Desai, KrishnaKant. 2006. Personal communication, January.

Desai, Krishnakant, Sunil Awatramani, and Madhu Pandit Das. 2004. "The No Change in ISKCON Paradigm," In *The Hare Krishna Movement: The Postcharismatic Fate of a Religious Transplant,* edited by Edwin Bryant and Maria Ekstrand, 194–213. New York: Columbia University Press.

Devi Dasi, Jyotirmayi. 2002 [1997]. "Women in ISKCON in Prabhupada's Times." Chakra website, November 29. Available at http://www.chakra.org/discussions/WomenNov29_02_02.html.

Devi Dasi, K. 1990. "Guru-kula." *A Confidential Report: The Hare Krishna Kids* 2 (January–May):1–2, 11–15.

Devi Dasi, Madireksana. 1994. "Why I Wear a Sari." *Back to Godhead,* November/December, 40–41.

Devi Dasi, Pranada. 2002. "Yesterday, Today, and Tomorrow." Chakra website, November 29. Available at http://www.chakra.org/discussions/WomenNov29_02_03.html.

Devi Dasi, Prtha. 1998. "Just Try to Understand." Vaisnava News Network (VNN) website, December 8. Available at http://www.vnn.org/editorials/ET9812/ET08-2634.html.

Devi Dasi, Radha. 1998. "Labeled a 'Feminist.'" Vaisnava News Network (VNN) website, November 26. Available at http://www.vnn.org/editorials/ET9811/ET26-2560.html.

Devi Dasi, Sita. 2002. "On Women Giving Class." Vaisnava News Network (VNN) website, January 11. Available at http://www.vnn.org/editorials/ET0201/ET11-7091.html.

———. 2005. "An Alternative Petition." *Hare Krishna Cultural Journal,* February 8. Available at http://siddhanta.com/archives/culture/2005_02.html.

Devi Dasi, Sitarani. 1982. "What's the Role of Women in Krsna Consciousness?" *Back to Godhead* 17(12):11–13, 26.

Devi Dasi, Sridhari. 2000. "When Women Are Protected." Vaisnava News Network (VNN) website, May 26. Available at http://www.vnn.org/editorials/ET0005/ET26-5965.html.

Devi Dasi, Urmila. 1992. *According to Religious Principles: A Guide to Sexual Relations in a Krsna Conscious Marriage.* Hillsborough, N.C.: ISKCON Education of N.C.

Devi Dasi, Yamuna. 2000. "Srila Prabhupada's Transcendental Sweetness and Beauty." *ISKCON Communications Journal* 8(1):6–7.

Dillon, Michele. 1999. *Catholic Identity: Balancing Reason, Faith, and Power.* Cambridge: Cambridge University Press.

Doktorski, Henry. 2003. "The Great Experiment: Sacred Music and the Christianization of the New Vrindaban Hare Krishna Temple Liturgies." Unpublished manuscript, Pittsburgh.

Downing, Michael. 2001. *Shoes outside the Door: Desire, Devotion, and Excess at San Francisco Zen Center.* Washington, D.C.: Counterpoint.

Durkheim, Emile. 1965. *The Elementary Forms of Religious Life.* New York: Free Press.

Eck, Diana. 2000. "Negotiating Hindu Identities in America," In *The South Asian Religious Diaspora in Britain, Canada, and the United States,* edited by Harold Coward, John Hinnells, and Raymond Williams, 219–37. Albany: State University of New York Press.

———. 2001. *A New Religious America: How a "Christian Country" Has Now Become the World's Most Religiously Diverse Nation.* New York: HarperCollins.

Ellison, Christopher, and Darren Sherkat. 1993. "Conservative Protestantism and Support for Corporal Punishment." *American Sociological Review* 58: 131–44.

Fantasia, Rick, and Eric L. Hirsch. 1995. "Culture in Rebellion: The Appropriation and Transformation of the Veil in the Algerian Revolution." In *Social Movements and Culture,* edited by Hank Johnson and Bert Klandermans, 144–59. Minneapolis: University of Minnesota Press.

Fenton, John. 1988. *Transplanting Religious Traditions: Asian Indians in America.* New York: Praeger.

Fine, Gary. 1995. "Public Narration and Group Culture: Discerning Discourse in Social Movements." In *Social Movements and Culture,* edited by Hank Johnson and Bert Klandermans, 127–43. Minneapolis: University of Minnesota Press.

Finke, Roger. 2004. "Innovative Returns to Tradition: Using Core Teachings as the Foundation for Innovative Accommodation." *Journal for the Scientific Study of Religion* 43(1):19–34.

Foster, Lawrence. 1991. *Women, Family, and Utopia: Communal Experiments of the Shakers, the Oneida Community, and the Mormons.* Syracuse, N.Y.: Syracuse University Press.

Friedman, Debra and Doug McAdam, 1992. "Collective Identity and Activism:

Networks, Choices, and the Life of a Social Movement." In *Frontiers in Social Movement Theory*, edited by Aldon Morris and Carol McClurg Mueller, 156–73. New Haven, Conn.: Yale University Press.

Gamson, William. 1975. *Strategy of Social Protest*. Homewood, Ill.: Dorsey.

Gamson, William, Bruce Fireman, and Steven Rytina. 1982. *Encounters with Unjust Authority*. Homewood, Ill.: Dorsey.

Garfinkel, Harold. 1967. *Studies in Ethnomethodology*. Englewood Cliffs, N.J.: Prentice-Hall.

GBC Executive Committee. 1998. "When Srila Prabhupada Is at the Center." Vaisnava News Network (VNN) website, December 20. Available at http://www.vnn.org/world/WD9812/WD20-2715.html.

"GBC Meetings, Day 3, March 1." 2005. Chakra website, March 4. Available at http://www.chakra.org/news/newsMar04_05.html.

GBC Resolutions. 1999. ISKCON Law 6.4.7.2 (unpublished).

———. 2000. *ISKCON Communications Journal* 8(1):21–22.

Geertz, Clifford. 1973. *The Interpretation of Cultures*. New York: Basic Books.

GHQ. 1999. "Notes from a Think Tank." Vaisnava News Network (VNN), February 21. Available at http://www.vnn.org/editorials/ET9902/5.html.

Glock, Charles, and Rodney Stark. 1965. *Religion and Society in Tension*. Chicago: Rand McNally.

Goffman, Erving. 1961. *Asylums*. Garden City, N.Y.: Doubleday (Anchor).

———. 1963. *Stigma: Notes on the Management of a Spoiled Identity*. Englewood Cliffs, N.J.: Prentice-Hall.

———. 1974. *Frame Analysis: An Essay on the Organization of Experience*. New York: Harper Colophon Books.

Goswami, Hrdayananda Dasa. 2000. "The Role of Guru in a Multi-Guru Society." *ISKCON Communications Journal* 8(1):45–53.

Goswami, Jagadisa Dasa. 1984. *Srila Prabhupada on Guru-Kula*. Los Angeles: Bhaktivedanta Book Trust.

Goswami, Satsvarupa Dasa. 1980. *Planting the Seed: New York City, 1965–1966*. Los Angeles: Bhaktivedanta Book Trust.

———. 1993. *Srila Prabhupada-Lilamrta*. 6 vols. Los Angeles: Bhaktivedanta Book Trust.

Goswami, Tamal Krishna. 1984. *Servant of the Servant*. Hong Kong: Bhaktivedanta Book Trust.

———. 1998. "The Perils of Succession." In his *A Hare Krishna at Southern Methodist University, Collected Essays 1995–1997*, 283–346. Dallas: Pundits Press.

Greeley, Andrew. 1992. Forward to *Lead Us Not into Temptation*, by Jason Berry. New York: Doubleday.

Greil, Arthur, and David Rudy. 1984. "Social Cocoons: Encapsulation and Identity Transformation Organizations." *Sociological Inquiry* 54:260–78.

Greven, Phillip. 1990. *Spare the Child: The Religious Roots of Punishment and the Psychological Impact of Physical Abuse.* New York: Knopf.

Gusfield, Joseph. 1981. "Social Movements and Social Change: Perspectives of Linearity and Fluidity." In *Research in Social Movements, Conflict and Change,* edited by Louis Kriesberg, 317–39. Greenwich, Conn.: JAI Press.

Hall, John. 1988. "Social Organization and Pathways of Commitment: Types of Communal Groups, Rational Choice Theory, and the Kanter Thesis." *American Sociological Review* 53:679–92.

Hickey, Nirmal, and Maya Carnell. 1997. "Perpetrators' Targets for Sexual Abuse." VOICE website (no longer operating).

Hickey Nirmal, Maya Carnell, and other anonymous contributors. 1997. "Our View of Prabhupad's Responsibility." VOICE website (no longer operating).

Holland, Dorothy, and Margaret Eisenhart. 1990. *Educated in Romance: Women, Achievement, and College Culture.* Chicago: University of Chicago Press.

Iannaccone, Laurence. 1988. "A Formal Model of Church and Sect." *American Journal of Sociology* 94:S241–68.

———. 1994. "Why Strict Churches Are Strong." *American Journal of Sociology* 99:1180–1211.

Introvigne, Massimo. 2000. *The Unification Church.* Salt Lake City: Signature Books.

ISKCON of Alachua Board of Directors. 2000. "Alachua Temple—Vote of No Confidence in GBC." July 20. Available at http://iskcon.krishna.org/Articles/2000/10/00191.html.

———. 2001. Letter to the GBC. April 19 (unpublished letter).

iskcon.com. 2005a. "ISKCON's Governing Body Discusses Gurus." No date. Available at http://www.iskcon.com/new/050311_gbc.html.

———. 2005b. "ISKCON's Governing Body Meets." No date. Available at http://www.iskcon.com/new/050301_gbc.html.

———. 2005c. List of U.S. ISKCON Communities. Available at http://www.iskcon.com/worldwide/centres/north_america.html.

Jacobs, Janet. 1984. "The Economy of Love in Religious Commitment: The Deconversion of Women from Nontraditional Religious Movements." *Journal for the Scientific Study of Religion* 23:155–71.

———. 1987. "Deconversion from Religious Movements: An Analysis of Charismatic Bonding and Spiritual Commitment." *Journal for the Scientific Study of Religion* 26:294–308.

Jenkins, Phillip. 1996. *Pedophiles and Priests.* New York: Oxford University Press.

Johnson, Gregory. 1976. "The Hare Krishna in San Francisco." In *The New Religious Consciousness,* edited by Charles Glock and Robert Bellah, 31–51. Berkeley: University of California Press.

Johnson, Hank, and Bert Klandermans. 1995. "The Cultural Analysis of Social Movements." In *Social Movements and Culture,* edited by Hank Johnson and Bert Klandermans, 3–24. Minneapolis: University of Minnesota Press.

Judah, Stillson. 1974. *Hare Krishna and the Counterculture.* New York: Wiley.

Kafle, Prajyumna. 2001. "The Destruction and Resurrection of My Hare Krsna Faith." *ISKCON Communications Journal* 9(1):43–50.

Kanter, Rosabeth Moss. 1968. "Commitment and Social Organization: A Study of Commitment Mechanisms in Utopian Communities." *American Sociological Review* 33(4):499–517.

———. 1972. *Commitment and Community.* Cambridge, Mass.: Harvard University Press.

Kent, Stephen. 2001. *From Slogans to Mantras: Social Protest and Religious Conversion in the Late Vietnam War Era.* Syracuse, N.Y.: Syracuse University Press.

Kephart, William. 1963. "Experimental Family Organization: An Historico-Cultural Report on the Oneida Community." *Marriage and Family Living* 25 (August):261–71.

Knott, Kim. 1987. "Hindu Temple Rituals in Britain: The Reinterpretation of Tradition." In *Hinduism in Great Britain: The Perpetuation of Religion in an Alien Cultural Milieu,* edited by Richard Burghart, 157–79. London: Tavistock.

———. 1995. "The Debate about Women in the Hare Krishna Movement." *ISKCON Communications Journal* 3(2):33–49.

———. 2004. "Healing the Heart of ISKCON: The Place of Women," In *The Hare Krishna Movement: The Postcharismatic Fate of a Religious Transplant,* edited by Edwin Bryant and Maria Ekstrand, 291–311. New York: Columbia University Press.

Kraybill, Donald. 1977. *Ethnic Education: The Impact of Mennonite Schooling.* San Francisco: R & E Research Associates.

———. 2001. *The Riddle of Amish Culture.* Baltimore: Johns Hopkins University Press.

Krebs, Theresa. 1998. "Church Structures That Facilitate Pedophilia among Roman Catholic Clergy." In *Wolves within the Fold,* edited by Anson Shupe, 15–32. New Brunswick, N.J.: Rutgers University Press.

KrishnaKant (Desai). 1996. *The Final Order: The Legal, Philosophical and Documentary Evidence Supporting Srila Prabhupada's Rightful Position as ISKCON's Initiating Guru.* Bangalore: ISKCON Revival Movement.

Kumar, Rasa. 2006. "Invitation to the 15th Annual Prabhupada Memorial Festival—Los Angeles May 27th and 28th." Available at http://www.chakra.org/announcements/eventsMay05_06.html.

Kurien, Prema. 1998. "Becoming American by Becoming Hindu: Indian Americans Take Their Place at the Multicultural Table." In *Gatherings in Dias-*

pora: *Religious Communities and the New Immigration*, edited by R. Stephen Warner and Judith Wittner, 37–70. Philadelphia: Temple University Press.

———. 2002. "'We Are Better Hindus Here:' Religion and Ethnicity among Indian Americans." In *Religions in Asian America: Building Faith Communities*, edited by Pyong Gap Min and Jung Ha Kim, 99–120. Walnut Creek, Calif.: AltaMira Press.

Labi, Nadya. 1998. "Not Doing as the Romans Do: A Woman's Place at the Altar Challenges a 2,000 Year-Old Catholic Tradition." *Time*, November 30. Available at http://www.time.com/time/magazine/article/D,9171,989688,DD.html.

Law Offices of Windle Turley. 2000. "'Hare Krishna' Sued for Child Abuse." Press Release, June 12. Available at http://www.wturley.com/news/2_News-HareKrishna.html.

Leonard, Karen, Alex Stepick, Manuel Vasquez, and Jennifer Holdaway. 2005. *Immigrant Faiths: Transforming Religious Life in America*. Walnut Creek, Calif.: AltaMira Press.

Levine, Adeline Gordon. 1982. *Love Canal: Science, Politics, and People*. Lexington, Mass.: Lexington Books.

Lofland, John. 1987. "Social Movement Culture and the Unification Church." In *The Future of New Religious Movements*, edited by David Bromley and Phillip Hammond, 91–108. Macon, Ga.: Mercer University Press.

Lofland, John, and Rodney Stark. 1965. "Becoming a World-Saver: A Theory of Conversion to a Deviant Perspective." *American Sociological Review* 30: 862–74.

Lorenz, Ekkehard. 2004. "The Gurus, Mayavadins, and Women: Tracing the Origins of Selected Polemical Statements in the Works of A. C. Bhaktivedanta Swami." In *The Hare Krishna Movement: The Postcharismatic Fate of a Religious Transplant*, edited by Edwin Bryant and Maria Ekstrand, 112–28. New York: Columbia University Press.

Mandelker, Ira. 1984. *Religion, Society, and Utopia in Nineteenth-Century America*. Amherst: University of Massachusetts Press.

Mansbridge, Jane, and Aldon Morris. 2001. *Oppositional Consciousness: The Subjective Roots of Social Protest*. Chicago: University of Chicago Press.

Mauss, Armand. 1994. *The Angel and the Beehive: The Mormon Struggle with Assimilation*. Urbana: University of Illinois Press.

McAdam, Doug. 1982. *Political Process and the Development of Black Insurgency, 1930–1970*. Chicago: University of Chicago Press.

Melton, J. Gordon. 1987. "How New Is New? The Flowering of the 'New' Religious Consciousness since 1965." In *The Future of New Religious Movements*, edited by David Bromley and Phillip Hammond, 46–56. Macon, Ga.: Mercer University Press.

Melton, J. Gordon. 2000. *The Church of Scientology*. Salt Lake City: Signature Books.

———. 2004. "Perspective: Toward a Definition of 'New Religion.'" *Nova Religio* 8(1):73–87.

Min, Pyong Gap. 2005. "Religion and the Maintenance of Ethnicity among Immigrants: A Comparison of Indian Hindus and Korean Protestants." In *Immigrant Faiths: Transforming Religious Life in America*, edited by Karen Leonard, Alex Stepick, Manuel Vasquez, and Jennifer Holdaway, 99–122. Walnut Creek, Calif.: AltaMira Press.

Min, Pyong Gap, and Jung Ha Kim. 2002. *Religions in Asian America: Building Faith Communities*. Walnut Creek, Calif.: AltaMira Press.

Muster, Lori. 2004. "Life as a Woman on Watseka Avenue: Personal Story I." In *The Hare Krishna Movement: The Postcharismatic Fate of a Religious Transplant*, edited by Edwin Bryant and Maria Ekstrand, 312–20. New York: Columbia University Press.

Nason-Clark, Nancy. 1998. "The Impact of Abuses of Clergy Trust on Female Congregants' Faith and Practice." In *Wolves within the Fold*, edited by Anson Shupe, 85–100. New Brunswick, N.J.: Rutgers University Press.

Nesbitt, Paula. 1997. *Feminization of the Clergy in America*. New York: Oxford University Press.

Niebuhr, H. Richard. 1929. *The Social Sources of Denominationalism*. New York: Meridian.

North Central Florida Krishna Community Resource Directory. 2001. "A History of *New Raman-reti*." Alachua, Fla.: KCF Publishing.

Numrich, Paul. 1996. *Old Wisdom in the New World: Americanization in Two Immigrant Theravada Buddhist Temples*. Knoxville: University of Tennessee Press.

Ofshe, Richard. 1980. "The Social Development of the Synanon Cult." *Sociological Analysis* 41(2):109–27.

Palmer, Susan. 1994. *Moon Sisters, Krishna Mothers, Rajneesh Lovers: Women's Roles in New Religions*. Syracuse, N.Y.: Syracuse University Press.

———. 2003. "Women's 'Cocoon Work' in New Religious Movements: Sexual Experimentation and Feminine Rites of Passage." In *Cults and New Religious Movements: A Reader*, edited by Lorne Dawson, 245–56. Oxford: Blackwell.

———. 2004. "Women in New Religious Movements." In *The Oxford Handbook of New Religious Movements*, edited by James Lewis, 378–85. New York: Oxford University Press.

Patel, Urvashi. 2006. "The Need for Diversity." Chakra website, June 8. Available at http://www.chakra.org/discussions/IntJun08_06.html.

Portes, Alejandro, and Rubén Rumbaut. 1996. *Immigrant America: A Portrait*. 2nd ed. Los Angeles: University of California Press.

Prabhupada, A. C. Bhaktivedanta Swami. 1974. "Varnasrama Walk Conversations." Vrndavana, India, March (unpublished).

——— 1992. *Srila Prabhupada Siksmrta: Nectarian Instructions from the Letters of His Divine Grace A. C. Bhaktivedanta Swami Prabhupada*. Los Angeles: Bhaktivedanta Book Trust.

Prabhupada Anti-Defamation Association. 1993. "Child Molesters Gurus? The False Krishna Gurus." California (typescript).

Prabhupada Disciple Database. 2006. Available at http://www.prabhupada.com/disciple.php.

Pullen, Elizabeth. 1998. "An Advocacy Group for Victims of Clerical Sexual Abuse." In *Wolves within the Fold,* edited by Anson Shupe, 67–84. New Brunswick, N.J.: Rutgers University Press.

Puttick, Elizabeth. 1996. *Women in New Religions*. London: Macmillan.

———. 2003. "Women in New Religious Movements." In *Cults and New Religious Movements: A Reader,* edited by Lorne Dawson, 230–44. Oxford: Blackwell.

Rangaswamy, Padma. 2000. *Namaste America: Indian Immigrants in an American Metropolis*. University Park: Pennsylvania State University Press.

Riley, Glenda. 1991. *Divorce: An American Tradition*. New York: Oxford University Press.

Robbins, Thomas. 2005. "Perspective: New Religions and Alternative Religions." *Nova Religio* 8(3):104–11.

Robbins, Thomas, and David Bromley. 1992. "Social Experimentation and the Significance of American New Religions: A Focused Review Essay." *Research in the Social Scientific Study of Religion* 4:1–28.

Rochford, E. Burke, Jr. 1985. *Hare Krishna in America*. New Brunswick, N.J.: Rutgers University Press.

———. 1987. "Shifting Public Definitions of Hare Krishna." In *Collective Behavior,* by Ralph Turner and Lewis Killian, 3rd ed., 258–60. Englewood Cliffs, N.J.: Prentice-Hall.

———. 1989. "Factionalism, Group Defection, and Schism in the Hare Krishna Movement." *Journal for the Scientific Study of Religion* 28(2):162–79.

———. 1991. "Re-membering Hare Krishna: Patterns of Disaffection and Reentry." In *Religion and Power Decline and Growth: Sociological Analyses of Religion in Britain, Poland and the Americas,* edited by Peter Gee and J. Fulton, 85–100. London: British Sociological Association, Sociology of Religion Study Group.

———. 1992. "On the Politics of Member Validation: Taking Findings Back to Hare Krishna." In *Perspectives on Social Problems,* vol. 3, edited by Gale Miller and James Holstein, 99–116. Greenwich, Conn.: JAI Press.

———. 1995. "Crescita, espansione e mutamento nel movimento degli Hare Krishna." *Religioni e sette nel mondo* 1(1):56–80.

Rochford, E. Burke, Jr. 1998a. "Prabhupada Centennial Survey Report." Submitted to ISKCON's International GBC, November 1998 (unpublished). Summary of the report was published in 1999, "Prabhupada Centennial Survey: A Summary of the Final Report." *ISKCON Communications Journal* 7(1):11–26. Available at http://www.iskcon.com/icj/7_1/71rochford.html.

———. 1998b. "Reactions of Hare Krishna Devotees to Scandals of Leaders' Misconduct." In *Wolves within the Fold,* edited by Anson Shupe, 101–17. New Brunswick, N.J.: Rutgers University Press.

———. 2000. "Demons, Karmies, and Non-Devotees: Culture, Group Boundaries, and the Development of Hare Krishna in North America and Europe." *Social Compass* 47(2):169–86.

———. 2007. "Social Building Blocks of New Religious Movements: Organization and Leadership." In *Teaching New Religious Movements,* edited by David Bromley. New York: Oxford University Press.

Rochford, E. Burke, Jr., and Kendra Bailey. 2006. "Almost Heaven: Leadership, Decline and the Transformation of New Vrindaban." *Nova Religio* 9(3): 6–23.

Rochford, E. Burke, Jr., Sheryl Purvis, and NeMar Eastman. 1989. "New Religions, Mental Health, and Social Control." In *Research in the Scientific Study of Religion,* vol. 1, edited by M. Lynn and David Moburg, 57–82. Greenwich, Conn.: JAI Press.

Rosen, Steven. 2004. "Who Is Shri Chaitanya Mahaprabhu?" In *The Hare Krishna Movement: The Postcharismatic Fate of a Religious Transplant,* edited by Edwin Bryant and Maria Ekstrand, 63–72. New York: Columbia University Press.

Sacks, Harvey. 1972. "On the Analyzability of Stories by Children." In *Directions in Sociolinguistics,* edited by J. Gumperz and D. Hymes, 325–45. New York: Holt, Rinehart & Winston.

Schneider, Joseph, and Peter Conrad. 1993. "In the Closet with Illness: Epilepsy, Stigma Potential and Information Control." In *Deviant Behavior,* edited by D. Kelly, 205–21. New York: St. Martin's Press.

Seligman, Adam. 1997. *The Problem of Trust.* Princeton, N.J.: Princeton University Press.

"Senior Devotees Speak about the Present and Future of ISKCON USA." 2002. Unpublished report (August).

Shepherd, Gordon, and Gary Shepherd. 2002. "The Family in Transition: The Moral Career of a New Religious Movement." Paper presented at the CESNUR International Conference, Salt Lake City and Provo, Utah, June.

Shinn, Larry. 1987. *The Dark Lord: Cult Images and the Hare Krishnas in America.* Philadelphia: Westminster Press.

Shupe, Anson. 1995. *In the Name of All That's Holy: A Theory of Clergy Malfeasance.* Westport, Conn.: Praeger.

Silver, Ira. 1996. "Role Transitions, Objects, and Identity." *Symbolic Interaction* 19(1):1–20.

Sivan, Emmanuel. 1995. "The Enclave Culture." In *Fundamentalisms Comprehended*, edited by Martin Marty and R. Scott Appleby, 11–68. Chicago: University of Chicago Press.

Skonovd, Norman. 1983. "Leaving the Cultic Religious Milieu." In *The Brainwashing/Deprogramming Controversy: Sociological, Psychological, Legal and Historical Perspectives*, edited by David Bromley and James Richardson, 91–103. New York: Mellen.

Slater, Phillip. 1963. "On Social Regression." *American Sociological Review* 28:339–64.

Spiro, Melford. 1958. *Children of the Kibbutz*. Cambridge, Mass.: Harvard University Press.

Snow, David, and Robert Benford. 1992. "Master Frames and Cycles of Protest," In *Frontiers in Social Movement Theory*, edited by Aldon Morris and Carol Mueller, 133–55. New Haven, Conn.: Yale University Press.

Snow, David, and Richard Machalek. 1982. "On the Presumed Fragility of Unconventional Beliefs." *Journal for the Scientific Study of Religion* 21:15–26.

———. 1984. "The Sociology of Conversion." *Annual Review of Sociology* 10: 167–90.

Snow, David, and Cynthia Phillips. 1980. "The Lofland–Stark Conversion Model: A Critical Reassessment." *Social Problems* 27:430–47.

Snow, David, E. Burke Rochford Jr., Steven Worden, and Robert Benford. 1986. "Frame Alignment Processes, Micromobilization, and Movement Participation." *American Sociological Review* 51:464–81.

Squarcini, Federico. 2000. "In Search of Identity within the Hare Krishna Movement: Memory, Oblivion and Thought Style." *Social Compass* 47(2):253–71.

Squarcini, Federico, and Eugenio Fizzotti. 2004. *Hare Krishna*. Salt Lake City: Signature Books.

Staff of the Boston Globe. 2002. *Betrayal: The Crisis in the Catholic Church*. Boston: Little, Brown.

Stark, Rodney. 1987. "How New Religions Succeed: A Theoretical Model." In *The Future of New Religious Movements*, edited by David Bromley and Phillip Hammond, 11–29. Macon, Ga.: Mercer University Press.

———. 1996. "Why Religious Movements Succeed or Fail: A Revised General Model." *Journal of Contemporary Religion* 11(2):133–46.

Stark, Rodney, and Roger Finke. 2000. *Acts of Faith: Explaining the Human Side of Religion*. Berkeley: University of California Press.

Stone, Gregory. 1981. "Appearance and the Self: A Slightly Revised Version." In *Social Psychology through Symbolic Interaction*, edited by Gregory Stone and Harvey Farberman, 187–202. New York: Wiley.

Swami, Bhakti Vikasa. 1998. "Bhakti Vikasa Swami Answers Conspiracy

Charge." Vaisnava News Network (VNN) website, November 24. Available at http://www.vnn.org/world/WD9811/WD24-2550.html.

Swami, Jayadvaita. 1987. "Several Grievances against the Members of the GBC." March 5; quoted in *Back to Prabhupada* 9:2 (2005).

Swidler, Ann. 1986. "Culture in Action: Symbols and Strategies." *American Sociological Review* 51:273–86.

———. 1995. "Cultural Power and Social Movements." In *Social Movements and Culture,* edited by Hank Johnson and Bert Klandermans, 25–40. Minneapolis: University of Minnesota Press.

Talmon, Yonina. 1973. "Family Life in the Kibbutz: From Revolutionary Days to Stabilization." In *Communes: Creating and Managing the Collective Life,* edited by Rosabeth Moss Kanter, 318–33. New York: Harper & Row.

Tarrow, Sidney. 1994. *Power in Movement.* Cambridge: Cambridge University Press.

Turner, Ralph. 1969. "The Theme of Contemporary Social Movements." *British Journal of Sociology* 20:390–405.

Turner, Ralph, and Lewis Killian. 1987. *Collective Behavior.* 3rd ed. Englewood Cliffs, N.J.: Prentice-Hall.

U.S. Bureau of the Census. 2000. "We the People: Asians in the United States." *Census 2000 Special Reports.* Washington, D.C.: U.S. Department of Commerce, Economics and Statistics Administration. Available at http://www.census.gov/prod/2004pubs/censr-17.pdf.

Vaisnava Family Resources. 2006. "Endorsement of the Grihastha Ashram and Community Development." Available at http://www.vaisnavafamilyresources.org/index.html.

Vaisnava Marriage Services Registry. 2006. Available at http://dasiziyadfamily institute.org/VaisnavaMarriageServicesRegistry.html.

Vaisnavas CARE, Inc. 2006. "Our Mission." Available at http://www.vaisnavas care.com/get_to_know_us.html.

Vande Berg, Travis. 2005. "Hindus, Indians, and Brown-Bodies: Three Subgroups of Indian Immigrants at ISKCON Temples." Unpublished manuscript, Ithaca College, Ithaca, N.Y.

Vande Berg, Travis, and Fred Kniss. 2005. "ISKCON and Immigrants: The Rise, Decline, and Rise Again of a New Religious Movement." Unpublished manuscript, Ithaca College, Ithaca, N.Y.

Vishnu, Swami Bhakti Bhavana. 2004. "The Guardian of Devotion: Disappearance and Rejection of the Spiritual Master in ISKCON after 1977." In *The Hare Krishna Movement: The Postcharismatic Fate of a Religious Transplant,* edited by Edwin Bryant and Maria Ekstrand, 170–93. New York: Columbia University Press.

Wallis, Roy. 1976. *The Road to Total Freedom: A Sociological Analysis of Scientology.* New York: Columbia University Press.

————. 1982. *Millennialism and Charisma*. Belfast: Queen's University Press.

————. 1984. *The Elementary Forms of the New Religious Life*. London: Routledge & Kegan Paul.

Warner, Stephen, and Judith Wittner. 1998. *Gatherings in Diaspora: Religious Communities and the New Immigration*. Philadelphia: Temple University Press.

West, Candace, and Don Zimmerman. 1987. "Doing Gender." *Gender and Society* 1(2):125–51.

Whitworth, John, and Martin Shiels. 1982. "From across the Black Water: Two Imported Varieties of Hinduism." In *New Religious Movements: A Perspective for Understanding Society*, edited by Eileen Barker, 155–72. New York: Mellen.

Williams, Raymond. 1988. *Religions of Immigrants from India and Pakistan*. Cambridge: Cambridge University Press.

Wilson, Bryan. 1976. "Aspects of Secularization in the West." *Japanese Journal of Religious Studies* 4:259–76.

————. 1982. *Religion in Sociological Perspective*. Oxford: Oxford University Press.

————. 1987. "Factors in the Failure of the New Religious Movements." In *The Future of New Religious Movements*, edited by David Bromley and Phillip Hammond, 30–45. Macon, Ga.: Mercer University Press.

————. 1990. *Social Dimensions of Sectarianism: Sects and New Religious Movements in Contemporary Society*. Oxford: Clarendon Press.

Wolf, David. 2004. "Child Abuse and the Hare Krishnas: History and Response." In *The Hare Krishna Movement: The Postcharismatic Fate of a Religious Transplant*, edited by Edwin Bryant and Maria Ekstrand, 321–44. New York: Columbia University Press.

Wright, Stuart. 1983. "Defection from New Religious Movements: A Test of Some Theoretical Propositions." In *The Brainwashing/Deprogramming Controversy: Sociological, Psychological, Legal and Historical Perspectives*, edited by David Bromley and James Richardson, 106–21. New York: Mellen.

————. 1984. "Post Involvement Attitudes of Voluntary Defectors from Controversial New Religious Movements." *Journal for the Scientific Study of Religion* 23:172–82.

————. 1988. "Leaving New Religious Movements: Issues, Theory and Research." In *Falling from the Faith: Causes and Consequences of Apostasy*, edited by David Bromley, 143–65. Newbury Park, Calif.: Sage.

Wuthnow, Robert, and Marsha Witten. 1988. "New Directions in the Study of Culture." *Annual Review of Sociology* 14:49–67.

Yearbook of Immigration Statistics. 2004. "Immigration by Region and Selected Country of Last Residence: Fiscal Years 1820–2004." Available at http://uscis.gov/graphics/shared/statistics/yearbook/2004/table2.xls.

Zablocki, Benjamin. 1971. *The Joyful Community.* Baltimore: Penguin Books.

———. 1980. *Alienation and Charisma.* New York: Free Press.

Zack, Arnold. 2002. "A Dispute Resolution Programme for ISKCON." *ISKCON Communications Journal* 10:1–11.

Zaidman, Nurit. 1997. "When the Deities Are Asleep: Processes of Change in an America Hare Krishna Temple." *Journal of Contemporary Religion* 12(3):335–52.

———. 2000. "The Integration of Indian Immigrants to Temples Run by North Americans." *Social Compass* 47(2):205–19.

Index

Pages numbers followed by "t" indicate tables.

Mass expulsion of householders from ISK-
CON communities, 162
Mayapura gurukula, 233n9; sexual abuse
of children at, 234n4
Mayapura temple, 241n9
Mayavada philosophy, 242n2
McAdam, Doug, 120
Melton, J. Gordon, 202, 215
Mennonite high school students, 99
Moonies (Unification Church), 204
Mormons, 54
Movement culture, 52
Movement failure, 161
Murder of New Vrindaban resident, 38,
230n5, 230n6
Muster, Lori, 117

Name changes, 11; among ISKCON youth,
109–10, 239n10
Narayana. *See* Maharaja, Narayana
Nason-Clark, Nancy, 94
Neglect of children at gurukulas, 76–78
Nesbitt, Paula, 145, 149
New Raman-reti (Alachua) community,
175–79, 214, 217, 236n15, 246n2,
250n11; ISKCON of Alachua Board of
Directors, 177–78
New religions. *See* Religions, new
New Vrindaban, 18–29, 34–38, 231n10;
adolescent girls at, 233–34n1; day-care
center, 82–83; evolution into interfaith
community, 44–46; Festival of Inspira-
tion, 210, 211; gurukula, 18–22, 27–
29; gurukula reunion, 239n10; jewelry
business, 50; Kulimela festival, 210–12,
250n7; murder at, 38, 230n5, 230n6;
privatization of, 45–46; Radha-Krishna
Temple of Understanding, 185–86; Var-
nashram College, 22–27
Niebuhr, Richard, 97
Nityananda, 195
North American Board of Education, 114
North American Grhastha Vision Team,
213–14
North American Office of Communications, 144, 250n5
North American Prabhupada Centennial
Survey. *See* Prabhupada Centennial
Survey
Noyes, John Humphrey, 53

Nuclear family: effect on ISKCON, 67–69;
rise of, 62–66
Numrich, Paul, 248n14

Occupational structure of ISKCON, 64t
Oneida community, 53; child rearing in,
54, 234n5
Oppositional cultural formation, 207
Oppositional religious culture, 203, 215–
16; characteristics of, 6–7; ISKCON's
abandonment of, 139
Organizational switching, 169–71
Oriental Exclusion Act, 183, 246n4

Parents: complaints about abuse, 87–88;
exclusion from gurukulas, 88–91,
236n11. *See also* Family life
Passing, 111–13, 239n13
Patel, Urvashi, 249n21
Paternalism, 143
Patriarchal framework of ISKCON, 116,
117
Peer-counseling, 213
Phillips, Cynthia, 237–38n3
Physical abuse in gurukulas: prevalence of,
75–76; at New Vrindaban, 19; at Vrndavana gurukula, 30–33. *See also*
Abuse of children
Picking (selling), 23–24, 230n4
Polygamy, 54
Prabhupada, A. C. Bhaktivedanta Swami:
authority of, questioning of, 153–60;
child abuse and, 235n9, 237n16,
243n12; cultural development and, 71–
73; death of, 14; disciplining of children and, 236n13; founding of ISKCON
and, 2–3, 9–10; Indian-Hindu immigrants and, 182–83, 188, 246n3; initiation and, 171–74; ISKCON Revival
Movement and, 171–72; legacy of,
217; marriage and family and, 79, 149–
50; publications of, 13, 126, 127, 148,
153–58, 182; sexual politics and, 55–
61; sexual relations and, 58; succession
problems, 171–75; teachings of,
preached by followers, 168; treatment
of women and, 126–29, 138–142,
145–51, 153–58, 160, 241n7, 243n9,
243–44n13, 244n14; on Varnashram
culture, 71–73, 141–43

About the Author

E. Burke Rochford Jr. is a professor of sociology and religion at Middlebury College in Vermont. He also is the author of *Hare Krishna in America*.